**RED SWAN**

# RED SWAN

How Unorthodox Policy Making
Facilitated China's Rise

**SEBASTIAN HEILMANN**

The Chinese University Press

*Red Swan:*
*How Unorthodox Policy Making Facilitated China's Rise*
   By Sebastian Heilmann

© The Chinese University of Hong Kong 2018

All rights reserved. No part of this publication may be reproduced or transmitted in any form or by any means, electronic or mechanical, including photocopying, recording, or any information storage and retrieval system, without permission in writing from The Chinese University of Hong Kong.

ISBN: 978-962-996-827-4

Published by   The Chinese University Press
               The Chinese University of Hong Kong
               Sha Tin, N.T., Hong Kong
               Fax: +852 2603 7355
               Email: cup@cuhk.edu.hk
               Website: www.chineseupress.com

Printed in Hong Kong

# CONTENTS

**vii** List of Tables and Figures

**1** Introduction
China's Policy Process and the Resilience of the Communist Party-State

**17** Chapter 1
China's Adaptive Governance as a "Red Swan" in Comparative Politics

**45** Chapter 2
From Local Experiments to National Policy: The Origins of China's Distinctive Policy Process

**73** Chapter 3
Policy Experimentation and Institutional Innovation in China's Economic Transformation

**115** Chapter 4
How to Combine Policy Experiments with Long-Term Priorities: Unorthodox Lessons from China

**131  Chapter 5**

Making Plans for Markets:
Policy for the Long Term in China

**147  Chapter 6**

The Reinvention of Development Planning in China

**197  Epilogue**

Changes in China's Policy Process under
General Secretary Xi Jinping

**221  Notes**

**255  Abbreviations**

**257  Glossary**

**261  Index**

# LIST OF TABLES AND FIGURES

**Tables**

| | | |
|---|---|---|
| 1.1 | Distinctive Contemporary Governance Techniques That Originated During the Revolutionary and Mao Eras (1927–76) | 37 |
| 1.2 | Transformative versus Protective Policy Styles and Adaptive Capacity | 40 |
| 2.1 | Establishing "Model Experiments": A Comparison of the Approaches in the Mao and Deng Eras | 67 |
| 3.1 | Major Types of Experimental Zones Designated by China's Central Government | 85 |
| 3.2 | Patterns of Experimentation in Crucial Areas of Economic Reform | 93 |
| 3.3 | "Experimental Point" Programs in China's State Sector, 1978–97 | 95 |
| 5.1 | Redirecting Plan Functions in China since the 1980s | 135 |
| 6.1 | Binding and Indicative Targets of the 11th and 12th Five-year Plans | 156 |
| 6.2 | Macro-regional Plans and Experimental Schemes | 161 |

| 6.3 | Plan Formulation in China: The Example of the 11th Five-year Plan | 175 |
| --- | --- | --- |
| 6.4 | Recombined Governance in Chinese Development Planning | 186 |
| 7.1 | Events That May Trigger a Crisis Mode | 202 |
| 7.2 | Characteristics of the Normal and Crisis Modes in Chinese Politics | 204 |
| 7.3 | A Stable Exterior with Underlying Fragilities: How Resilient is China's Political Order to Unexpected Shocks? | 207 |
| 7.4 | Characteristics and Methods Attributed to a "Chinese Development Model" | 212 |

## Figures

| 3.1 | Experimental Regulation in China, 1979–2016 | 82 |
| --- | --- | --- |
| 3.2 | China's Experimentation-based Policy Cycle | 88 |
| 7.1 | China's Path to Political and Economic Transformation | 199 |

# RED SWAN

# Introduction

## China's Policy Process and the Resilience of the Communist Party-State

China stands as a major "Red Swan" challenge to the social sciences. The political resilience of the Communist party-state, in combination with a rapidly expanding and internationally competitive economy, represents a significant deviant and unpredicted case with a huge potential impact not only for the global distribution of political and economic powers but also for global debates on models of development. China's exceptional and unexpected development trajectory thus challenges conventional wisdom as well as conventional models of political change. For such a cognitive challenge Nassim Taleb has coined the term a "Black Swan."[1] Due to the revolutionary red colors that continue to dominate state flags and political symbols in the People's Republic of China (PRC), China's approach to governance should instead be characterized as a "Red Swan," and it requires a rethinking of conventional assumptions and models in comparative politics.

Traditional models of political systems predominantly concentrate on classifying types of regimes on a spectrum that ranges from "democracy to dictatorship"[2] and pointing to a large gray area of "hybrid" or "fragile" systems.[3] Based on the experiences of the collapsed socialist systems in the former Soviet Union and Eastern Europe, political systems in which Communist parties maintain a monopoly on power are only credited with a marginal ability, if any ability at all, to adapt. Communist one-party systems not only show fundamental political defects (a lack of checks and balances, suppressed pluralism of opinion, and violations of civil and political rights), but historically they have also been extremely inflexible in terms of institutions, political objectives, and state activities. The standard literature on socialist systems therefore disputes their ability to make improvements with respect to administrative organization, economic coordination, technological innovation, as well as their ability to compete on the international stage.[4]

This traditional approach to systemic classification, however, is not helpful to understand the dynamics in the PRC, a system that is unexpectedly adaptable and versatile in many policy fields, particularly in regard to economic and technology policies. The observation that many official institutions in the PRC are similar to those in the former Soviet Union or the former German Democratic Republic does not contribute to an understanding of the completely different capacities and outcomes of state activities. A better feel for China's development dynamics requires the use of analytical perspectives that go beyond preconceived regime typologies.

To avoid the inherent limitations of typological approaches, this book uses analytical approaches drawn from policy studies. One methodological principle of policy studies disaggregates political systems into policy subsystems, each of which is characterized by very different dynamics.[5] The focus is on the manner in which action programs in China's governmental system can be developed, formulated, implemented, adjusted, and revised. Therefore, policy making is seen as an open-ended process with an uncertain outcome, driven by conflicting interests, recurrent interactions, and continuous feedback. It is not regarded as being determined in a straightforward way by history, regime type, or institutions. The discovery of policy and institutional alternatives in a constantly changing political-economic context is the most uncertain and demanding part of the policy process.⁶ The keys are the political and administrative methodologies as well as the capacity to deal with both existing and emerging challenges, the correction mechanisms when things go wrong and conflicts arise, and the adaptive capabilities in constantly changing economic or international contexts.

Such process- and action-based studies of the dynamics of state activity over time go beyond abstract, generalized, systemic, or institutional perspectives. Thus this book is not concerned with the "hardware" of the political system (constitutional bodies, leading party organs, bureaucratic organizations, and so forth), nor does it focus on examining isolated variables on their own (the concentration of power, hierarchical control, legal certainties, inclusive versus extractive institutions, and so on). Instead, the focus here is on the "software" with which action requirements and action programs are processed in Chinese politics.

Consequently, the chapters in this book deal with the typical mechanisms that bring otherwise cumbersome bureaucracies and static constitutional rules to life. The analysis centers on observable patterns of interaction and feedback, methods for dealing with problems, adaptive capacities, as well as policy outcomes and potential novel approaches in specific action areas.

A key advantage of this kind of policy analysis is that it provides an open perspective: when new requirements for government action or regulation emerge (and in their wake, new problem definitions and new interests and conflicts), these policy studies can grasp such shifts in a straightforward manner. However, preconceived regime and institutional analysis tends to be blind to new and divergent observations and developments that do not fit into predefined analytical frameworks. From a teleological view, social-science research is often fixated on the search for signs of a "real" market economy or a "real" democracy in China. This perspective tends to shut its eyes to surprising observations, unexpected features, and unorthodox mechanisms that may provide a non-democratic system, such as that in China, with surprising agility and capacity with respect to policy innovation.

## The revolutionary origins of China's policy process

Unlike in Russia and Eastern Europe, the imposition of a national Communist regime in China required nearly three decades of revolutionary mobilization and struggle. This protracted process gave rise to a particular "guerrilla-style policy-making" approach[7] that proved capable of generating an array of creative—proactive as well as evasive—tactics for managing sudden change and uncertainty. This policy style allows constant adaptation to changes in the surrounding environment and justifies continual adjustments during implementation. It produces maximum creativity because policy makers are required to:

- test and constantly push the limits of the status quo and seize every possible opportunity to change the situation to their advantage;
- keep the core strategic objectives firmly in mind, yet to be as agile and pragmatic as possible in choosing tactical and operational means;
- tinker with a full range of available operational tactics and organizational approaches, be they traditional, non-traditional, or even foreign;
- search for and exploit random opportunities and discoveries that promise to promote political power and strategic goals.

The guerrilla policy style of policy making that enabled success in the unpredictable military-combat settings of revolutionary times bequeathed a dynamic means of navigating the treacherous rapids of transformative governance during both the Mao era ("socialist construction," "permanent revolution") and the post-Mao era ("reform and opening," "socialist market economy," "joining the WTO"). Its core features continue to shape present-day policy making and contribute to the flexibility and volatility of Communist Party rule.

At the same time, a guerrilla policy style has fundamental flaws: a lack of democracy and political accountability, undue administrative discretion, and the single-minded pursuit of strategic policy goals (e.g., economic growth or demographic controls), with little regard for the deleterious side-effects that often emerge only over time (e.g., environmental degradation or gender imbalances). As demands from Chinese society for political accountability, legal entitlements, and a social safety net increase, public tolerance for guerrilla-style policy making may well decline. Chapter 1 in this volume thus focuses on the mechanisms that characterize guerrilla-style policy making.

## Experimental programs and policy innovation

Since 1978, decentralized reform initiatives and local reform experiments capable of becoming nationwide political programs have had the utmost importance for China's economic development. This represents a special methodology for policy experimentation (*zhengce shiyan*) that is able to open up a wide range of unimaginable opportunities for action in a cumbersome, bureaucratic, and authoritarian system of government.

This special methodology, which also finds expression in the rather idiosyncratic Chinese terminology used to describe it, essentially consists of three steps. First, local "experimentation points" (*shidian*) or local "experimentation zones" (*shiyanqu*) are established. Second, successful "model experiments" (*dianxing shiyan*) are identified under these pilot experimental projects and expanded "from point to surface" (*you dian dao mian*, or *yidian daimian*) to test the extent to which the new policy options can be generalized or need to be modified. Third, the policies are not implemented in national legislation until they have been thoroughly tried and tested in a real-life administrative environment, a process that usually takes a number of years. As an example, it took twenty-three years from the first experiments with insolvent state-owned enterprises (SOEs) in 1984 until the national Bankruptcy Law entered into force in 2007, during which time many experimental regulations were tested in this controversial policy area, initially in individual cities, industries, and companies.

The internationally best-known variants of such experimentation are China's special economic zones (SEZs) (*jingji tequ*), which were explicitly set up to be open to the outside world and to be governed by modern economic regulations. Almost without exception, the most important policy reform measures—ranging from rural decollectivization, to management reforms in SOEs and the setting up of stock markets, to reforms in the rural health system—were initiated in decentralized experiments that remained subject to selective intervention by high-level leaders of the Chinese Communist Party (CCP) and the government. The essential interplay between decentralized and centralized initiatives stimulates the experimental-policy procedures in China: some phases of the experimentation process are strongly decentralized (the initiation of local experiments and the execution of official experimental programs), whereas other phases (the identification of successful, local "model experiments" and the initiative to expand "from point to surface") are centralized. Overarching policy targets are set centrally, but policy instruments are developed locally and then tested before they are applied throughout the country.

In practice, the experimental approach allows new solutions to be identified and adapted for continually emerging requirements during the permanent search process. This particular approach of step-by-step policy making is a critical prerequisite for China to have been able to carry out such comprehensive political and institutional changes since the 1980s—in spite of the many institutional, policy, and ideological forces of inertia—without resulting in the collapse of the party-state.

The Chinese approach to developing reform and innovative measures is unconventional because the testing of new action programs routinely occurs ahead of the national legislation. In the policy cycle of democratic constitutional states, a law or regulation generally kicks off policy implementation, and as a matter of principle administrative activity is bound by statute. However, the experimental state activity practiced in China is incompatible with the strict standards for the legality of administrative actions. Testing out reforms before enacting legislation is, however, key to understanding the ability to adapt and innovate that China's system of government has demonstrated in many policy areas since 1978—not only with respect to economic and technology policies but also in the expansion of its social-security systems. Policy experimentation as a key driver of policy innovation in the Chinese polity is the subject of Chapters 2–4.

## Development planning and long-term priority-setting

The Chinese leadership regards one of the greatest strengths of the PRC's political system as the opportunity to set long-term development priorities and to "concentrate power" (*jizhong liliang*) on large, national projects. In contrast, it is felt that one of the greatest weaknesses of democratic political systems is that they cannot pursue long-term development targets and programs due to the frequency of election campaigns and changes in government.

In fact, medium- and long-term development planning (*zhongchangqi fazhan guihua*) plays a key role in coordinating and directing state activity across various policy areas in the PRC. The most visible features of this development planning continue to be the national five-year plans in which the CCP and the government establish their priorities. In administrative practice, these national frameworks are inconsistently coordinated and therefore they are a rather contradictory package of thousands of specific action programs at various administrative levels. This web of programs continues to evolve before, during, and even after the official term of the national five-year plan, and hence over staggered, uncoordinated periods. Multi-year plans in present-day China do not consist of a single, standardized planning period for all policy areas and administrative levels; rather there is a variable and continuous cycle of coordination and evaluation. Since the year 2000, China's development plans have included complex lists of indicative targets (*yucexing zhibiao*, that is, targets that are desired by the government, but at the same time remain flexible) and strictly binding targets (*yueshuxing zhibiao*) that serve both as administrative benchmarks and sources of cadre assessments.

The functions, procedures, and instruments of development planning have diverged dramatically from the traditional socialist economic planning that China's Communists originally borrowed from the Soviet Union. Since the 1990s, China's development plans have been explicitly targeted at planning for and with national and international markets in order to open up new growth potentials for the Chinese economy and to redirect economic organization and social and environmental development over the long term. Development planning represents the political leadership's aspirations to perpetuate "macro-management" (*hongguan tiaokong*) through the CCP and the government.

Since the 1990s, the process of drawing up, evaluating, and adjusting development plans has included many more government departments and scientific advisers as well as corporate and social interests than in previous decades. Even foreign economists and environmental experts and organizations (such as the World Bank) are included in regular consultations to formulate and evaluate the Chinese government's multi-year programs.

China's medium- and long-term development planning is a state activity designed to go beyond individual policy areas. It focuses on the following core functions:

- *Strategic policy coordination* in the sense of prioritizing and coordinating state action programs in many policy areas from an anticipatory, long-term perspective;
- *Resource mobilization* in the sense of mobilizing and pooling limited resources with the aim of bringing about structural changes that are identified by the government as necessary to achieve sustainable and lasting economic, social, or environmental development;
- *Macro-management* in the sense of controlling the level of, and changes in, key economic variables, with the aim of achieving set priority development targets, preventing serious economic downturns, and mitigating the effects of external shocks that may be driven by global trading and financial systems.

However, the effectiveness of such development planning is disputed, even within China. Although there is much evidence of efficient planning implementation with respect to infrastructure development, the fight against poverty, and technology policy, as examples, there are also cases of planning failures, particularly with respect to efforts to introduce a new growth model that is not investment- and export-led. Due to this significant variation in the efficiency of state development planning in China, it is advisable to refrain from making general judgments about China's planning system (for instance, "China's state planning is effective and up-to-date" or it is "ineffective and obsolete") and instead to differentiate according to the different policy areas and the different outcomes over time. The particular approach to long-term priority-setting and planning that has taken shape since the 1990s is elaborated upon in Chapters 5 and 6.

## Adjusting priorities by means of target-setting in the cadre system

In most political systems, the overarching lists of targets and priorities set by governments and parliaments are framed in vague and selective terms (often only immediately after a new government has come to power) or for narrowly defined policy areas based on consensus (environment and technology policy, for instance). In everyday governance, however, the list of goals is usually implemented incrementally in national legislation, as the process tends to be diverted or obstructed by domestic compromises, constraints, or a constant stream of urgent new action requirements (crisis management).

Governments and the parliamentary majorities that support them very rarely define the quantitative performance targets against which government activity can subsequently be periodically measured. In fact, legislators usually avoid committing to quantitative performance targets in transparent and verifiable ways. Plausible reasons are given to justify this reasoning, arguing that governments are unable to control or influence many of the economic and social development variables in an open market economy. At the same time, there is a strong political interest for government performance not to be measurable using quantitative guidelines because this will leave the government open to political attack in the event of negative developments.

In terms of governance, this procedure means that vaguely defined goals, as laid down in the laws, are unable to provide effective guidance. A legitimate administration abides by the procedural rules that have been set, but these fail to give clear directions or to indicate priorities when it comes to achieving the most pressing goals. Many industrial and emerging countries have administrative systems that are organized according to the principles and practices of a corporate form of management ("New Public Management"), whereby quantitative performance targets play a crucial role within departmental bureaucracies to steer administrative actions. These performance targets generally relate only to narrow bureaucratic departmental guidelines (in line with their remit for fiscal or environmental administration, for example) and do not relate to key goals, such as providing all-round support for structural change in the economic system, maintaining social stability, or supporting investments in technology.

In contrast, governments and administrations in China attempt to channel the activities of leading cadres (*lingdao ganbu*) within party and state bodies based on a broad spectrum of quantitative targets (*ganbu zhibiao*). These goals are not restricted to the specific responsibilities of individual departmental administrations ("mission-based targets"); instead, they include overarching national and political objectives ("non-mission-based targets") that are determined by the high levels of the party and the government. This ranges from advancing the organization of the CCP and the fight against corruption, to innovation in the economy and administration, right up to maintaining social stability.

Targets and performance goals for leading cadres are designed to enforce national policy at the lower levels of government. Administrative actions in China are guided by people and party-based (cadre-based) responsibility and accountability. An assessment of administrative performance is primarily based on political specifications and interventions by means of the CCP cadre system rather than based on state statutory or bureaucratic rules.

The system of cadre evaluation based on political priorities and target-setting is the central mechanism for accomplishing the priorities of the national political leadership. These priorities are partially adjusted during the medium- and long-term and partially adjusted during the short term. Promotions, demotions, and dismissals of state-sector employees are formally dependent on regular (generally annual) assessments of cadre performance (*ganbu kaohe*). In addition, promotions and recommendations by high-ranking inner-party patrons are essential for a career as a leading party cadre. Since the 1990s, the CCP organization departments responsible for cadre administration have continuously adjusted the lists of goals and assessment processes in line with the priorities of the party leadership. However, quantitative performance benchmarks are susceptible to manipulation of both the results and the data reports (for instance, those containing economic, social, or environmental statistics), which can then be used to systematically distort or to gloss over the results.

It is evident that government and administrative activities in the PRC are driven by completely different mechanisms, criteria, incentives, and sanctions than those in other industrial and emerging economies. Policy priorities set for the long term or added at short notice and predetermined by the party leadership take precedence over legal and departmental criteria. The CCP's action priorities are implemented through the performance targets of the leading cadres. Compared with international benchmarks, this administrative management practice produces special opportunities for action and creates unique outcomes.

On the one hand, work priorities are clearly indicated and can be adjusted at short notice by means of the cadre performance targets. Since the 1990s, the national party leadership has been taking advantage of this by setting quantitative targets that require all government authorities to actively attract foreign investors in order to expand China's physical infrastructure, introduce new environmental standards in industry, and abolish special rural levies.

On the other hand, strict quantitative targets give rise to state interventions that do not consider the interests and rights of the concerned societal groups and individuals. For example, quantitative targets for birth control (strict upper limits for domestic birth rates) and in the fight against crime (arrest quotas and conviction rates) regularly lead to excessively violent legal enforcement and serious human rights violations. This is a legacy of the authoritarian planning and campaign regime that is incompatible with law-abiding actions subject to judicial review.

## Conclusion:
## Strengths and weaknesses of policy making in China

From a comparative perspective, the Chinese approach to policy making appears rather unorthodox: plans of action are frequently initiated as experiments—without appropriate legislation and regulation put in place beforehand—and are subsequently further developed during their implementation, adaptation, revision, and re-implementation. Consequently, policy making is in a constant state of flux, approved plans of action are subject to change, and corridors for action by the state can be modified. Thus, China's policy process is much more unpredictable than the legislative processes we encounter in constitutional democracies.

There is one basic pattern in the policy-making process that is enduring and essential to Communist Party rule: key political goals are defined centrally; the policy instruments, however, are regularly developed and tested locally, and they are only later applied on a national scale. A policy-making process driven by constant experiments and feedback in a country as multifaceted as China gives rise to a broad range of policy instruments and organizational patterns. This process allows government headquarters to resort to a host of alternative policy options in order to respond to changing conditions and needs for action. The interplay between centralized power and political hierarchy on the one hand, and local initiative, experiments, and deviation from official norms on the other, is a critical part of China's political system. This perpetual interplay is not rigid or ossified; instead, it is simultaneously both highly flexible and fragile.

In sum, in the Chinese political system decisions, policies, and plans cannot be regarded as a single, distinct, or formalized outcome but rather as a chain of statements, documents, and iterative rounds of implementation trials and adjustments. This feedback-driven process has contributed to an authoritarian flexibility, adaptability, and assertiveness. At the same time, however, it is the basis for a lack of administrative accountability and inadequate checks on political power.

Seen from a historical perspective, unusual for a one-party regime, China's policy process is supportive of an ability to learn lessons. However, such learning takes place within narrow constraints, remaining strictly instrumental and reversible, and defined by the parameters of one-party rule. It is by no means a capacity for learning that might lead to changes in the system of party leadership, or even to a new political order in the sense of constitutional learning. Major shortcomings in the Chinese system of government—a lack of checks and balances and a lack of legal security—although they may be somewhat compensated for, cannot be alleviated by an unexpectedly productive process of policy making.

# 1

# China's Adaptive Governance as a "Red Swan" in Comparative Politics*

Observers have been predicting the imminent demise of the Chinese political system since the death of Mao Zedong more than forty years ago. Such forecasts gained currency and urgency with the Tiananmen Uprising almost thirty years ago, when it did appear that the regime was tottering on the verge of collapse.[1] Although the People's Republic of China (PRC) managed to outlast both the Eastern European and Soviet variants of communism, predictions of its impending demise did not disappear. In the last several years we have seen a steady parade of books with titles such as *The Coming Collapse of China*, *China's Trapped Transition*, *China: Fragile Superpower*, or, more optimistically, *China's Democratic Future: How it Will Happen and Where it Will Lead*.[2]

---

\* This is a revised version of an analysis that was co-authored with Elizabeth J. Perry and originally published under the title "Embracing Uncertainty: Guerrilla Policy Style and Adaptive Governance in China," in Sebastian Heilmann and Elizabeth J. Perry, eds., *Mao's Invisible Hand: The Political Foundations of Adaptive Governance in China* (Cambridge, MA: Harvard University Asia Center, 2011), pp. 1–29, republished here with permission from Harvard University Asia Center and Elizabeth J. Perry.

The rapid economic growth of the post-Mao era generated expectations of a commensurate political transformation. It was widely believed that to sustain such economic progress in the face of mounting social unrest would require jettisoning an outmoded Communist Party in favor of liberal democratic institutions. With each passing decade, however, the characterization of the Chinese Communist system as exhausted and about to expire rings more hollow. Far from decrepit, the regime, having weathered Mao's death in 1976, the Tiananmen Uprising in 1989, Deng's death in 1997, and large-scale ethnic riots in 2008–9, seems over time to have become increasingly adept at managing tricky challenges, ranging from leadership succession and popular unrest to administrative reorganization, legal institutionalization, and even global economic integration. Contrary to expectations, the PRC regime has proven surprisingly capable of surviving serious unanticipated crises, from the Asian Financial Crisis of 1997–99 through the SARS epidemic of 2003 to the global economic downturn in 2008–9. These challenges would have sounded the death knell to many a less hardy regime.

To be sure, the phenomenon of rapid economic growth without political liberalization comes at a high price. The absence of civil liberties for ordinary Chinese citizens is perhaps the most obvious and egregious of these costs. But the lack of political restraints also contributes to numerous other serious problems in contemporary China, from cadre corruption to weak consumer protections and environmental degradation. It is certainly conceivable that some combination of these vulnerabilities sooner or later might lead to systemic change.

We has no predictions about how long Communist Party rule in China may persist. The vagaries of historical contingency render any such exercise of limited utility. Nor do we speculate on what an alternative future political system might be. Such prescriptions are better left to Chinese policy makers and political reformers. Instead, as social scientists we will take a fresh look at the reasons and, more precisely, the policy mechanisms[3] behind the staying power of Communist Party rule up to this point: How has the Communist Party in China achieved such rapid and profound organizational, economic, and social change over the last four decades? What political techniques and procedures has the authoritarian regime employed to manage the unsettling impact of the fastest sustained economic expansion in world history—a transformation that has been accompanied not only by greater wealth and global clout but also by political-ideological contestation, growing income and regional inequalities, and rampant popular protest?

## China as a "Red Swan"

Conventional political science models of regime types and regime transitions, constructed around dichotomous systemic categories stemming from the Cold War period ("from dictatorship to democracy," "from plan to market," and so forth) assign almost no adaptability to Communist party-states. Institutionally, Communist political systems are judged to be inflexible and incapable of continuous improvements in administrative organization, economic coordination, technological innovation, and international competitiveness.[4] However, this explanatory framework is not particularly useful to understand the complex dynamics of an innovative, competitive, and powerful China. In light of the country's unusual development record, it has become increasingly problematic to try to fit China into the shop-worn categories of Cold War regime types, even if we add new attributes to the original categories.[5]

China has not taken the road anticipated by Western social scientists and desired by the Western public. Marketization has not produced democratization. Although the intense ideological pressures, struggle campaigns, and organized dependency of the Mao era have given way to a more regularized administrative and technocratic, and in some fields even consultative, mode of governance, China has not made a transition in the direction of electoral, pluralist democracy.[6] It remains an authoritarian party-state, characterized by Leninist institutions. Yet China's Soviet-inspired formal institutions have been combined with distinctive governance methods shaped by the Chinese Communists' own revolutionary and post-revolutionary past, and during the post-Mao era complemented by selective borrowing from "advanced" foreign organizational and regulatory practices. It is these governance techniques, we argue, that account for the otherwise puzzling pattern of spectacular economic success under the aegis of an institutionally unreformed Communist system.

Though market coordination has gained a considerable foothold in China's economy, the state still controls the "commanding heights" in key industries (from infrastructure, to telecommunications, and to finance) through public property rights, pervasive administrative interference, and Communist Party supervision of senior managers. China's political economy thus diverges fundamentally from the Anglo-American marketization-cum-privatization paradigm. Moreover, Chinese capitalism guided by the Communist Party also deviates from core features of the Japanese and South Korean "developmental states," in which state enterprises, public property, and political control over senior executives played a very limited role and in which the liberalization of foreign trade was introduced at a much more mature state of development than that in China.[7]

As we will detail, many contemporary methods of governance crucial to sustaining Communist Party rule in a shifting and uncertain environment can be traced back to its formative revolutionary experiences. China's governance techniques are marked by a signature Maoist stamp that conceives of policy making as a process of ceaseless change, tension management, continual experimentation, and ad hoc adjustments. Such techniques reflect a mindset and method that contrast sharply with the more bureaucratic and legalistic approaches to policy making in many other major polities.

Due to its idiosyncratic developmental pathway during the past forty years, contemporary China presents an enigma to the field of Chinese politics, which did not predict the surprising resilience of the Communist system under reform and has yet to provide a convincing explanation for it. It also poses a major puzzle to the field of comparative politics, where prevailing theories of modernization, democratization, and regime transition offer little illumination for the case of post-Mao China.[8]

China stands as a "Red Swan" challenge to the social sciences.[9] The political resilience of the Communist party-state, in combination with the rapidly expanding, internationally competitive, and integrated economy, represents a significant deviant and unpredicted case, with a huge potential impact not only for the global distribution of political and economic power but also for global debates about models of development. Framed in terms of social-science methodology, China's exceptional development trajectory represents an "extreme value on an independent or dependent variable of general interest."[10] As such, it challenges conventional wisdom as well as conventional models of political change.

In relying upon concepts and theories derived from more familiar historical trajectories (e.g., the triumph of Western liberal democracies over the Communist regimes during the last decade of the twentieth century) to examine a political economy that emerged from very different experiences, analysts have tended to dismiss potentially powerful innovations as irregularities, deviations, externalities, or simply dead-ends. But what if China is in fact pursuing a unique path, and—due to its size, history, and surprising success—introducing important unconventional, non-Western techniques to the repertoire of governance in the twenty-first century? Whether the PRC's institutional and policy solutions during the past four decades turn out to be transitional remains uncertain, but in any case so far they have served the Communist Party's management of economic and social change remarkably effectively, and for that reason alone they deserve our serious attention as social scientists. If these techniques continue to persist, they will surely command both widespread public interest as well as concern.

We wish to sound a cautionary note against the common tendency among Western observers to trivialize the contributions of political leadership and policy initiatives in China by reducing Chinese politics to an unremitting interplay of repression and resistance. We seek not to celebrate the reform record of the PRC but to understand it. In the first instance, such an understanding requires an investigation of its origins. Identifying the roots of contemporary methods of governance is important to analyze both the genesis and the generalizability of the specific array of solutions, institutions, and processes at work in China today. These roots are firmly planted, we will argue, in the fertile soil of China's Maoist past. The usual practice of restricting the study of contemporary Chinese political economy to the reform period has had the unfortunate effect of obscuring key sources of its dynamism. Therefore, here we focus on the formative legacy of revolutionary (1927–49) and early PRC (1949–76) techniques of policy creation and implementation that we label, in shorthand, "Maoist."[11]

To be sure, there were important variations within that eventful half-century of "Maoist" political history. At certain moments, both before and after the political victory of 1949, Mao Zedong's distinctive mass mobilization methods were challenged by a more orthodox Soviet style of bureaucratic control. That

Mao's approach repeatedly won out in these conflicts did not redound to the benefit of the Chinese people. The more disastrous effects of the Great Leap Forward exemplify the negative consequences of an unbridled Maoist mode of development. Leadership and ideology proved decisive in determining whether the power of revolutionary governance would be put to destructive or productive ends.

## Prevailing institutional explanations

By highlighting the importance of the revolutionary experience for contemporary practices, we depart from mainstream explanations of regime resilience. As scholars have begun to seek an answer to the puzzling vigor of the Chinese Communist system, they have generally concentrated on the role of institutional factors. According to Andrew Nathan, the Chinese regime's surprising resilience can be attributed to its institutionalization of the elite succession process, its containment of factionalism, and its success in fostering a "high level of acceptance" through various "input institutions"—local elections, letters-and-visits departments, people's congresses, administrative litigation, mass media, and so forth.[12] David Shambaugh sees the Chinese Communist Party as "a reasonably strong and resilient institution" and suggests that "a range of intraparty reforms, as well as reforms affecting other sectors of the state, society and economy" have contributed to the party's ruling capacity.[13] Barry Naughton and Dali Yang point out that "China has retained a core element of central control: the *nomenklatura* system of personnel management" and they argue that "this nomenklatura personnel system is the most important institution reinforcing national unity."[14] As Andrew Walder has observed, although the composition of the political elite has changed dramatically since Mao's day (reflecting, among other things, the exponential growth in its educational credentials), its organizational structure has remained remarkably stable.¹⁵

Whereas the above scholars have looked to formal institutions as the basis of regime resilience, others have emphasized the role of informal institutions. Kellee Tsai, for example, credits the contribution of "informal adaptive institutions," such as the transitional practice of private entrepreneurs registering their enterprises as collectively owned and pressuring the central authorities to adopt new measures (e.g., admitting private entrepreneurs as members of the Chinese Communist Party) that have inadvertently served to strengthen state stability.¹⁶ Lily Tsai notes the value of local "informal institutions of accountability" (e.g., temple associations and lineages) for the provision of public goods in rural China. According to her analysis, these solidary groups (which include local officials as well as ordinary villagers) generate increased support for the government in the Chinese countryside.¹⁷

A complete answer to the contemporary resilience of the Chinese Communist system is of course complex, varying over time, under different leaders, and with respect to different challenges. We do not discount the role of either formal or informal institutions in this process. But why has only China benefited from such institutions? After all, a defining feature of Communist systems is their common institutional structure: a Leninist party, collectivized production, a command economy, a centralized propaganda apparatus, a coercive public security apparatus, and so forth. What, then, accounts for the glaring difference between China's contemporary experience and the experiences of other formerly Communist countries? Why has China proven to be more tolerant of informal institutions than many of its erstwhile counterparts elsewhere in the world? And why did China—in contrast to the Soviet Union and Eastern Europe—not only survive the 1989 crisis with its party-state system intact, but then in the space of a single generation manage to engineer an economic and social transformation of such stunning proportions?

We believe that much of the explanation for this singular achievement lies in its creative adaptation of key elements of China's revolutionary legacy. Unlike Russia and Eastern Europe, the imposition of a national Communist regime in China required nearly three decades of revolutionary mobilization and struggle. In the course of such a protracted process, which moved the Communists from the major cities to the rural hinterland and then on the Long March from the southern to the northern regions of the country, invaluable lessons in adapting to a wide range of different environmental conditions and challenges were learned. That these rich revolutionary experiences led directly to the dramatic successes, as well as to the devastating failures, of Chairman Mao's radical programs during the initial years of the PRC is well recognized.[18] The origins of the mass campaigns of the 1950s and 1960s, which brought improved literacy and basic health care but also the worst famine in the twentieth century and serious environmental damage,[19] are easily traceable to the revolutionary policies of the war-time base areas.

Less widely acknowledged, however, is the continued importance of revolutionary precedents in the techniques of rule and policy making employed by Mao's successors. Instead, reform-era China is usually characterized as a post-revolutionary society in which, with the notable exception of the Leninist party-state, Maoist ideas and initiatives have been thoroughly discredited and dismantled.[20] In the aftermath of the Cold War, with ideological conflict seemingly having been superseded by economic competition, at most the revolutionary past is generally regarded as a historical curiosity.

Despite the institutional commonalities among the Communist countries, from its revolutionary days to the present China has embarked on a singular path. Unlike the Soviet Union and its Eastern European satellites, Mao's China exhibited a trademark policy style that favored continual experimentation and transformation (or "permanent revolution") over regime consolidation. To be sure, the erratic and idiosyncratic course navigated by the Great Helmsman in his quixotic quest to continue the revolution after 1949 was terribly disruptive and destructive, but the underlying protean approach was also available for more productive uses. China's long revolution gave rise to a "guerrilla-style policy-making"[21] approach that was capable of generating an array of creative—proactive as well as evasive—tactics for managing sudden change and uncertainty. With new political leadership and new policy priorities, these familiar practices could lead to very different outcomes.

The formula in the wartime base areas to encourage decentralized initiatives within the framework of centralized political authority proved highly effective when redirected to the objectives of economic modernization on the part of Mao's successors. Unlike other countries saddled with the rigid top-down legacies of Leninist parties and command economies, some of whose leaders also proposed bold reforms, the Chinese polity has been singularly adept in adjusting to the demands of domestic economic reforms and global market competition. A major reason for this glaring difference is China's unusual receptivity to on-the-ground generation of new knowledge and new practices—a feature, we believe, that is derived in large measure from many of the same policy mechanisms that propelled the Chinese Communists' protracted revolutionary struggle.

From an institutional perspective, the Chinese polity fits the standard definition of an authoritarian Communist party-state. Yet China's vast and bureaucratically fragmented political system is animated by policy processes that allow for far greater bottom-up input than would be predicted from its formal structures. These processes are fundamental to the PRC's resilience and adaptability.

## Political resilience and adaptive governance

What do we mean by resilience and adaptability? Resilience can be defined as the capacity of a system to experience and absorb shocks and disturbances "while retaining essentially the same function, structure, feedbacks, and therefore identity."[22] Adaptability can be defined as "the capacity of actors in a system to further resilience" through their actions and interactions, either intentionally or unintentionally. The foundation of adaptability in this sense is response diversity: a variety of reactive, digestive, pre-emptive, and proactive operations and procedures that facilitate continual adjustment to and absorption of endogenous and exogenous challenges. In such agency-oriented definitions of resilience and adaptability, institutional mechanisms are only one, and sometimes only a minor, element. Behavioral and cognitive processes are critical; adaptiveness depends on a readiness to venture forth into unfamiliar environments to act, experiment, and learn from changing circumstances.

Historical institutionalist Douglass North places adaptive capacity at the center of his explanation of developmental success. He notes that both in political and economic systems, adaptive capacity is facilitated by formal and informal institutions and norms that enable actors in the system to try out various options. A broad spectrum of plausible alternative solutions is needed to escape developmental blockages, tackle emerging challenges, and grasp new opportunities.[23] Nassim Taleb provides a new twist to the discussion on adaptive governance by proposing that innovative strength varies not according to systemic features (market versus plan, democracy versus authoritarianism) but by the opportunities afforded for "maximum tinkering." The prerequisite to such tinkering in any political economy is an openness to random discoveries of novel solutions on the part of its institutions, processes, and actors. Intensive tinkering can take place in non-democratic systems as long as the rulers are willing to encourage a decentralized generation of new knowledge.[24] In this chapter and the following chapters, I seek to show why China has provided a political setting conducive to the kind of broad-based tinkering that development theorists such as Dani Rodrik identify as essential for discovering policy alternatives that, if built into specific domestic conditions and adapted to a changing global environment, have the potential to propel economic and social development.[25]

## The potential of retrospective governance studies

To explain the adaptive capacity of the Chinese polity, we must look to the historical experiences and techniques of Communist Party rule under Mao Zedong, and their retention, reinvention, and renovation under Mao's successors.

The approach adopted here bears some similarity to that of historical institutionalism inasmuch as we monitor continuities and changes in political trajectories over time. But in important ways we also depart from that approach. Rather than trace the "path-dependent" evolution of an institution as it unfolds seamlessly from some previous "critical juncture,"[26] we begin our analyses with prominent features of China's contemporary political scene and then work backwards in search of their (often tortuous) historical origins.

A major advantage of retrospective governance studies is their open research design. When new actors, interests, or ideologies enter the scene, the approach easily accommodates such additions—in contrast to the more deterministic, prestructured models of institutional political economy. Moreover, our approach promises to avoid the teleological tendency so pervasive in social-science debates about China's transformation (ever on the outlook for signs of a "real" market economy or a "real" democracy) by leaving open the future possibility of unorthodox mechanisms, overlooked actors, unexpected interactions, and random interventions. Rather than biased expectations in light of familiar Western models, we adopt an inductive outlook that views modern and contemporary Chinese history as an uncertain process of discovery and not as a trajectory pre-ordained by past experiences (or present-day social-science paradigms).

In adopting this open-ended approach, one discovers in contemporary China a complex amalgam of governance mechanisms that combine Maoist, post-Maoist, and borrowed foreign elements. Moving from "socialist construction" of the Mao era to "reform and opening" of the post-Mao era, China has not simply jettisoned its revolutionary past as it "transits" toward a democratic future. Rather, a succession of post-Mao leaders have managed to fashion a surprisingly adaptive pattern of authoritarian rule that so far has been capable of withstanding challenges, including grievous and growing social and spatial inequalities, which surely would have undone less robust or flexible regimes. We obviously do not claim that its revolutionary origins tell us everything we need or want to know about the Chinese regime's resilience. But we do believe that this particular focus provides an important complement—and in some cases corrective—to prevailing approaches.

## Institutional plasticity and policy-style continuity

Institutional and policy instability were prominent features of Chinese politics throughout the last century. Except for a small number of crucial core institutions, such as the Communist Party's hierarchical cadre system that Naughton and Yang rightly identify as a pillar of the Chinese polity, few organizational arrangements functioned continuously over the entire history of the PRC.[27] Party, government, and legal institutions have been subject to frequent and sometimes wild shake-ups and reorganizations.[28] Policy volatility was extreme by any comparative standard until at least 1992 when China's leadership settled on the formula of a "socialist market economy."

If institutions and policies were so unstable under Communist rule, where then do we look for continuities and guiding principles? How have Chinese policy makers responded when facing challenges or initiating programs that could not be handled by bureaucratic "autopilot" procedures? The common ground that connects the chapters in this volume, beyond the historical legacy argument, is a focus on policy style—or the government's guiding methodology for tackling shifting policy tasks.[29] An important concern in public administration theory, the concept of "policy style," opens a revealing window on the issue of continuity and change in contemporary China. Although PRC institutions and policies have been subject to frequent shifts over time, major components of the Communist Party's policy style have remained surprisingly stable, even across the watershed years of the Mao and post-Mao eras.

In adopting a policy-style perspective, we are not simply imposing yet another abstract Western concept on China. The term "work-style" (*zuofeng*) permeates Chinese administrative practice. Pointing to durable policy-making routines and administrative habits that are neither formalized nor reflected upon, yet encompass a set of generally accepted problem-solving techniques, *zuofeng* is very similar to the concept of "policy style" in public administration studies.[30] Here we have a rare case where technical terms in Western social-science theory and the discourse of Chinese administrative practices actually intersect.

Once a mainstay of scholarship on Chinese politics, policy studies have been overshadowed in recent years by a fascination with "civil society," "social movements," "rights consciousness," and other phenomena often associated with the rise of a market economy. The research accessibility of such phenomena, when contrasted to the opaqueness of the Chinese political elite, has understandably contributed to a shift in scholarly priorities. The decline of policy studies is unfortunate, however, because in China's state-heavy political economy, administrative coordination and state intervention remain at least as decisive as market exchanges. The policy process holds special importance to explain not only political interactions and rule-making but also Chinese economic markets and social trends that are not independent of state interference. The policy process is a key mechanism for connecting (both empirically and analytically) formal hierarchies, informal networks, market transactions, and social interactions.

## Guerrilla policy style

The exceptional institutional and policy instability of PRC history is usually attributed to the erratic and divisive behavior of the paramount leaders.[31] Such behavior, we propose, reflects a deeper policy style whose basic components stem in large measure from the formative experiences of guerrilla warfare and revolutionary mobilization. In the course of surviving and surmounting seemingly impossible odds, Mao and his colleagues came to appreciate the advantages of agility over stability.

The guerrilla policy style of the PRC leadership includes a shared understanding[32] about political agency and a distinctive methodology of policy generation that enabled success in the unpredictable military-combat settings of revolutionary times and that bequeathed a dynamic means of navigating the treacherous rapids of transformative governance during both the Mao era ("socialist construction," "permanent revolution") and the post-Mao era (the "four modernizations," "reform and opening," "socialist market economy," "joining the world" [world economy/World Trade Organization] [*rushi*]). Core features of what we call guerrilla policy style continue to shape present-day policy making and have contributed to the flexibility, and volatility, of Communist Party rule.

The proven ability of mobile guerrilla warfare to reap unexpected gains in a highly uncertain and threatening environment left an indelible imprint on Chinese policy makers who took part in the revolution (including the cohorts of Mao, Deng, and Hu Yaobang, who dominated Chinese politics until at least the early 1990s). The Maoist guerrilla approach to problem-solving stemmed from almost thirty years of incessant political and military struggles that the Communists fought from a militarily inferior—and at times seemingly hopeless—position. It was marked by secrecy, versatility, speed, and surprise. Over the course of the revolution, continuous improvisation became a defining feature of Chinese Communist tactics. Moreover, Mao made abundantly clear that war and politics were to be played according to the same rules. As he stated in 1959: "Military affairs are politics under special conditions. They are a continuation of politics. Politics are also a type of war."[33]

The legacies of the guerrilla policy style in China have attracted scant attention from Western scholars.[34] Yet core features of contemporary Chinese policy making are also defining characteristics of Chinese guerrilla warfare.[35] Beyond the well-known combination of centralized leadership and intensive popular mobilization (the "mass line"), the guerrilla mode of political leadership and policy making revolves around the following shared understandings:

- the political world and its power constellations are subject to eternal flux and ceaseless change that cannot be effectively halted or channelled by political-legal institution-building;
- policy making should be kept fluid by trying to avoid binding constraints (e.g., personal pre-commitments or legal-contractual obligations) so as to retain room for political initiative and policy revision;
- policy making is a process of continual improvisation and adjustment that "shapes itself in the making";[36]
- recurrent standard operating procedures that can be discerned by enemy forces should be avoided;
- advice derived from theory and abstract models is not to be trusted; instead, new methods of action are derived from pilot efforts and practical experience in concrete settings;
- strategic decisions are the preserve of the top leadership; yet operationalization and implementation require substantial latitude for local initiative and independence;
- tensions among political forces and within society should be actively manipulated to take full advantage of political opportunities;[37]
- unexpected opportunities should be ruthlessly exploited to weaken or eliminate political enemies; alliances should be forged or broken as conditions dictate;
- risks should be minimized by launching new campaigns and staging direct confrontations only under the most favorable environments.

The policy style that emerges from these stratagems is fundamentally dictatorial, opportunistic, and merciless. Unchecked by institutions of accountability, guerrilla leaders pursue their objectives with little concern for the interests of those who stand in their way.

But with regard to adaptive capacity, the approach allows for maximum creativity since policy makers are required to:

- test and constantly push the limits of the status quo and seize every possible opportunity to change the situation to their advantage;
- keep the core strategic objectives firmly in mind, yet be as agile and pragmatic as possible in choosing tactical and operational means;
- tinker with a full range of available operational tactics and organizational approaches, be they traditional, non-traditional, or even foreign;
- search for and exploit random opportunities and discoveries that promise to promote political power and strategic goals.

The policy style shaped by these basic features can be characterized as a change-oriented "push-and-seize" style that contrasts with the stability-oriented "anticipate-and-regulate" norm of modern constitutional governments and rule-of-law polities (which typically support a predictable environment in which political leaders are held accountable for their actions). It shares, however, certain affinities with the "business as warfare" theme that permeates recent writings on market competition by today's captains of global capitalism.[38]

In the guerrilla policy style, political accountability is sacrificed for the goal of leadership flexibility, expressed in the Maoist formula of "politics in command" (*zhengzhi guashuai*). In theory, lower-level leaders are subject to supervision by their Communist Party superiors. However, since oversight is sketchy and episodic, local policy makers are not credibly constrained. In post-Mao local government we find widespread evidence at the grassroots levels of entrepreneurial, experimentalist, opportunistic, and ruthless policy makers who simultaneously advance their careers as well as their material interests. In so doing, they embody classic features, including the downsides and risks, of the guerrilla policy style. The guerrilla fighter is a populist, not a democrat.

Mao's conversion of guerrilla warfare into a mode of political governance was driven by Machiavellian calculations. As Michel Oksenberg observes, "Mao's pattern of rule… [was an]… effort to control… the process of policy making by determining communication channels, personnel appointments and military deployment… [to] avoid becoming the captive of the administrative apparatus. … Mao had to use informal means (such as the use of personal ties) or counter-institutions (such as campaigns) in order to make the formal mechanisms which he only partially created responsive to his will."[39]

The guerrilla policy style stands in stark contrast to democratic norms of political accountability, legal consistency, and procedural stability. It also exists in clear tension with the formal bureaucratic norms that are an important part of the Soviet Communist tradition that during the Mao era competed with Mao's free-wheeling style.[40] Although bureaucracy has gained a more secure status in post-Mao China, comprehensive rounds of "rectification" and restructuring remain a conspicuous feature of Chinese politics.[41] Forceful top-down policy initiatives, and interventions and campaigns that disrupt bureaucratic routines and shake up bureaucratic organizations, continue to occur.

In addition to its negative impact on political accountability and procedural predictability, the guerrilla policy style generates difficulties for central-local interactions and interregional distribution. To maximize flexibility and reduce the burden (and accountability) of the central leadership, the division of labor among different levels of command is not clarified and it is under-institutionalized. In effect, localities are generally left to fend for themselves, receiving only erratic and episodic central support. Although this may work to boost local policy creativity and operational autonomy, the lack of centrally coordinated redistribution also generates stark interregional disparities and underequipped "local government[s] on a shoestring."[42]

Guerrilla policy making consists of malleable stratagems that are employed in multiple variations and applications in response to shifting constellations of political forces. These stratagems only work if they are used in ways as to surprise one's competitors. Guerrilla-style policy making calls for circumventing existing rules, overcoming constraints, and maximizing one's own maneuverability, while minimizing or eliminating the influence of one's opponents on the course of events.

Moving back beyond Communist Party history to probe more deeply into the Chinese past, one may observe that basic features of the guerrilla policy style are congruent with a long and influential line of traditional thought that stressed fluid, dialectical, and tactical approaches to managing ubiquitous tensions and contradictions.[43] The ancient *Book of Changes* presents an image of the world subject to continuous flux and driven by ceaseless interactions among opposing elements. The military prescriptions in Sun Zi's *Art of War* reflect a similar view: "All warfare is based on deception. Hence when able to attack, we must seem unable; when using our forces, we must seem inactive; when we are near, we must make the enemy believe we are far away; when we are far away, we must make him believe we are near." What Iain Johnston has labeled the dominant "*parabellum* paradigm" of Chinese strategic culture assumes the ubiquity of conflict and the attendant advantages of "absolute flexibility" in the application of violence.[44] Perhaps due in part to these powerful cultural and intellectual legacies, Chinese leaders seem inclined to adopt a strategic outlook that differs markedly from that of many Western democratic politicians.

## Conclusion

Whether the particular Maoist legacy under consideration is presented in more negative or more positive terms, we agree on the value of investigating its continuing impact on contemporary practices. A range of governing techniques—political-administrative, legal, social, and economic—owe their origins to the Maoist past (see Table 1.1).

Table 1.1 Distinctive Contemporary Governance Techniques That Originated During the Revolutionary and Mao Eras (1927–76)

| Political-Administrative | Legal | Social | Economic |
|---|---|---|---|
| institutional plasticity; strong informal networks; weak bureaucratic rules | law and adjudication as malleable instruments to advance party policies | grassroots practices and on-site investigations as inputs into national policy making | policy objectives set by the Party Center; policy instruments developed by the localities |
| shifting balance in central-local policy initiatives; experiment-based policy generation | priority of party decrees over law in policy implementation | managed campaigns for policy implementation | policy implementation according to local circumstances |
| weakly institutionalized central-local interactions; prohibitions against collective actions by local governments | emphasis on mediation, informality, and morality in dispute resolution | controlled social polarization; careful targeting and staging of political repression | generating economic policy change from experimental sites |
| extensive propaganda work; active construction of public opinion | judicial populism vs. judicial professionalism | discretionary approaches for dealing with social groups and organizations | achieving "hard targets" (e.g., the GDP growth rate) through cadre-system incentives |
| political campaigns; circumvention of bureaucratic inertia through populist appeals | experimental regulation and legislation | guiding and educating society through model experiences | production and investment campaigns as short-term fixes to economic bottlenecks |

Source: Selected findings in Heilmann and Perry, eds., *Mao's Invisible Hand: The Political Foundations of Adaptive Governance in China.*

Despite these authors' emphases on the continued salience of Maoist influences, no one claims that the guerrilla policy style explains everything or that it remains unchanged. No one denies that this policy style has had a dreadful impact on political accountability and the legal system. And no one asserts that this policy style will save the Communist Party from political and social pressures that may result in a future systemic transformation. Two core components of the guerrilla policy style—ideological control and mass mobilization—have been substantially diluted during the reform era. Under Mao, as Chung observes, centralized ideological control was so effective at times that "even in the middle of organizational breakdown and administrative disruption, the self-policing Maoist norms operated effectively to ensure mechanical conformity and to detect even slight deviations at the local level."[45] That reservoir of popular enthusiasm, or ideological conformism, facilitated the regime's reliance on mass campaigns—in place of bureaucratic methods—during the Great Leap Forward and the Cultural Revolution. Ideological indoctrination and mass upheaval were regarded by post-Mao leaders as among the most problematic elements of the Maoist legacy, responsible for preserving Communist Party rule at the expense of economic modernization. It was this conclusion that prompted Deng Xiaoping to declare an end to mass campaigns. However, although ideologically-inspired mass mobilization today no longer plays the same central role in routine policy making and administration as it did in the past, the ambitious propaganda effort to shape and manipulate public opinion has never ceased, even if, as Thornton suggests, the goal has changed from mobilizing the masses for political action and personal sacrifice to promoting passive compliance and commercial consumerism.[46]

The guerrilla policy style competes today (as it did intermittently even under Mao) with more conventional approaches:

bureaucratic and law-based policy making and implementation. "Regularizing" governance has become a core theme of the Chinese leadership since the 1980s. China's bureaucratic and legal systems have been extended and modernized to a degree well beyond anything envisaged during the Mao era. But inherited and adapted elements of guerrilla policy still play a vital role in dealing with crucial policy tasks, from mobilization in times of perceived crisis to managing central-local interactions to facilitating economic policy innovation and reorganizing public health care. Designed to handle a changing, complex, and unpredictable environment in a pro-active manner, the guerrilla policy approach—for better or for worse—remains politically potent.

What emerges from studying the legacies of revolutionary and Mao-era policy styles in contemporary Chinese governance is not a ready-made "Chinese model" defined by replicable institutional variables. Instead, we find a fluid, context-, situation-, and agency-based *modus operandi*: a method of policy generation and implementation based on an acceptance of pervasive uncertainty, a readiness to experiment and learn (even from enemies and foreigners), an agility to grasp unforeseen opportunities, a single-mindedness in pursuing strategic goals, a willingness to ignore ugly side-effects, and a ruthlessness to eradicate unfriendly opposition.

Because the guerrilla approach to policy generation and implementation is experimental and non-repetitive, it is not best conceptualized as an "informal institution."[47] Whether formal or informal, institutions are designed to contain uncertainty and stabilize actors' expectations about future interactions by specifying certain norms and rules. In contrast, the rationale behind guerrilla policy making is to embrace uncertainty in order to benefit from it. The guerrilla policy approach is driven by a determination to overcome or eliminate existing constraints rather than to work within them.

The guerrilla policy style pursues a decidedly change- and agency-oriented agenda. It constitutes a type of transformative governance geared to overcoming the status quo. Unlike polities that consider themselves to be advanced or mature systems and that therefore cling to an implicitly protective type of governance, the guerrilla policy style is not directed to systemic and institutional consolidation. Table 1.2 juxtaposes as ideal types the transformative and protective policy styles.

Table 1.2 Transformative versus Protective Policy Styles and Adaptive Capacity

|  | Transformative (Guerrilla) Policy Style | Protective Policy Style |
|---|---|---|
| overriding policy goal | overcoming the status quo | defending/incrementally improving the status quo |
| institutional structure | fluid institutional arrangements | fixed institutional arrangements |
|  | shifting the division of labor among different administrative levels | constitutionally defined division of labor among different administrative levels |
| policy process | agency-oriented ("politics in command"; "push and seize") | structure-oriented (rigid institutional checks; "anticipate and regulate") |
|  | policy makers with considerable discretionary powers | policy makers bound to formal rules |
|  | experimental | legalistic |
|  | active management of uncertainty through policy experimentation | attempt to contain uncertainty through extensive legal provisions |
|  | maximum exposure to random discoveries of novel policy solutions | minimal exposure to random discoveries of novel policy solutions |
| adaptive capacity | policy-driven (ad hoc, periodically volatile) | law-based (pre-stabilized), market-driven |
|  | possibility of swift, "big leap" adaptation and innovation | incremental, "small step" adjustments |
| political accountability | cast aside to facilitate maximum policy flexibility | emphasized as the foundation of rule of law |

Trump populists

To reiterate, the Chinese guerrilla policy style is not a generic feature of Communist countries. In contrast to the PRC, after their Stalinist phases, the socialist states of the Soviet Union and Eastern Europe attempted to defend, and improve only incrementally, the status quo. They made every effort to solidify their rule, not to repeatedly reinvent it. The former is a uniquely Maoist imperative. Since the guerrilla policy style rests on fluid institutional arrangements, the adaptation of party-state institutions to new economic priorities proved much less problematic in China than it was in the former Soviet and Eastern European Communist party-states, despite a series of reform efforts from Khrushchev through Gorbachev.[48]

These important differences between the PRC and the other Communist systems suggest that the preoccupation with institutional analysis and regime typologies characteristic of many Western studies of the Chinese political economy may be misplaced. Chinese Communist Party rule has proven to be adaptive not because of its institutional foundations (which were as clumsy and fragmented as those in the former Communist party-states of Eastern Europe) but because of a pervasive policy style that encourages diverse and flexible responses to fundamentally redefined development priorities and to large-scale changes in the domestic and global environments.

The difficulties in trying to force China's development experience into the procrustean bed of conventional institutional categories are not accidental. The dynamics and capacities of China's political system are driven by particular patterns that are ill-suited to such a taxonomic exercise. A methodological alternative is to expand research on the deviant (unconventional or even unique) and varying policy mechanisms that have propelled change in important sectors of China's government, economy, society, and international relations. More generally, the power of policy creativity deserves greater emphasis in discussions on how to facilitate change in developing, emerging, and even advanced political economies.[49]

A serious analysis of China's transformative style of governance not only helps to explain the peculiarities of the Chinese case (by going beyond static and linear institutionalist, path-dependency perspectives). It also poses a potential challenge to current more-developed political economies struggling to keep up with the accelerated pace of change in the twenty-first century, while they remain saddled with a strong institutional status-quo bias[50] and weak policy corrective mechanisms. The adaptive capacity of China's non-democratic political system offers a radical alternative to the bland governance models favored by many Western social scientists who seem to take for granted the political stability and economic superiority of the capitalist democracies. To increase policy agility and strengthen the resilience of democratic rule in the twenty-first century may require an intellectual effort that questions twentieth-century assumptions about Western systemic superiority by taking a sober look at the foundations of innovative capacity displayed by non-democratic challengers such as China.

Again, the Chinese guerrilla policy style has fundamental flaws: lack of political accountability, undue administrative discretion, and distributive deficiencies that contribute to severe regional and social tensions. The most serious long-term shortcoming, beyond its fundamentally undemocratic nature, may lie in the single-minded pursuit of strategic policy goals (e.g., economic growth or demographic controls) with little regard for the deleterious side-effects that often emerge over time (e.g., environmental destruction or gender imbalances). As demands from Chinese society for political accountability, legal entitlements, a social safety net, and environmental protection grow, public tolerance for guerrilla-style policy making may well decline. The difficult test for China's adaptive capacity will be some massive crisis in which not only economic and social learning but also political-institutional responsiveness and popular support for the government are stretched to the limit. As Andrew Nathan warns in a recent essay on "authoritarian impermanence":

> What keeps such crises of government from becoming crises of the regime are cultures of open dissent, the robust rule of law, and the institutional capacity to change leaders in response to public discontent without changing the system.... Without them, the authoritarian regime must perform constantly like a team of acrobats on a high wire, staving off all crises while keeping its act flawlessly together. Today... the regime is managing to do that. But it cannot afford to slip.[51]

Again, we make no predictions about the future of China's high-wire performance. Taking a page out of the Chinese policy makers' playbook, we too may be well advised to "embrace uncertainty." But, however long before the curtain closes on China's virtuoso acrobatic act, we do insist that to date it has been sufficiently sure-footed to merit a more complete explanation of its origins.

# 2
# From Local Experiments to National Policy: The Origins of China's Distinctive Policy Process*

To explain the capability of China's party-state to generate institutional and policy innovations for economic reform and to adapt to a rapidly changing economic environment, many studies point to the crucial role of decentralized experimentation.[1] A policy process in which central policy makers encourage local officials to try out new ways of problem-solving and then feed the local experiences back into national policy formulation has been a pervasive feature of China's economic transformation. It has decisively shaped policy making in areas ranging from rural decollectivization, foreign economic opening, and promotion of private business to state-sector restructuring and stock market regulation. In some intensely disputed policy areas, such as state-sector bankruptcy, experimental programs with varying priorities continued for more than twenty years before a finalized national law was eventually passed. Over and over, those national policy makers who attempted to change the way the economy was run instrumentalized the results from experimental

---

\*  This is a revised version of an analysis that was originally published under the title "From Local Experiments to National Policy: The Origins of China's Distinctive Policy Process," in *The China Journal*, No. 59 (January 2008), pp. 1–30, republished here with permission from *The China Journal*.

programs to take initiatives and to overcome opposition from rival policy makers who tried to defend the old rules of the game.

The existence of a sophisticated indigenous methodology of "proceeding from point to surface" in making policies suggests an entrenched legitimacy of decentralized experimentation that far exceeds the sporadic experiments that were carried out in other authoritarian polities or in the paradigmatic party-state of the Soviet Union. The Chinese point-to-surface approach entails a policy process that is initiated from individual "experimental points" and is driven by local initiative with the formal or informal backing of higher-level policy makers. If judged to be conducive to current priorities by party and government leaders, the "model experiences" (*dianxing jingyan*) that are extracted from the initial experiments are then spread through extensive media coverage, high-profile conferences, intervisitation programs, and appeals for emulation to other regions. This expansion process requires progressive policy refinement and produces a search for generalizable policy solutions. If they gain broad acceptance among top policy makers, the tried-and-tested novel approaches emerging from this process are integrated, after further revisions, into national policies. Thus, the point-to-surface technique allows room for local officials to develop models on their own, while ultimate control over confirming, revising, terminating, and spreading model experiments rests with the top-level decision-makers. Importantly, the mode of experimentation practiced in the People's Republic of China (PRC) focuses on finding innovative policy instruments, and it not designed to define the policy objectives that remain the prerogative of the party leadership.[2]

Although it is rarely disputed that experimentation constitutes a crucial mechanism for institutional and policy innovation, the origins of the experimental policy process observed in China remain unexplained. Research undertaken thus far does not explain how the Chinese pattern of policy experimentation took shape and became an entrenched approach to generate new policy options. To make decentralized experimentation work in an authoritarian party-state, there must be a special mechanism that legitimizes local initiative while leaving hierarchical control intact. As a consequence, the patterns of central-local interactions differ from explanatory models that are derived from the context of the advanced democratic polities, such as the "laboratories of federalism" or "decentralization."

The methods and terminology used in experimental programs in China are comparatively so idiosyncratic and unconventional that an exploration of their political origins may provide important clues as to why, and under what conditions, local experimentation came to be accepted and legitimized as a general method of leadership and policy making in China. The core elements of experimentation, such as "experimental points" or "proceeding from point to surface," may serve as identifiers in our search for the origins of China's experiment-based policy process.

In the first section of this chapter, I elaborate on the Chinese Communists' experience in experimentation to develop transformative policies during their revolutionary struggle. Second, I turn to the non-Communist intellectual context and the pioneering policy-experimentation practice in the Republic of China. In the third section, I explain core features of China's contemporary policy process based on the revolution-era repertoire that policy makers can draw upon in their search for new policy instruments to facilitate rapid economic modernization.

## Revolutionary antecedents of experiment-based policy making

The mode of policy experimentation of the Chinese Communist Party (CCP) attests to the persisting importance of formative historical experiences to China's contemporary policy process. The methodology and terminology of policy experimentation that continue to be used by present-day policy makers (albeit often unconscious of their historical roots)[3] date from the revolutionary experience of the CCP and are not inventions of reform-era leaders who after 1978 made energetic pleas for "vigorous" (Deng Xiaoping) or more "cautious" (Chen Yun) experimentation.

## Experiments with land reform (1928–43)

An elaborate mode of local policy experimentation under central guidance was developed in the context of experiments with land reform in the Communist base areas before the founding of the PRC in 1949. The experiments with alternative approaches to land reform that were undertaken by Mao Zedong in Jinggangshan and Deng Zihui in Minxi in 1928 constituted a pioneering experience for later Communist land policy. Recent research by Chinese historians and recollections by party cadres involved in early land reform work suggest that Deng Zihui, not Mao, may have been the first to initiate the point-to-surface type of controlled experimentation based on the establishment of "model villages," dissemination of "model experiences," and progressive refinement of policies in the course of expansion.[4] In Minxi area Deng Zihui made serious efforts to develop novel policies from the bottom up by consulting with the local populace and absorbing their suggestions on practical measures, while reserving decisions on policy acceptability and expansion for party bodies. By 1930, the Minxi experiences were already widely known in Communist publications and they served as an important reference for land policies applied in the Jiangxi Soviet from 1931 to 1934. Moreover, the Minxi methods were later summarized in an official report that circulated in Yan'an beginning in February 1943, at a time when the point-to-surface methodology was intensively discussed and eventually elevated to an official leadership technique of the Communist Party.[5] Though Deng Zihui apparently did not coin the point-to-surface terminology, his consistent efforts for bottom-up experimentation, gradual model dissemination, and constant revision of policy instruments certainly influenced intra-party debates on policy-making approaches and more directly influenced the views of Mao.

During the Communist Party's Jiangxi Soviet period (1931–34), implementation of agrarian policies varied considerably from place to place. The party leadership, internally divided and insecure about concrete ways to make revolution in the countryside, came to accept the stark variations in policy implementation, encouraging party organs at each level to experiment with unconventional measures and to produce diverse models for emulation by other localities. On this basis, Mao Zedong drafted detailed reports on "model Soviet governments" that contained long sections on organizational techniques and their applicability to other locations. The "Xingguo Model" (*mofan xingguo*), describing a county in the Jiangxi Soviet area that was praised by Mao in 1934 for its pioneering achievements in organizational, educational, and land reform work, became a reference for many other experimental sites in the late 1930s and 1940s. Yet the proliferation of emulation campaigns undertaken in the Jiangxi Soviet did not result in systematic and uniform policy making. There were myriads of model experiments, but the expansion of novel local approaches to larger areas remained patchy and piecemeal. In spite of these constraints, Mao refined an organizational technique during his Jiangxi years that would later become a principal revolutionary method: dispatching work teams consisting of "strong cadres" to selected sites so as to test and demonstrate methods of land reform in one small spot; simultaneously training party activists and potential new cadres in this spot; bringing the "masses" from other places to the model demonstration site; sending cadres and activists from the model spot to adjacent areas, thereby spreading those practices that had been identified by top leaders as conducive to current party policies. One of Mao's collaborators during these early land reform endeavors retrospectively depicted this technique as "experimental point" work.[6] Yet the experimentalist terminology that would emerge in the 1940s was not yet used in the Jiangxi Soviet.

After the central leaders of the Communist Party established their headquarters in Yan'an, and with the intensification of the Japanese military campaigns, the many scattered guerrilla bases behind Japanese lines (mainly in North China) became centers of the Communist Party–led peasant movement and sites of a large variety of mass mobilization and land reform experiments. One major center of revolutionary experimentation, where numerous Chinese Communist leaders who would later become top reform-era policy makers were involved, was the Taihang Base Area (at the border of Shanxi and Henan provinces).

This base area operated under constant military threats and political uncertainties inflicted by Japanese attacks, an erratic provincial warlord (Yan Xishan), and Kuomintang (KMT) forces. In autumn 1939, taking the 1934 Xingguo Model as a reference, two "experimental counties" (*shiyanxian*), reporting directly to the base area party committee, were expected to provide a "model demonstration" (*dianxing shifan*) to guide the entire area to introduce new methods of mass mobilization and recruitment of party activists. The experimental sites were required to test a new "bottom-up work-style" based on consultation with the populace. "Contests on experimental work" were held among different party branches. Less successful branches were required to visit and learn from the successful branches. Local party activists were expected to become "labor heroes in creating experiments." To achieve the objectives of strengthening the Communist Party's local mass base, the envisaged experimental period of six months was subdivided into two-month phases, each with clearly stated work objectives to be accomplished according to schedule.[7] Because Deng Xiaoping was a prominent leader in this base area, it is very likely that the opportunistic but active experimentation in Taihang may have exerted considerable influence on his approach to policy making during later stages of his political career.[8]

## Elevating experimentation to a method of political leadership (1943–53)

During the 1942–43 Rectification Movement, which resulted in major restatements of revolutionary leadership and strategy, decentralized policy experimentation was confirmed as a standard method of "creating model experiments" and "proceeding from point to surface." An authoritative, yet still vague, guideline for this method was published under the name of Mao in June 1943. In a general statement on "methods of leadership," Mao stressed that for any task party cadres must "make a breakthrough at some single point, gain experience, and use this experience for guiding other units."[9] In successive statements on this leadership method, Mao made it clear that it was not meant to justify unfettered trial and error and it had to be geared to the creation of "model experiments" that demonstrated effective and novel ways to realize the policy objectives established by the party leadership.[10] In line with his practice-based epistemology, Mao held that policy implementation, not policy debate, provided the crucial device for learning and innovation.[11] In a 1948 directive to the party, he went so far as to proclaim that the "model experiences" produced by several Communist-controlled base areas were "much closer to reality and richer than the decisions and directives issued by our leadership organs" and they should serve as an antidote against tendencies toward "commandism" within the party.[12]

That designing methods of effective implementation was largely left to local initiative was one of the practical lessons derived from the Communists' protracted land reform efforts. Broad discretionary powers were given to basic-level party organs to experiment with diverse measures of rural transformation, ranging from brutally repressive to more conciliatory approaches. Even on the eve of the Civil War victory, Mao stressed that land reform could not be achieved in a mere few months or by one-size-fits-all measures. Instead, it had to be based on a carefully designed point-to-surface approach; first by obtaining experience on the ground in a small number of selected sites and then by spreading the experience in a succession of increasingly broader and stronger wave-like movements.[13] During this time, as Vivienne Shue writes, the point-to-surface method emerged as "one of the standard devices of the Party and the government for implementing important rural policies" in a "consciously experimental" but carefully controlled manner.[14]

The pursuit of an experiment-based policy approach resulted from necessity. The CCP simply did not have a sufficient number of well-trained rural cadres to dispatch to the hundreds of thousands of villages. Furthermore, because the revolutionary process was driven from scattered base areas, the party lacked an integrated apparatus and capacity for standardized policy implementation. Model villages and other basic-level model units were designated, supervised, and propagandized by higher-level party bodies that often did not have the means to give consistent material support from above. Thus model units were forced to support themselves and to come up with creative local problem-solving for many endeavors. It was not the lack of political power or ideological determination on the part of the Party Center, but the lack of resources and personnel that forced the Party Center to give room to local initiative and even to tolerate ideological deviations as long as they strengthened overall Communist Party control in the respective localities.

CCP-controlled experimentation was elevated to a general method of leadership by Mao's statements. But the concrete techniques and terms were specified by other party leaders based on their practical experiences. By 1951, party guidelines for land reform had been consolidated into six steps, of which steps 2 to 6 have been crucial to Chinese-style policy experimentation to the present day: (1) train work team cadres and send them down to the localities; (2) carry out model experiments; (3) accomplish breakthroughs in a key point; (4) broaden the campaign from point to surface; (5) integrate point and surface with regard to the applied measures; and (6) unfold the campaign in steady steps.[15]

By the early 1950s, the terms "model experiment," "experimental point," as well as "model demonstration," "proceeding from point to surface," and "integrating point and surface" (*dianmian jiehe*) had emerged as key terms in the Chinese Communists' repertoire of policy experimentation. All these terms are still widely used in official language today. However, "experimental point" has by far become the most prevalent term in reform-era policy experimentation. Beginning in the 1950s, the term "experimental point" was used as a synonym for the more formal term "model experiment," both of which have the meaning of obtaining experience through concrete work in one spot so as to guide general policy.[16]

In an earlier analysis, I characterize the term "experimental point" as an indigenous neologism introduced by the Chinese Communists.[17] After the article was published, Peter Kuhfus (a sinologist specializing in the history of interactions between the Soviet and Chinese Communist parties) pointed out that the Russian term *opytnyi punkt* ("trial point," or "experimental point") had at least occasionally been used in local pilot projects of the 1930s and

1940s in the Union of Soviet Socialist Republics (USSR).[18] Whereas "experimental point" has remained a widely used official term in China from the early 1950s to the present day, Soviet sources did not prominently use the term after the 1940s.[19] Most importantly, the Soviet Communists did not use the "point-to-surface" terminology that plays a crucial role in Maoist experimentation. For Soviet policy making, the "experimental point" method never had the significance that it gained for the Chinese Communists' policy process. When economic reforms were considered in the Soviet Union during the 1960s, even very modest local experiments in the planning and allocation systems were met with stiff resistance from the bureaucracy and violent criticism from prominent economists who castigated economic experimentation as a retreat from systematic theoretical analysis and comprehensive planning.[20] The centralized planning bureaucracy and rigid economic order that were founded on detailed laws and decrees in the Soviet Union were clearly a much less hospitable context for decentralized and informal experimentation than in the PRC where there was more room for decentralized tinkering due to the constantly shifting institutional and legal environments.

According to a 1953 cadre education journal, the goals of the "experimental point" method were defined as to prevent "blind" implementation of unfamiliar policies; to give cadres an opportunity to learn and overcome old habits by first trying out new solutions on a small scale; to "educate the masses" and win their support for new policies through active participation in local experiments; and to help save resources, manpower, and time to carry out new policies. At the same time, it was emphasized that the success of "experimental point" work depended on appropriate preparation and timing (premature establishment would lead to failure), the selection of "typical" experimental sites that could teach credible lessons to "the masses" in other sites, a contingent of strong cadres and activists at the test spots, and sophisticated analyses to extract generalizable lessons.[21]

In sum, the "experimental point" and point-to-surface methodologies were firmly established through a series of statements by top Communist Party leaders, and they were refined and re-defined by practical application during the 1943–53 period. Although these methodologies were the product of the distinctive historical context of revolutionary struggle, they came to be seen by the economic reformers of the 1980s as the "concretization" of the CCP's best traditions in "seeking truth from facts.[22] Deng Xiaoping, Chen Yun, and other powerful veterans, though holding differing views on the desirable extent, direction, and speed of the economic reforms, were in agreement that the successes of the large-scale experimentation during the 1943–53 period provided valuable lessons about flexible and risk-minimizing methods of policy innovation that could be employed to modernize the country. This is why the terminology of experimentation was taken from its revolutionary context and made to serve the purpose of reforming the Chinese economy.

## Embedded revolutionaries: Non-Communist sources of policy experimentation

As Donald Munro succinctly states, the point-to-surface technique "differs fundamentally from Soviet socialist emulation theory"[23] in terms of its decentralized and informal character. Strikingly, experimentation is a blind spot in the Marxist-Leninist canon. Developing methods of revolution through experiments was neither debated nor proposed by Marx, Lenin, or Stalin.[24] In Lenin's entire collected works, the need for experimentation to find new policy solutions is only mentioned once and in a very specific context.[25] Stalin was vehemently hostile to "spontaneous" and "blind" local initiative.[26]

A commandist top-down approach to policy generation and implementation represented the legitimate revolutionary strategy and administrative practice in the Soviet Union. Since revolution meant making the laws of history into a reality, revolutionaries knew what to do in advance of implementing policy and they were not supposed to be distracted by experimentation.

Nevertheless, Chinese political intellectuals and activists came to perceive the Russian revolution as a huge experiment. Qu Qiubai, a prominent figure in the early Chinese Communist movement, characterized Soviet Russia as "a laboratory of communism" in which Bolshevik "chemists" remolded the Russian people in the "test tubes" of the Soviets and produced new "socialist compounds."[27] Soviet Russia's New Economic Policy (NEP) attracted much interest among Chinese Communists. But the books that introduced the NEP to the Chinese public did not mention experimentation as a key element of Soviet governance. In fact, the NEP was never conceived of as an experiment for developing policy tools in an open-ended manner. Rather, it was seen by Lenin as a package of emergency measures for economic survival and as a transitional arrangement that was to lead to "correct" socialist economic policies as soon as Communist power was consolidated.[28] Since an experimentalist approach to making revolution was therefore not developed in the Marxist-Leninist classics, it is even more remarkable that the Chinese Communists turned to the experimental point-to-surface approach in their efforts to transform China.

In explaining the revolutionary experience and legacies of the Chinese Communists, Benjamin Schwartz and many others in his wake point to the distinctive circumstances, social forces, and political dynamics at work in the Chinese revolution that virtually forced unorthodox solutions onto the Communist leaders and provoked major deviations from the standard Marxist-Leninist and Soviet recipes. From the perspective of official party historiography, it is clear who invented Chinese-style policy experimentation: Mao Zedong raised the basic concepts while other party leaders developed Mao's concepts further through practical application. However, this interpretation of the emergence of the point-to-surface methodology in China is untenable in the face of the ample evidence of social and administrative experimentation that preceded the Communists' activities. The findings presented in the following paragraphs are unequivocal. The transformation of social, political, and economic conditions by way of decentralized but controlled experimentation was not pioneered by the Communists. Instead, Communist experimentation was part of a much bigger story about widespread efforts at experimentation in extremely uncertain times during China's Republican era.

## *The Deweyan imprint on Mao's experimental approach*

The impact of John Dewey's pragmatist philosophy on political debate in China during the 1920s has been the subject of numerous scholarly works. The series of lectures that Dewey presented in major Chinese cities and universities in 1919 and 1920 influenced the thinking of a generation of political intellectuals and activists, including the founders of the Chinese Communist Party and Mao Zedong. One core theme in Dewey's lectures was the experimental method, which he presented as the central innovative feature of modern science and the most important method for obtaining scientific knowledge. Chinese political activists eagerly picked up his statements on experimentation which, according to Dewey, "is guided by intentional anticipation instead of being blind trial and error.... it is experience marked by the intent to act upon the idea." Dewey contrasted classical philosophies that tended to be "isolated from the cold, hard facts of human experience" with modern approaches that stressed that ideas and theories had to be tested through practical application and experimentation: "There can be no true knowledge without doing. It is only doing that enables us to revise our outlook, to organize our facts in a systematic way, and to discover new facts."[29]

Dewey's Chinese followers presented experimentation as the core of the Deweyan approach to social reform and rendered Dewey's philosophy as "experimentalism" (*shiyan zhuyi*).[30] The most prominent interpreter and popularizer of Deweyan thinking, the American-trained philosopher Hu Shi, gave a decisive twist to the Chinese debate on pragmatism by extracting Dewey's methodological prescriptions from their Western normative context and stressing a one-sidedly instrumentalist understanding of pragmatist philosophy. Hu Shi presented Dewey's "experimentalism" as a methodology of social engineering that proved to be extremely attractive to a very broad spectrum of young Chinese intellectuals, ranging from American-inspired reformers to Soviet-leaning radicals. According to Yu Yingshi, Hu Shi's "reductionist" rendering of Deweyan philosophy exerted a lasting influence on modern Chinese political thinking, including Mao's steady emphasis on learning through practice and debates on "practice as the sole criterion of truth" that served to justify the initiation of the economic reform and opening.[31] Indeed, Mao also once admitted that he was an ardent admirer of Hu Shi during the early May Fourth period.[32]

The influence of Deweyan ideas on Mao Zedong's epistemology, with its emphasis on learning through direct practical experience, has been noted in a number of academic works. With regard to Mao's article "On Practice," Herbert Marcuse holds that "there is more Dewey than Marx in all this."[33] Certain formulations and arguments appearing in "On Practice" are strikingly similar to what Dewey stated in his China lectures.[34] Recent works reveal that in 1920 Mao attended at least one of Dewey's China lectures, and he had read and recommended the Chinese edition of Dewey's *Five Major Lectures* and had stocked this book when he opened a bookstore in the same year.[35] Dewey's 1920 dictum on modern science, "everything through experimentation"[36] (translated by his disciples into Chinese as *yiqie dou cong shiyan xiashou*) was echoed in a 1958 directive by Mao that stated "everything through experimentation"[37] (*yiqie jingguo shiyan*).

Along with Mao, most other founding members of the CCP were deeply attracted to Dewey's epistemology that conveyed the message that learning and acting, that is, obtaining knowledge about the world and bringing change to the world, could be achieved through a well-conceived process of practical experimentation. In the early version of Chinese communism, "experimentalism both as a philosophy and as a scientific method, had ... an upper hand over dialectic materialism." Even the idea of class struggle was initially rejected by most early Communist protagonists.[38] Dewey's "emphasis on methodology, logic, and practicality made it irresistibly attractive to the leaders of the intellectual revolution ... and highly useful in promoting many social, ethical, and economic reforms."[39]

### Non-governmental reformists: Experimental sites in the Rural Reconstruction Movement

During the May Fourth era, as a result of Dewey's 1919–20 pleas for social experimentation and his disciples' vigorous application efforts, numerous experimental sites were established throughout China, with a focus on schools, agriculture, health care, and local administration. According to KMT government statistics, about 600 different para-governmental and non-governmental organizations (NGOs) (many supported by foreign funds) were involved in rural reform efforts and in more than 1,000 experimental sites that were scattered all over the country in the mid-1930s. In addition to many small experimental sites, such as schools, agricultural stations, or health centers, about twenty full-scale, though mostly failing and short-lived, experimental counties were officially recognized by the central government prior to 1937.⁴⁰ Thus, before the Japanese invasion social experimentation had become a popular activity in which Chinese political activists took an active interest.

NGO-funded American agricultural reformers were pioneers in introducing the idea and practice of experimentation to Chinese administrators. The American system of establishing one agricultural experiment station in every state was transferred to the provincial-level units in China.⁴¹ Although American advisers raised serious doubts about the success of China's experiment stations in trying out new agricultural methods and varieties,⁴² the general approach of setting up one experimental unit per province was taken up in the experimental county program of the 1930s. Moreover, the Chinese terminology of experimentation was introduced in the 1910s and 1920s by those involved in agricultural experimentation who popularized "experimental extensions" (*shixing tuiguang*) of technological and organizational innovations.⁴³

Those most prominent in the social experimentation during the Republican era emerged from the Mass Education movement (MEM) and the Rural Reconstruction movement (RRM) which established influential non-Communist antecedents for the point-to-surface approach in rural reform. In June 1925, the Yale-educated Chinese founder of the MEM, Yan Yangchu (James Yen), established the basic principles of what later would become essential elements of the Communists' point-to-surface technique:

> The general plan of the [Mass Education] Movement is to select one or two typical rural districts in north, south, east, west and central China, respectively, for intensive and extensive

experimentations ... to make it a model district in education and in general social and economic improvement, so that it may be used as a demonstration and training center for other districts. While intensive experiments of this kind are being undertaken in the chosen areas, the Movement promotes its program extensively to as many villages as possible and as rapidly as possible.[44]

As early as the late 1920s, the terms "experimental county" and "experimental zone" were already employed by MEM/RRM leaders and other NGO initiators who were active in rural China.[45] The experimental sites managed by the MEM and RRM exerted considerable influence on the Communists for a number of reasons that are not readily conceded by official party historiography. From the very beginning of MEM activities, there existed close personal relationships that crossed the boundaries between the Communist Party and the non-Communist MEM. One co-founder of the MEM who became the closest collaborator of James Yen from the 1920s to 1949 was an uncle of Qu Qiubai, one of the most eminent Communist Party leaders of the 1920s.[46] More importantly in terms of experimental practice, in the 1930s local MEM and RRM associations were systematically used as cover organizations by underground branches of the Communist Party. When rural reconstruction experiments reached their climax in the mid-1930s, the CCP was at a low point in its history. At that time, the MEM and RRM had become big players in rural reform. In May 1937, CCP strategist Liu Shaoqi encouraged party organs that operated in areas controlled by the Japanese or by the KMT to take an active part in MEM and RRM rural work. Therefore, numerous CCP cadres became MEM activists who worked for the non-Communist rural reform movement during the day and held meetings with their CCP underground comrades during the evening.[47]

At the leadership level, on several occasions MEM and RRM leaders engaged in political exchanges with Mao Zedong in Yan'an. When Mao received a delegation in 1938, he spoke of the MEM as a "friend" of the Communist Party, and, certainly for tactical reasons, he expressed his appreciation of their endeavors.[48] In the same year, Mao met for several days of lively chats with RRM leader Liang Shuming, and he obviously held Liang in high regard at the time.[49] Several Communist delegations visited Ding experimental county to study the social programs initiated there, and Mao certainly was well informed about the basic ideas and diverse experiments conducted by the RRM and MEM. In their search for policies that might generate mass support, Communist leaders used the MEM/RRM efforts at reorganizing rural production, education, and health care as instructive references and in some cases they appeared to directly copy social programs that originally had been developed in Ding experimental county.[50] In utilizing novel policies, recruiting political activists, and addressing the most pressing needs of the peasants, there was clearly a lot to learn from those non-Communists involved in experimentation.[51]

Remarkably, it was not only the Communists who were inspired by the MEM and RRM experimental sites; between 1932 and 1937, the KMT also undertook some prominent efforts to test new ways of governing the countryside. Scores of KMT politicians and administrators visited and inspected the experimental sites managed by the RRM and MEM as part of policy tourism in search of new organizational models for the Chinese countryside.[52] Although the objectives and policies involved in the KMT-led efforts at county administrative reconstruction met with much distrust, at least two experimental counties (of altogether twenty counties in eleven provinces) set up by the KMT, Jiangning in Jiangsu province and Lanxi in Zhejiang province, that focused on administration, education, welfare, and security were promoted by determined county leaders with high-level backing.[53] These two government-sponsored rural reform efforts "from above" were thought to have produced much useful experience. But since these experiments relied on very generous subsidies and had to be terminated in the face of the Japanese invasion, they did not serve as models for other jurisdictions.[54]

## Lessons of widespread experimentation during China's Republican era

Seen from the perspective of the widespread experimental programs in Republican China, it can be said that the Communists merely joined the strong trend of experimentation that had gained momentum since the May Fourth era. The Communists, however, learned from these other experimental efforts only for tactical reasons and they were determined to redirect rural experimentation toward their revolutionary goals. From the Communist point of view, the experiments of the Deweyans, liberal reformers, and NGOs had failed because they had ignored the issue of political power and had tried to work from within the inimical political environment.[55] The reformists never had the authority to transform their experimental projects into a general operational program for a larger jurisdiction. Even if individual non-Communist experiments appeared to work and were widely judged to be successful, they remained isolated and confined to one small area. The novel policy instruments generated in such places could never be spread systematically due to the reformists' lack of political authority.

In the course of the 1940s, the Communists gained power to proceed with policy implementation from one experimental spot to the entire area under their control, thereby obtaining a crucial capacity that had never been enjoyed by the reformists of the 1930s. Communist leaders made it clear that they did not see any meaning in experiments unless the Communist Party was in control of the overall experimental process. Thus, although the Communists' unorthodox experimental terminology as well as their individual policies dealing with land reform, rural education, and health care may have been influenced by the non-Communist experience, the point-to-surface technique of controlled experimentation by way of sent-down cadre teams, mass mobilization, struggle sessions, and wave-like extensions to neighboring areas constituted a thoroughly Maoist creation.

According to the Communists' conception, experimentation was about finding innovative policy instruments, not about defining policy objectives, which remained the exclusive task of the party leadership. A revealing internal directive, dating from 1940, on one Communist "experimental county" in the Taihang Base Area (then under the leadership of Deng Xiaoping) frankly stated that "this experimental county was not established for experimenting" per se but for becoming an exemplar that generates and demonstrates successful leadership methods and policies.[56] Cadres in charge of model experiments were allowed to try out various ways and means to realize the policy goals set by the CCP leadership. But they were not authorized to redefine policy objectives on their own, and their experiments were subject to termination, curtailment, or revision by higher-level party organs at any time.

In sum, experimentation has been a core feature of the Maoist approach to policy making since revolutionary times. In drawing lessons from the non-Communist experimental programs of the Republican era, Communist leaders developed an extremely instrumentalist understanding of policy experimentation that was compatible with the principle of hierarchical party control.

## Maoist methods of revolution and post-Mao reform

After a serious understanding of the formative historical experience of CCP leaders and their methods of rule, it becomes clear that experimenting with concurrent local policy alternatives in post-Mao China was not an issue of random choice by enlightened leaders. When searching for new policy approaches to facilitate economic modernization in the late 1970s, China's veteran leaders shared their knowledge and appreciation of the "experimental point" method. They redefined the main mission of the party (from achieving communism to achieving rapid economic growth) and reverted to the experience of the 1946–53 period, which they regarded as the most successful and splendid period of large-scale controlled structural change and economic policy in the history of the Communist Party.

Deng Xiaoping and Chen Yun became the most prominent advocates of applying the point-to-surface technique to economic modernization, even though they came to differ substantially with regard to the speed and extent of change. From 1978 to 1992, Deng repeatedly characterized reform and opening as a "large-scale experiment" that could not be carried out with the help of textbook knowledge but instead required vigorous "experimenting in practice."[57] Chen Yun propagandized the "experimental point" technique as a way of controlled and cautious policy innovation.[58] However, in contrast to Deng, Chen took a very sceptical stance toward the introduction of non-socialist special economic zones whose creation Deng Xiaoping justified as an "experiment," pointing to the pre-1949 Communist base areas as a precedent. Deng was an impatient advocate of rapid economic growth. Contrary to common perception,[59] however, Deng personally never cited the gradualist slogan "crossing the river by groping for the stones" to describe the logic of reform. In actuality, this formula was introduced by Chen Yun in December 1980 as an antidote to what he saw as reform exuberance, and it was only thereafter that the slogan became a popular characterization of the Chinese reform approach.[60]

In its 1981 decision on party history, China's post-Mao leadership identified certain Maoist methods as lasting and indispensable elements of official doctrine. The point-to-surface technique was paraphrased, as in Mao's 1943 article on leadership methods, as the combination of guidance through concrete work on individual issues (*gebie zhidao*) with the making of general policy appeals (*yiban haozhao*).[61] In the 1980s and 1990s, individual party theoreticians made efforts to establish experimentation as an original Chinese contribution to Marxist theory and argued that "a scientific socialist viewpoint can be established only through social experiments."[62] Others identified experimental points as "social-science laboratories" and as a powerful scientific instrument for linking the processes of obtaining knowledge and implementing policy.[63] In 1992, the importance of experimentation was even inserted into the CCP constitution, stipulating that the whole party "must boldly experiment with new methods, ... review new experience and solve new problems, and enrich and develop Marxism in practice."[64]

However, with respect to the central role of "model experiments" and "proceeding from point to surface" in policy generation and implementation, there was no systemic shift from the Mao era to the Deng era. Though the approaches to policy experimentation differ in important individual features (the role of outside work teams, local cadres, and legislation), the overall continuities that can be observed in nine of the twelve typical steps of experiment-based policy formation are striking (see Table 2.1).

Table 2.1 Establishing "Model Experiments": A Comparison of the Approaches in the Mao and Deng Eras

| | | Maoist Mass Mobilization Approach ([1928]–1943–1976) | Dengist Administrative Approach (1979–) |
|---|---|---|---|
| Steps in establishing "model experiments" | 1 | Conduct a thorough investigation of several locations | |
| | 2 | Select a location conducive to successful experimentation | |
| | 3 | Dispatch a cadre "work team" | *Rely on local cadres* |
| | 4 | Nurture new activists and cadres in the location | |
| | 5 | Regularly report to higher-level party organs | |
| Steps in "proceeding from point to surface" | 6 | Send in investigation teams from the higher-level authorities | |
| | 7 | Confirm/revise/terminate local model experiments | |
| | 8 | Reassign the original work team and local activists to surrounding locations | *[No work teams used]* |
| | 9 | Promote local model leaders to leading provincial or national positions | |
| | 10 | Launch an emulation campaign and intervisitation program | |
| | 11 | Give speeches and issue documents to spread the model experience | |
| | 12 | *[Formal legislation rarely enacted, 1957–78]* | Enact national regulation/legislation |

Drawing lessons from what went wrong during the earlier decades, the post-Mao leadership carried out a radical turn away from ideological fever and single models for emulation. It instead acknowledged regional variations and promoted concurrent experiments and multiple models. Locally produced institutional and policy innovations were taken up by reformist policy makers eager to bolster their political standing and to keep their rivals at bay by godfathering "model experiments" that could demonstrate the success and superiority of their policy preferences. If experiments went wrong in the eyes of their supporters, they typically were phased out and silently brought to an end by no longer giving them any attention.[65] In the background interviews conducted for this study,

Chinese officials in charge of "experimental point work" unanimously stated that failing experiments typically are not terminated in a clear-cut way by a formal administrative decision or document. Instead, administrators are used to reading the subtle signals from above and they tacitly stop working on those projects that have lost the attention and support of the policy makers. Only in very rare cases did failing "models" come under public scrutiny, typically in the context of criminal or corruption investigations that did not implicate top policy makers but targeted local or corporate misconduct as the root cause of their failure.

Decentralized experimentation facilitated "guerrilla-style policy making" (this is how Roderick MacFarquhar referred to it in his comments during the conference on "Adaptive authoritarianism: China's party-state resilience in historical perspective" held at Harvard University, July 14–16, 2008) and "government on a shoestring" (as Lily Tsai commented during the same conference): a low-cost way of local problem-solving and policy generation that has constituted the only constructive option for underequipped local governments from revolutionary times to the present day and that has, at the same time, served as a convenient technique for the Party Center to avoid accountability for local policy failures while receiving recognition for economically successful policy innovations generated by local initiatives. In a paradoxical turn, China's experiment-based policy process has helped to circumvent severe deficiencies in administrative integration, fiscal capacity, policy coherence, and political accountability, while allowing to build up systemic adaptive capacity and national economic strength.

Clearly, at every stage, from setting policy objectives to selecting model experiments and identifying generalizable policy options, "proceeding from point to surface" has always been an intensely politicized process driven by competing interests, ideological frictions, personal rivalries, tactical opportunism, or ad hoc compromises.

For policy makers who wanted to change the way the economy was run, experimentation turned out to be a good way to deal with uncertainty (the inability to predict the precise impact of specific reforms in a rapidly changing economic context) and ambiguity (the ambivalence, vagueness, or even confusion in policy-makers' thinking about their policy priorities). In such an often volatile policy-making context, the "experimental point" method helped to release broad-based policy entrepreneurship that contributed to economic innovation and expansion. Though this process along the way also produced costly fake and failed "models," the costs of failed local experiments were clearly much less serious, at least from the perspective of national policy makers and the majority of unaffected jurisdictions than the costs attached to failed national reform legislation. Moreover, because experimentation mobilized local knowledge and problem-solving, it produced a wealth of previously unavailable information on the workings and the potentials of the local economies.[66] Yet post-Mao experimentation did not stop with the search for individual models and policy options. Rather, it resulted in serial, and cumulatively radical, redefinitions of policy parameters for economic activity over time.

## Conclusion

In the Chinese approach to policy making, the "experimental point" and "point-to-surface" methodologies enjoy systematic significance. The pattern of experimental governance that we find in China has distinctive foundations in a hierarchical party-state and differs from models of decentralization or federalism that are frequently applied to explain the dynamics of central-local interactions in China's economic reforms.[67] The findings presented in this chapter support Elizabeth Perry's proposition that "certain elements of China's revolutionary inheritance have actually furthered the stunningly successful implementation of market reforms."⁶⁸ This paradox can also be seen in the case of reform-era experimentation that has been crucial in facilitating policy innovation, yet is rooted in Maoist techniques of rule.

One of China's core strengths in reforming its economy has been its distinctive process of central-local interactions to generate a policy that enjoys an entrenched legitimacy within the Communist Party and can be put to work for the shifting policy priorities of the post-Mao era. Explanations that stress central-local factional machinations as the paramount driving force behind policy innovation do not appreciate the extent and importance of local initiative in generating novel policy instruments and in transforming the parameters and priorities of central policy makers over time. Furthermore, the effectiveness of experimentation is not based on all-out decentralization and spontaneous diffusion of policy innovations. China's experiment-based policy making requires the authority of a central leadership that encourages and protects broad-based local initiative and filters out generalizable lessons, but at the same time contains the centrifugal forces that necessarily come up with this type of policy process.

Conceptual dichotomies such as centralization vs. decentralization, or constitutional concepts such as federalism that suggest a stability of vertical checks and balances that is not a given in China's polity, cannot capture the oscillating dynamics of China's policy-making approach. It is experimentation under hierarchy, i.e., the volatile, yet productive combination of decentralized experimentation with ad hoc central interference, resulting in selective integration of local experiences into national policy making, that is the key to understanding China's policy process.

In searching for the prerequisites for China's unexpectedly adaptive authoritarianism during the last three decades, this distinctive policy process may provide a more powerful explanation than static factors (such as the initial economic structure or the state's enforcement capacity), explanations that ignore the process of policy making and policy implementation (arguments based on quasi-natural economic liberalization and inevitable convergence with market principles), or explanations that treat policy experimentation merely as a derivative feature of factional rivalries. It is China's historically entrenched process of policy generation through local experiments and model demonstrations that has provided a productive link between central and local initiative and has allowed policy makers to move beyond policy deadlock in spite of the myriad conflicts over strategy, ideology, and interests.

# 3
# Policy Experimentation and Institutional Innovation in China's Economic Transformation*

## Introduction

Due to the institutional turn that has taken place in development studies over the last two decades, we now understand much more about the impact of diverse institutional arrangements on economic growth. However, institutionalist research has not produced many concrete answers to one crucial challenge: how to facilitate institutional change despite the massive inertia and opposition that block structural reform and inhibit economic development in many political economies without imposing foreign blueprints and thereby ignoring the intricacies of local conditions.[1] A critical undercurrent within the institutional turn, represented for instance by Peter Evans and Dani Rodrik, has consistently stressed that it is insufficient to understand and

---

\*   This is a revised version of an analysis that was originally published as "Policy Experimentation in China's Economic Rise," in *Studies in Comparative International Development*, Vol. 43, No. 1 (March 2008), pp. 1–26, republished here with permission from Springer Science+Business Media.

propagandize the institutional prerequisites and international "best practices" for economic growth and good governance. We also must identify the political and administrative processes that help to mobilize bottom-up initiatives, stimulate institutional experimentation, and apply viable local experiences to national policy making. As Charles Lindblom bluntly notes, the real challenge of policy making lies in "smuggling" changes into often uninviting and resistant political economies.[2]

This chapter attempts to contribute to the study of policy processes that can bring about administrative, legislative, and economic institutional innovation—even in the context of a rigid authoritarian-bureaucratic environment and regardless of strong political opposition. The focus is not what institutions must be established to fulfil certain tasks from a predictive functionalist perspective. Instead, I concentrate on how existing, and initially deficient, institutions can be put to work, transformed, or replaced to bring about economic and social development in an open-ended process of institutional innovation that is based on locally generated solutions rather than on imported policy recipes.

One country that potentially can provide important lessons about this is China. Judged by Evans's emphasis on the need to "expand the range of institutional strategies explored,"[3] China has advanced the most among the large emerging countries in achieving such an objective economically. During the last three decades, China's political economy has become highly innovative in finding policies and institutions to master the complex challenges of large-scale economic change while at the same avoiding systemic breakdown. Mukand and Rodrik[4] place the Chinese experience, together with that of India, at the center of their analysis, stressing the unorthodox policies, regulatory practices, and unclarified property rights regime that have accompanied strong economic growth. China's economic transition has been facilitated by an unusual adaptive capacity that, according to North, entails an institutional structure that, despite ubiquitous uncertainties, enables it to try out alternative approaches to overcome long-standing impediments to economic development, tackle newly emerging challenges, and grasp new opportunities.[5] That this was possible in the Chinese context was unexpected because throughout the course of its economic reform, China's policy makers and administrators had to work with the institutions of a Communist party-state—an institutional context that has proven to be extremely inflexible in almost every other place where such a polity exists.[6]

I argue that a distinctive policy cycle, experimentation under hierarchy, is the key to understanding the emergence of an unexpectedly adaptive authoritarianism in China. Though ambitious central state planning, grand technocratic modernization schemes, and megaprojects have never disappeared from the Chinese policy agenda, an entrenched process of experimentation that precedes the enactment of many national policies has served as a powerful corrective mechanism.

First, I propose a definition of transformative experimentation that helps to understand why this approach to reform differs fundamentally from conventional policy making and is not confined to merely incremental change. Next, I examine the specific tools and processes that facilitated experimentalism in China. Then I turn to case studies of experimentation in crucial economic reform areas that, although sharing the same basic processual patterns, reveal very different political dynamics and innovative effects due to a starkly varying constellation of actors, interests, and risks that promote or inhibit change in different policy subsystems. The following section synthesizes the insights that China's experience provides about the interrelation between policy learning and rent-seeking in experimentation. In the conclusion, I discuss the applicability of the experimental approach to reform-making in other political economies.

## Policy experimentation as a distinct mode of governance

Several prominent scholars have pointed to policy experimentation as an effective mechanism that may help to determine what works on the ground, induces behavioral changes, and produces institutional innovations that are conducive to entrepreneurialism, investment, and economic growth.[7] Though the importance of experimentation is often highlighted in academic studies, it remains a surprisingly ill-defined and vague concept. It often merely paraphrases the cycles of policy reversals and policy re-prioritization that are characteristic of all political systems when established policies are regarded as failing, too costly, or politically risky. Experimentation in a stricter definition, as used here, implies a policy process whereby experimenting units try out a variety of methods and processes to discover imaginative solutions to predefined tasks or to new challenges that emerge during the experimental activity. Policy experimentation is not equivalent to  free-wheeling trial and error or spontaneous policy diffusion. Rather, it is a purposeful and coordinated activity geared to produce novel policy options that are injected into official policy making and then replicated on a larger scale or even formally incorporated into national law.

In more technical terms, experimentation aims "to inform policy by using experiments with direct interventions and control groups instead of observational studies or theoretical analyses."[8] If experimentation is designed and evaluated by social scientists as part of government-sponsored pilot programs, it is usually limited to narrowly defined trial measures and preselected target groups. It often is confined to the fine-tuning of implementation technicalities (such as testing the suitability of a new social security card in a pilot site) and only very rarely does it apply to substantive policy formulation (such as the extent, focus, or budgeting of social policies) that is the object of complex bargaining processes in which tactical political considerations are more important than outside expertise.[9]

In contrast, the transformative policy experimentation described in this chapter is much more comprehensive and ambitious because it attempts to alter economic and administrative behavior and institutions. Such experimentation also opens up entirely new market segments and establishes new types of corporate organization, thereby regularly moving beyond the originally defined test groups and procedures and involving policy makers at different levels of the political system. Mosteller sees such "reorganization experiments" as most difficult to carry out because they depend on a chain of complex interrelations, may require a great deal of time and resources, tend to provoke stiff political opposition, must deal with ongoing contextual changes, and are subject to political-administrative interference and changes in the rules of the game at the middle of the experimental process. Transformative experimentation usually comes in the shape of demonstration projects taking place in a politically realistic, i.e., fluid, disturbed, and contested, context that escapes strict scientific controls, but it can provide a fuller view of the workings of novel policies and their impact on major social, market, or administrative actors.[10]

Policy experimentation in this variant constitutes a distinct mode of governance that differs in one fundamental way from standard assumptions about policy making. The conventional model of the policy process, which is widely taken for granted by jurists, economists, and political scientists, holds that policy analysis, formulation, and embodiment in legislation precede implementation.

But policy experimentation, as presented in this study, refers to innovation through implementation first, and then, later, the drafting of universal laws and regulations.

At first glance, policy experimentation displays commonalities with what Lindblom characterizes as the incremental method of successive limited comparisons in making public policy: the exploratory, reversible character of policy making and the prior reduction of political antagonisms by avoiding drastic change at the outset.[11] Yet, under certain conditions identified in the following analysis, experimentation may transcend incrementalist tinkering with existing practices and lead to drastic policy departures and transformative changes marked by the emergence of new configurations of actors, interests, institutions, ideologies, and goals.

The pursuit of extensive, continuous, and loosely institutionalized experimentation can be understood as a crucial policy mechanism in China's economic rise. Several students of China's political economy have already emphasized the importance of experimentation in facilitating institutional innovation and economic efficiency gains.[12] However, the specific origins, tools, processes, and effects of experimentation in major areas of Chinese economic reform have largely been unstudied. Chinese policy makers and their advisers, in public statements and in interviews conducted for this study, tend to explain the pervasive use of experimental programs as a product of reform entrepreneurship, either as a controlled "scientific" generation of novel policies or as a way to pioneer policy change by circumventing political and bureaucratic constraints. In social-science explanations, Chinese-style policy experimentation is treated either as a product of specific structural preconditions that allows for sectoral and spatial gradualism,[13] as an outcome of administrative decentralization and jurisdictional competition,[14] or as a second-best approach forced upon the reformists in order to broaden their base of political support and to avoid ideological controversies and to keep factional rivals at bay.[15]

Each of these explanations captures important specific aspects of China's economic reform policy. Taking a broader view that includes the entire policy cycle, the processes that are at the heart of large-scale experimentation in China do not easily fit into standard assumptions of central-local interactions and policy implementation that are largely based on the experiences of democratic and federalist systems in advanced political economies where constitutional government produces vertical checks and balances. In the hierarchical setting of China's party-state, there is a different causal relationship underlying central-local interactions during experimentation. In China, the process from experimental programs to national policy is shaped by a policy terminology and methodology that stem from the formative revolution-era experience of the CCP, which legitimated developing policy by "proceeding from point to surface" and implementing policy "in accordance with local circumstances."[16] The pattern of experimental governance that we find in China's party-state today, experimentation under hierarchy, has distinctive foundations and is unlike what is treated conventionally under sweeping headings such as decentralization or federalism. Although hands-on experimentation is delegated to local officials, China's central government plays an indispensable role in scaling up and generalizing local innovations, thereby coordinating the reform process. This approach to experimentation resembles the modes of social program replication that have been discussed in the development community,[17] in particular, the approach of "staged replication," which moves from local pilot testing through implementation in a broader selection of demonstration sites to universal application. In contrast to the experience of other countries, including India, where the "corpses of pilot projects litter the development field,"[18] Chinese-style experimentation managed to transform many pilot projects into full-scale operational programs that cover a broad policy spectrum ranging from economic regulation to organizational reforms within the Communist Party.

## Tools of experimentation

In democratic polities, policy experimentation generally refers to small-scale exploratory pilot projects, such as pioneering legislation by individual states in federal systems ("states as laboratories"), experimental or sunset clauses incorporated into formal legislation, or, more rarely, a special dispensation for local administrative districts to be exempt from certain provisions of national law.[19] The approach in China's party-state is very different. Experimentation comes in three main forms as (1) experimental regulation (provisional rules made for trial implementation), (2) "experimental points" (model demonstrations and pilot projects within a specific policy domain), or (3) "experimental zones" (local jurisdictions with broad discretionary powers).

### *Experimental regulation*

An examination of regulations dealing with the economy (including health services and social insurance reform) during the first two decades of China's economic reforms reveals that throughout this period, well over 30 percent of such regulations were marked as provisional, experimental or as regulating experimental points and zones (see Figure 3.1). In 1985, the national legislature issued a formal decision, giving the central government power to formulate interim regulations with respect to economic structural reforms. Since then, the government has made full use of this prerogative and has issued thousands of economic regulations that bypass the legislative bodies. Corne points to a proliferation of experimental regulations in China's economic policy making, characterizing it as "a form of 'quasi-law'" that is revised and finalized by formal legislation only after sufficient experience has been obtained during the trial period.[20] Since 1997, the share of experimental economic legislation has declined due to the growing institutionalization of economic administration and World Trade Organization (WTO)-driven harmonization with international regulatory standards. From 2001 to 2006, the share of experimental economic regulation fluctuated between a low of 13 percent (2001, 2002) and an extraordinary peak of 28 percent in 2003, when rural and welfare experimentation were pushed energetically by the newly installed leadership. From 2004 to 2014 the share of experimental economic regulation fluctuated between 17 percent and 21 percent but it suffered a steep drop beginning in 2015 when the official turn from local initiative toward "top-level design" took effect. Considering that the main burden for policy experimentation was formally delegated to regional governments in 1998, the share of experimental regulations issued by the central government since then remains significant. The increasing comprehensiveness of economic legislation and the impact of the WTO have clearly reduced, but not terminated, the role of experimental legislation in policy innovation. Although experimental regulations have lost the striking importance they enjoyed in the 1980s and 1990s, they are still particularly important in certain policy domains, such as rural and welfare reform, that attract strong attention from top policy makers. In actuality, the distribution of reformist ambitions over the specter of policy domains is still derived from the concentration of experimental regulations in individual sectors.

Figure 3.1   Experimental Regulation in China, 1979–2016

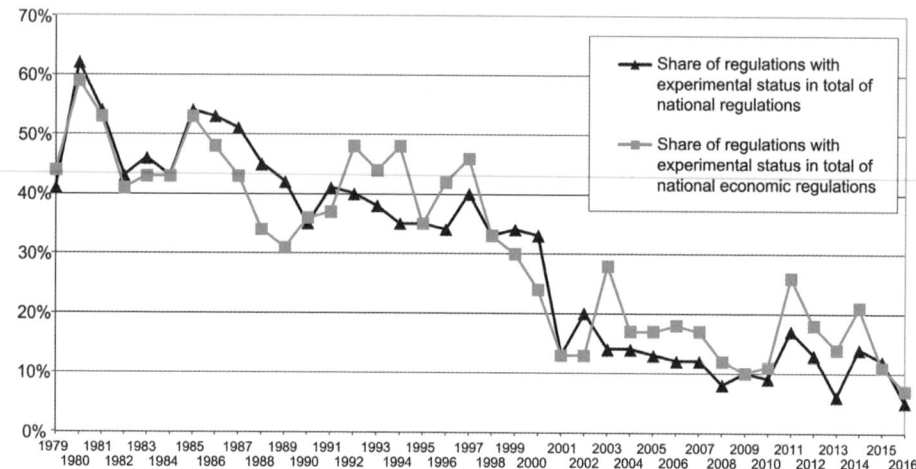

Database: Beijing University Law School, at http://www.pkulaw.cn, accessed January 26, 2017. Based on an analysis of ordinances, stipulations, and measures issued in the name of the State Council and ministerial-level central government organs that are marked in their titles as "provisional," "experimental," or as regulating "experimental points/zones." Regulatory documents with a lesser legal and administrative status (classified as "normative documents," *guifanxing wenjian*) are not included in this quantitative analysis.

## *Experimental points*

Even more pervasive than formal experimental regulation is the use of a particularly Chinese governance technique to prepare, test, and revise policies and regulations: "experimental points" or "proceeding from point to surface." The term "experimental point" indicates experimentation with new policies or institutions, limited to a certain policy area or economic sector and carried out in limited experimental units. Most major reform initiatives in post-Mao China were prepared and tried out by means of experimental points before they were universalized in national regulations. At the end of the 1980s, the experimental point method became fully institutionalized at the central government level. Within the National Commission for Economic Structural Reform, a high-level Bureau for Comprehensive Planning and Experimental Points was established in 1988. This bureau, in existence until 1998, was charged with guiding and coordinating the various departmental and local experimental points in economic reform as well as with drafting related economic regulations. When the bureau was overwhelmed by the administrative complexity and political controversies inherent in this task, experimental point work was officially delegated to the regional governments in 1998.[21] However, individual central-government bodies continue to coordinate experimental point work to promote major national reform initiatives. General implementation guidelines are issued for every experimental point that is authorized by the central government. Initially, these guidelines were vague, simply establishing guiding thoughts and general demands. But in recent years, provisions regarding the establishment, objectives, and legal embedding of individual experimental points have become much more elaborate. A series of recently designated experimental points dealing with the rural reforms, for example, has been established by the issuance of a formal State Council circular for each pilot program.[22] Between 2003 and 2006, a total of 138 experimental point programs coordinated by 31 ministerial-level State Council organs can be documented, with a special focus on rural economic and societal policies, financial regulation, social security, health care, and education. Each of these experiments was implemented in several locations concurrently. Notwithstanding the overall regularization of legislative procedures since the mid-1990s, experimental points continue to be emphasized by national ministries as indispensable to optimize the implementation of national policies.

## Experimental zones

Whereas experimental points in a narrow sense involve testing specific measures in only a specific policy area, experimental zones are geographical units and jurisdictions that are provided by the central authorities with broad discretionary powers, for example, to streamline the economic bureaucracy or to promote foreign investment, and thereby generate or test new policy approaches.[23] Every new reform push has been characterized by the establishment of a new batch of special zones (see Table 3.1), "creating a new system alongside, or in the interstices of, the existing one" that served as a test ground for entire new sets of unorthodox policies and institutions.[24] The internationally best-known examples of this reform approach are China's special economic zones, which were also authorized to draft and enact their own legislation. The Shenzhen Special Economic Zone (SEZ), due to its proximity to Hong Kong, was the most active laboratory of such legislation. It issued more than 400 economic regulations from 1979 to 1990 and exerted a strong influence on national economic legislation with regard to foreign trade and investment.[25] The SEZ experiments are characterized by testing in a Chinese context controversial policies that were often inspired by experiences in neighboring East Asian or Western advanced economies. The actual content of many major experimental policies pioneered in the SEZs, for example those dealing with land auctions, wholly foreign-owned companies, or labor market liberalization, far exceeded the reform limitations that at the time still applied to the rest of China. Thus, the SEZs were distinct from the conventional experimental points that remained fully integrated in the domestic economy and were subject to strict political constraints.

Table 3.1   Major Types of Experimental Zones Designated by China's Central Government

| | | |
|---|---|---|
| 1. | Special Economic Zones (from 1979) | 5 |
| 2. | Cities with a status as "Experimental Point for Compre¬hensive Reform" (from 1981) | 72 |
| 3. | Economic and Technological Development Zones (from 1984) | 54 |
| 4. | Coastal Economic Development Zones (from 1985) | 7 |
| 5. | Experimental Zones for Rural Reform (from 1987) | 30 |
| 6. | Experimental Zones for Developing the Commodity Economy (Wenzhou, 1987–1989) | 1 |
| 7. | High-Tech Industrial Development Zones (from 1988) | 53 |
| 8. | Investment Zones for Taiwanese Investors (from 1989) | 4 |
| 9. | Shanghai Pudong New Zone (1990) | 1 |
| 10. | Bonded Zones (special customs regulations) (from 1990) | 15 |
| 11. | Border-Area Economic Cooperation Zones (from 1992) | 14 |
| 12. | "Experimental Zones for Comprehensive Coordinated Reform" (from 2005) | 2 |
| 13. | "Experimental Zones for Coordinated and Balanced Development between Urban and Rural Areas" (from 2007) | 2 |
| 14. | Experimental Zones for Free Trade (from 2013) | 11 |
| 15. | Experimental Zones for Comprehensive Innovation and Reform (from 2015) | 8 |

Sources: Data as of February 2017. Data compiled from: State Council General Office, ed., *Zhongguo jingji gaige kaifang shiyanqu* [China's Experimental Zones for Economic Reform and Opening] (Beijing: Zhongguo qingnian chubanshe, 1992); *Zhongguo jingji tizhi gaige nianjian* [China Economic Systems Reform Yearbook] (Beijing: Gaige chubanshe, various years). Homepages of the Ministry of Agriculture/Research Center for Rural Reform, at http://www.rcre.agri.cn, accessed November 17, 2017; Taiwan Affairs Office of the State Council, at http://www.gwytb.gov.cn, accessed November 17, 2017and media coverage.

Due to China's deep integration into the international economy, constraints on experimental policy solutions have been growing. WTO rules have placed restrictions on experimental regulations in the SEZs.[26] China's national legislature has taken an increasingly critical stance toward government experimentation that bypasses formal legislation. The CCP also emphasizes law-based policy implementation. Despite these recent constraints, institutional and policy experimentation continues to be employed vigorously in China. The government's ambitious plan to create a "new socialist countryside" has become a new field of intensive decentralized experimentation. During the 2000–2007 period, a huge variety of experimental point programs and point-to-surface replication efforts dealt with pressing rural issues, such as the marketing of rural products (from 2000), reduction of taxes and levies (2000–2004), land management (2001–4), cooperative health care (since 2003), and rural credit cooperatives (since 2003). Experimental programs resulted in major policy changes with respect to the elimination of entire categories of rural taxes and levies and the introduction of central government co-funding of rural health services. Beyond the rural reforms, in 2005 and 2006 two "experimental zones for comprehensive coordinated reform" in Shanghai and Tianjin were designated by the central government to deal with the issue of institutional complementarities between economic, social, and administrative development. Experimental policy tools continue to be used for pioneering reforms that are at the top of the policy agenda.

## The experimentation-based policy cycle

In rule-of-law systems, the principle of law-based administration rules out discretionary and experimental administrative measures before the enactment of laws and regulations. One striking feature of the legislation-centered policy process in liberal democracies is that the potential impact of policies under deliberation must be largely assessed beforehand, without first being able to refine novel policies through implementation at experimental sites. Even the much-quoted state-level policy innovation in federalist systems ("laboratories of federalism") firmly rests on issuing laws and regulations and rarely involves pre-legislation administrative experiments.

Conversely, discretionary experimentation through implementation in advance of legislation plays a crucial role in China's policy cycle. The analytical model depicted in Figure 3.2 synthesizes common features that can be identified across the different areas of reform experimentation and also lie at the heart of the policy cases examined in the following sections of this chapter. In terms of their content and sequence, these patterns differ starkly from the standard models in the policy cycle.

As can be expected in an authoritarian party-state, initiation of experimental programs from inside the government is by far the most frequent starting point of policy experimentation. Based on findings obtained from a series of interviews with senior officials who have been in charge of experimental point work during the last three decades, most experimental efforts are initiated by local policy makers who, to tackle pressing problems in their respective jurisdiction and at the same time to pursue personal career and material interests, seek informal support for their pilot efforts by higher-level policy patrons. Contacts are usually made during inspection tours by senior leaders to the localities or through secretaries, advisers, and researchers who serve as go-betweens for policy makers at different administrative levels. Encouragement and protection extended by senior leaders to those involved in local experimentation, a mechanism of informal "policy hedging," are major determinants of pioneering behavior at the local level because unhedged individual initiative can be risky in terms of one's career or simply futile within the Chinese polity. Even in cases such as rural decollectivization and private business growth, in which popular entrepreneurship at the outset triggered local policy adjustments, the informal rules of policy hedging and senior patronage turned out to be decisive in legitimating, defending, and scaling up the local experiments. In a hierarchical system, bottom-up experimentation will not succeed without higher-level patrons or advocates who are indispensable in disseminating and introducing locally-generated policy innovations. In essence, as the following case studies will demonstrate, distinguishing between bottom-up ("spontaneous") and top-down ("mobilization-style") initiation of experimentation is nearly meaningless since there is a strong element of both, local initiative and central sponsorship, during the initial stages of major experimental efforts. One will not work without the other. The dynamics of the experimental process rest precisely on this interplay (Figure 3.2 [I]).

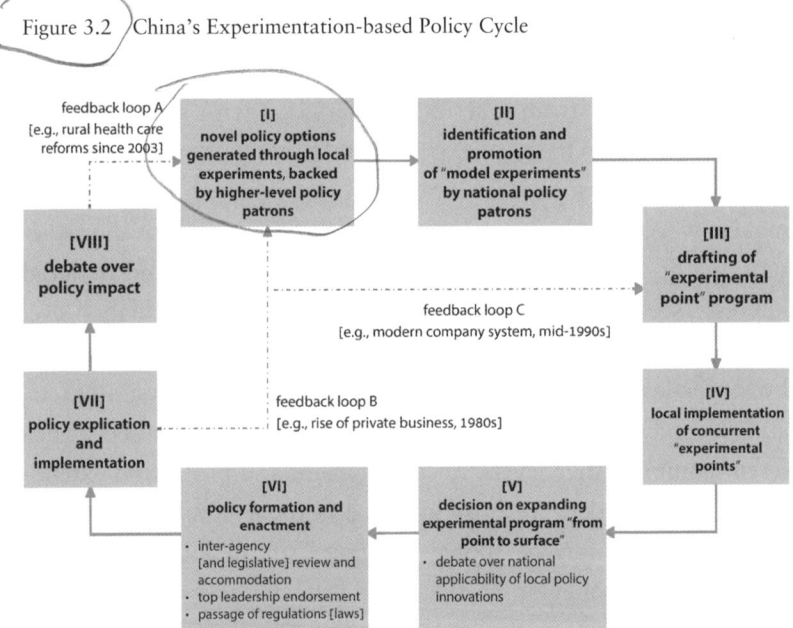

Figure 3.2 China's Experimentation-based Policy Cycle

After the results and means of local experimentation have been endorsed by a powerful policy maker as a model for others, veritable campaigns to broaden support for the new policy option are initiated by top-level policy advocates and their followers. Policy advisers and researchers are typically asked to conduct systematic studies that take into account domestic and foreign experiences. Foreign experts from economically advanced countries and international organizations are invited to contribute to policy intelligence and to drafting concrete proposals (Figure 3.2 [II]). If positive results of local experiments and potential benefits of policy innovation can be successfully communicated among the policy-making community, and if other top-level decision-makers join the policy initiative, national guidelines for piloting in a larger number of "experimental points" will be formulated. This action leads to an intensification of lobbying efforts by local officials who seek to obtain official "experimental point" status to gain access to central preferential treatment and to improve their career prospects (Figure 3.2 [III]).

The central government authorizes the jurisdictions that have been selected as official experimental points to try out new policy solutions. The center also selectively extends generous subsidies (at least to the end of the 1990s) and discretionary powers to the designated pilot projects that must report regularly to higher-up authorities (Figure 3.2 [IV]). Inspectors are sent in to conduct official evaluations. Feedback and consultation between national policy makers and those involved in local experimentation are facilitated during official conferences that deal with the lessons learned from the local experiments. Policy makers identify successful innovations produced by the experimental units. These innovations then become the subject of internal and often also public debate. If several major national policy makers support the "model experience" of specific experimental points and agree to "proceed from point to surface," a new wave of pilots based on the "model experiment" is extended to many more local jurisdictions. Simultaneous emulation campaigns are introduced, frequently triggering a veritable policy tourism, with hundreds of outside delegations converging on the sites of the officially designated "model experiments" (Figure 3.2 [V]).

National policy makers order the drafting of formal government regulations or laws and provide detailed directives to the drafting group. Thereafter begins a complex process of interministerial review and accommodation, which is similar to bureaucratic regulation-making in most other polities. Top national policy makers can still stall the new policy initiative. But if none of them organizes energetic opposition, the new policy will be accepted by the Politburo and the State Council and will be imposed nationwide through central party directives, government regulations, or the law (Figure 3.2 [VI]). Yet the adoption of new regulations or laws is not the end of the policy process since the ensuing explication and implementation of policy (Figure 3.2 [VII]) may yield a new round of experimentation, as indicated by feedback loops B and C in Figure 3.2. Those government regulations that are marked as "provisional" or "experimental" in their titles expressly invite policy modification. Feedback loop A, through which a new round of experimentation is initiated in response to the impact of new policies (Figure 3.2 [VIII]), is the standard feedback mechanism. All three basic types of feedback processes are found in the case studies presented below.

It is the distinctive interaction of generating national and local policy that is essential for continuing the experimental policy cycle. Those involved in hands-on experimentation in local governments are the most critical, not those in the central government whose role is to filter out generalizable models and policy lessons derived from the local experiences. Centrifugal forces that naturally come up in such a policy process are contained by the hierarchical nature of the Communist Party's system of top-down cadre appointments, which include all important leading positions in the polity and the state-controlled parts of the economy. Due to its segmented character, policy experimentation prevents collective action by local governments that, instead of collaborating to demand all-out decentralization, lobby the central government for individual concessions.²⁷ The atomistic character of intrastate lobbying essentially bolsters the political authority of the center.

In their study of central-local interactions in China's reform process, Cao, Qian, and Weingast draw analogies with federalism but they neglect the central role of higher-level policy makers in granting local experiments a go-ahead through non-intervention, informal patronage, or public advocacy.²⁸ In a hierarchical system of official appointments, the authority of the higher levels must be taken into account even by the boldest local-level pioneers of reform. The "federalism, Chinese style" approach suggests that hierarchical governance has been replaced by administrative decentralization, jurisdictional competition, and central-local bargaining. Although these factors play an important role in central-local interactions and local governments clearly feel more confident and secure today in making local policies, none of these changes has eliminated the weight of hierarchy and the ad hoc central interference in China's political economy.

As an organizational approach, the Chinese "point-to-surface" approach in policy development is devised to ensure local initiative while maintaining ultimate hierarchical control.²⁹ Since this method is decidedly open with regard to the means of reform, it naturally leads to decentralized initiatives that cannot be anticipated by the center. In the process of policy conception, implementation, and revision, governments at various levels thereby become participants, sometimes leaders, and sometimes followers of reform initiatives. The entire policy process must be conceptualized as an oscillating multi-level interaction rather than as a dichotomized process of centralization versus decentralization.

## The impact of experimentation in major policy domains

The pervasive use of special tools and patterns of experimentation substantiates the importance of unorthodox policy mechanisms in China's approach to economic reform but it does not tell us much about the actual interests behind, and effects resulting from, experimental regulations, points, or zones during the policy process. To clarify the functions and effects of experimentation in China's economic transformation, we must take a closer look at crucial contested areas of reform-era policy making.

As the discipline of policy studies has amply demonstrated, policy making is "taking place in policy domain-specific subsystems, which operate more or less independently of one another in a parallel fashion."[30] Thus the specific configuration of institutions, actors, interests, ideas, issues, and risks in a policy subsystem determines the chances for generating and revising policy. Moreover, policy subsystems tend to reveal durable patterns of interaction, which undergo major changes if systemic or sectoral crises destroy core elements of the old configuration or, less dramatically, if new actors with differing interests and ideologies manage to enter the subsystem and modify the customary rules of the game.

To classify the major domains of China's economic reform according to their dynamics of experimentation, Table 3.2 is structured along two key variables: (1) newly emerging economic actors and their opportunities for interest articulation in national policy making, and (2) the policy risk attached to experimentation, which is narrowly defined as the extent of uncertainty among national policy makers regarding the impact of experimentation on core properties of the political economy (state control and the dominant position of state-owned enterprises) and on essential systemic outputs (economic growth and social stability).

Table 3.2  Patterns of Experimentation in Crucial Areas of Economic Reform

|  | Denial and delay of the entrance of new actors to national policy making | Entrance of new actors to national policy making |
|---|---|---|
| Extensive policy risks in experimentation | restructuring of state-owned enterprises (1978–mid-1990s) | liberalization of foreign investment and trade (1992–2000) |
|  | incentivized bureaucratic experimentation results in tinkering of the policy repertoire | central policy pushes trigger for runaway local experimentation |
| Limited policy risks in experimentation | toleration and promotion of private business (1978–2004) | introduction and regulation of stock exchanges (1990–2005) |
|  | low-key local experimentation sets off successive national policy adjustments | technocratic grand experimentation allows extension of the policy repertoire |

Political macro-conditions that were particularly volatile during the first phase of economic reform (1978–91) clearly had an immediate impact on all policy subsystems discussed here. Before the 1992 turning point, economic policy was strongly contested and "reforms seemed to advance strongly in certain years and retreat in other years."[31] In spite of the changing "macro-climate" in China's polity, the four policy subsystems studied here (state-owned enterprises, private business, foreign trade and investment, and stock markets) reveal "micro-climates" that diverged considerably from overall policy moods. Each policy subsystem worked according to a distinct logic of policy making. Yet policy change through experimentation still played a crucial role in each of them.

The following case studies do not do justice to the entire sequence and intricacies of the reform measures in the respective policy domains. The case studies focus instead on the factors that help to understand the contribution of experimentation to facilitating policy change: the configurations of policy actors, risk perceptions, conflict ("factionalism") and consensus among national policy makers, the interplay between local initiative and central support, and the type and extent of policy renewal, ranging from policy tinkering to strategic departures.

## Policy tinkering in a closed subsystem: State-owned enterprises

From 1978 to the mid-1990s, reforms at the core of China's socialist economy, the state-owned enterprise (SOE) sector, took place in a virtually closed policy subsystem, dominated by powerful entrenched state bureaucratic and enterprise actors with strong vested interests and shored up by official ideological adherence to state control over strategic economic assets. Under such restrictive conditions, policy experimentation was confined to tinkering with a policy repertoire that continued to be based on bureaucratic instruments and incentives for making SOE management less wasteful. SOE managers and their patrons in the industrial bureaus continued to be successful in lobbying top policy makers to refrain from exposing SOEs to harder budget constraints. These factors worked to delay for almost two decades the entry of new actors and new regulatory frameworks into the national policy-making arena until the subsystem was forced open by mounting perceptions of financial crisis and the imposition of a new policy paradigm that aimed at "grasping the big, releasing the small [SOEs]."

Experimental programs in the 1980s (see Table 3.3), designed as a response to chronic SOE deficits, were mainly oriented to improving the performance (less waste, better products, fewer state subsidies) of the SOEs by providing additional incentives and decision-making powers to SOE managers, albeit without transforming the bureaucratic institutional set-up outside of the companies.[32] But reformist experimentation met with strong reservations from parts of the policy-making community, industrial bureaucracies, and the national legislature. In effect, SOE restructuring that went beyond changes in the bureaucratic incentives and aimed at full-scale corporate reorganization turned out to be unsuccessful.[33]

Table 3.3 "Experimental Point" Programs in China's State Sector, 1978–97

| | |
|---|---|
| delegation of greater autonomy to enterprises | 1978–80 |
| delivery of contract profits to the state | 1981–82 |
| substitution of profits with taxes | 1983–86 |
| transformation of SOEs into shareholding companies | 1984–97 |
| bankruptcy regulation | 1984–97 |
| preparation of the national SOE law | 1984–88 |
| SOE responsibility contracts | 1987–93 |
| establishment of enterprise groups | 1991–97 |
| modern company system (formal corporatization of large SOEs) | 1994–97 |

Source: *Zhongguo jingji tizhi gaige nianjian* [China Economic Systems Reform Yearbook] (Beijing: Gaige chubanshe, various years).

In the mid-1990s, an ambitious new attempt to transform SOE operations was undertaken with the "modern company system" (MCS) experimental program. Confronted with an accelerating accumulation of state-sector debts, top policy makers agreed on the need for a thoroughgoing SOE restructuring. As a result, a new Company Law was passed in 1993, which envisaged the transformation of SOEs into modern business entities with transparent corporate-governance structures, while still shunning the privatization of state assets. Policy implementation was then based on "post-law experimentation" (see Figure 3.2, feedback loop C): MCS experiments were designed to smooth the implementation of a reformist national law. Experimental points established between 1994 and 1997 revealed how tacit resistance by SOE managers and their supervisory agencies produced a heavily bureaucratized design for experimentation and consequently meager results. An evaluation of MCS implementation in the 100 centrally-supervised experimental companies at the end of 1996 concluded that "almost no experimental enterprise has achieved the minimum standards of a modern corporation."[34] Overall, the MCS program appeared heavily inhibited and clumsy in comparison to the pioneering experimentation that was possible in more open policy subsystems.

Policy tinkering in SOE reform helped to contain political and ideological controversies, but it allowed only incremental change. By the mid-1990s, SOE management had moved away from the earlier rigid administrative coordination, but it was still dominated by the socialist legacy of soft budget constraints. The closed and sluggish policy regime in China's state sector was finally broken up in response to the mounting financial risks that were perceived as an immediate threat due to the Asian Financial Crisis. Beginning in 1997, China's central policy makers moved beyond incremental reform and adopted a package of transformative policies to turn around the SOEs. These policies included large-scale mergers, management and employee buyouts, takeovers of small SOEs by private investors, the inclusion of foreign strategic partners, closures, mass layoffs, and exposure to international competition through WTO accession.

## Successive policy adjustments in a curbed subsystem: Private business

From 1978 to 2004, the promotion of private business took place in a curbed policy subsystem. For ideological reasons, private business was one of the least acceptable emerging elements in China's reforming socialist economy and, at the outset, it was tolerated only as a marginal, temporary, and controlled supplement, which was not allowed to disrupt the public sector and therefore did not pose a major policy risk.[35] The lack of official recognition severely restricted the articulation of private-sector demands at the level of national policy making until the mid-1990s. Locally, business interests were curbed by officials who first obstructed the emergence of the private sector but who then quickly learned to extract new resources (most importantly taxes, fees, kickbacks, and employment) from private companies. Private business underwent a gradual political ascent, beginning locally and then progressing from a "dependent clientelism" to varying patterns of "symbiotic clientelism" in which those involved in private business managed to further their interests through collusive relations with local officials who had a strong interest in opening up a new source of levies that were not subject to central controls.[36] During the early stages of reform, central-state policy toward the private sector was confined to vague policy statements that had to be "stretched" by local governments to justify ideologically-dubious private-business experimentation. Therefore, policy change in this reform domain was driven by unregulated, low-key, yet broad-based, bottom-up initiative. We find a sequence of "unpublicized experimentation, followed by a general 'in principle' approval, then by ratification and specific regulations" only after the new type of economic activity was already widespread and flourishing locally.[37]

Moving beyond low-key local experimentation, reformist central policy makers undertook a prominent initiative to elevate a powerhouse of self-propelled private business development to a national model when, in late 1986, they designated the coastal Wenzhou district as an "experimental zone for developing the commodity economy." After obtaining the official label of an "experimental zone," the local government pioneered in formulating China's first regulations on joint stock cooperative firms and non-state financial institutions, both ideologically contested innovations that attracted much national publicity for about two years. Reformist policy makers and their advisers used the Wenzhou experimental zone to demonstrate the potential advantages of private business growth and to question official adherence to the dominance of public enterprise. The debate over the Wenzhou private-sector pattern prepared the ground for new national regulations in 1987 and a constitutional amendment in 1988, which improved the legal standing of private firms. The Wenzhou experiments had a major impact on national policy debates until the political winds blowing from Beijing changed drastically in 1989 and de facto terminated the official legitimation of the "experimental zone."[38]

Local policy making in relation to the emerging private sector generally was strongly discretionary. Myriad provisional regulations and temporary permits were extended to private businesses. One crucial informal institutional innovation utilized by local governments throughout China was the registration of private companies as "collective" enterprises to conceal the true extent of the private sector and to avoid the political pitfalls involved in the open promotion of non-socialist businesses. This transitional institutional arrangement was tacitly tolerated by central policy makers for most of the 1980s and 1990s, and it faced heavy political fire only briefly during the ideologically charged years between 1989 and 1991. Pretending to belong to the socialist "collective" economy was crucial to the private sector's spectacular, yet concealed, growth until the mid-1990s when most entrepreneurs began to feel sufficiently safe to stage their public "coming out" and to officially register as private businesses. Local experience with promoting and regulating private business provided the basis for successive national policy adjustments between 1987 and 2004. Official access to the national policy arena was obtained from the mid-1990s through the reactivation of the Federation of Industry and Commerce that had represented the private sector in the 1950s but since then had been mainly dormant. However, private enterprise and private property did not enjoy full legal protection until 2004, when the state constitution eventually guaranteed a credible legal and political status.

The ascent of China's private sector is a remarkable example of how, over time, bottom-up experimentation promoted a gradual, yet transformative change of policy parameters and priorities in a politically curbed subsystem. From the central government's perspective, a problematic legacy of locally-driven policy innovation exists in the entrenchment of collusive networks between local officials and entrepreneurs that continue to pose a challenge to unified national regulation and taxation of the private sector.

*Policy departures in a partially open subsystem:*
*Foreign investment and trade*

As opposed to the 1978–91 period when foreign opening, and in particular the SEZs, were the subject of major political controversy, the promotion of foreign trade and investment took place in a policy subsystem that was effectively cracked open by the strong reformist initiative launched by Deng Xiaoping in early 1992. Consequently, China's integration into the world economy became driven by a drastic policy departure consisting of redefinitions of the goals, instruments, and rules guiding foreign economic relations. Economic opening was officially extended from the coastal regions to all of China,[39] thereby accepting the extensive risks inherent in downgrading central state control over the external economy and in inviting powerful foreign investors and companies. Ideological debates and factional rivalries that had accompanied the market-oriented reforms in the 1980s were effectively silenced by Deng's injunction to end discussion of the economic reforms in rigid antagonistic (socialist versus capitalist) categories. The shockwaves from the disintegration of the Soviet Union contributed to elite consent as much as Deng Xiaoping's fierce reformist determination.

The ambitious central policy packages formulated in 1992–93 called for "breakthroughs" in transforming the economic system into an internationally competitive "socialist market economy", and amounted to a comprehensive overhaul of economic strategy. This forceful central policy push, which signaled a strategic opportunity for policy entrepreneurs, was immediately understood locally. The pushes in reform in 1992–93 triggered runaway "policy grabs" and spontaneous experimentation by local officials who were eager to benefit from the new dynamism in transnational economic exchanges. Local policy makers started to lobby and compete fiercely to establish special trade and development zones and to obtain preferential conditions, which were extended selectively by the central government to boost foreign trade and investment. In securing policy privileges, formal bureaucratic application procedures proved to be much less important than the support of individual national policy makers who could serve as advocates for the establishment of particular zones.[40] Because many local policy makers did not wait for proper approval to establish special zones, the central government undertook several retrenchments, forcing the closure of illicit zones that consumed huge public investment funds and offered generous tax breaks to investors without considering the effects on macroeconomic stability.

During the post-1992 policy rush, economic exchanges with the outside world were transformed from a supportive measure of reform to a core pillar for China's modernization. The proliferation of special trade and development zones broadened support among local officials for market-oriented reform.[41] Because the special zones provided foreign-trade opportunities to countless domestic firms, which conducted their transactions through the zones, the role of the zones exceeded that of local experimental sites and they became crucial to the rise of new foreign trade–oriented actors across China's domestic economy.[42]

The preferential policies, bestowed by the central government on trade and development zones, provided economic incentives. The policies also allowed much room for experimenting with novel administrative and business practices as well as for generating new policies and regulations,[43] whereas most other jurisdictions still had to play by the established rules. This "segmented deregulation" created a policy regime in which central decision-makers, not market forces, determined "which localities had a comparative advantage in foreign and domestic trade."[44] From an economic perspective, this approach created severe distortions and opportunities for rent-seeking. But viewed in terms of policy reform, segmented deregulation was highly conducive to reorienting policy makers and administrators toward foreign trade and investment.

Joint central-local initiatives achieved the post-1992 policy departure in China's foreign economic relations. Central policy making determined the speed and extent of deregulation, but keen competition for preferential policies from the localities exerted new types of pressures on central policy makers. Remarkably, China's economic opening before WTO accession was "accomplished not by liberalization but by a series of administrative arrangements that achieved a bureaucratic consensus and accommodated the individual incentives of central and local political officials."[45] The post-1992 policy rush prepared the ground for the next, much more formalized, treaty- and law-based policy departure in 2001 when WTO accession deepened and liberalized China's participation in world trade and investment flows.

*Extension of the policy in an alien subsystem: The stock market*

In the construction and regulation of stock exchanges in Shanghai and Shenzhen since 1990 we find rare constellations of a policy subsystem that represents a radically alien element in China's political economy. The stock market had to be "squeezed into an economy still based on state planning and the absence of private ownership."[46] Insiders from China's newly emerging financial industry, using their excellent connections to top national policy makers, had launched the policy initiative to establish stock exchanges in a socialist economy on an experimental basis. Limited experiments with issuing shares and trading had already been approved by the central government and udertaken locally during the 1980s. Remarkably, giving stock exchanges a hand in financing and restructuring enterprises was judged to be a low-risk initiative and therefore was supported even by otherwise staunch sceptics of capitalist methods because this experiment was designed to open new channels for SOE financing without relinquishing state control over the listed entities.[47] Operating under these basic political constraints, financial reformers managed to insert a new set of policy instruments—stock exchanges with their accompanying institutions and organizations—into a political economy that lacked a credible legal definition and protection of private property and equity rights. The introduction of stock exchanges represented a grand technocratic experimentation that produced an odd combination of state control over most listed assets and the volatile dynamics of equity trade and speculation.

Whereas the Shanghai and Shenzhen stock exchanges were under the supervision of the respective municipal governments in the early to mid-1990s, national regulatory institutions were only gradually established between 1993 and 1997. After 1997, responding to a series of shocking domestic scandals and to the challenge of the Asian Financial Crisis, the central government brought the stock exchanges under its control, affirmed their legitimate role in the socialist market economy, and made them serve the purposes of national industrial policy and SOE restructuring.

The overall history of the stock market in China is marked by a series of experimental schemes. Most important were the repackaging of SOEs into listed shareholding companies (early 1990s), selected transfers of legal person shares to new owners (1992),

Hong Kong listings of SOEs (1993), the creation of "national champions" (from the second half of the 1990s), and several attempts to reduce the holdings of state shares (1999, 2001, and 2005). The two stock exchanges were classified as "experimental points" from 1990 to 1997.

The novel set of policy instruments that was introduced through the stock market experiments brought much less substantive change to the Chinese economy than might be expected. The stock market has remained dominated by government agencies and government-linked companies that are eager to raise capital by going public, but they share a common interest to block the access and ascent of private corporate competitors. Politically well-connected companies continue to dominate the market, and since market growth is generally subject to strict regulation and supervision, the officially sought-after benefits of the shareholding experiment (better corporate governance, greater competitiveness, etc.) have largely remained unattainable.[48] Overall, the fundamental policy parameters guiding the stock market experiment from the beginning have not been transformative. The exchanges were not designed to become a vehicle of privatization but rather to raise capital for government-linked companies. Whether the institutions and practices of the stock markets can be credibly adapted to China's corporate world, which is dominated by state actors and shaped by constant political interference, remains an unresolved issue.

## *Limits to elite-sponsored experimentation: Social goods and societal participation*

In such case studies in areas of major economic reforms, initiatives from inside the government played a dominant role in beginning experimentation, as to be expeced in an authoritarian polity. Yet outside initiation—that is, bringing policy issues to the national agenda through social demands and public criticism—has become more prevalent during China's recent reform experience.

The Chinese practice of elite-sponsored experimentation, geared toward opening new channels for profit-seeking and rent-seeking opportunities, does not solve the problems of those segments of society that have been left behind in terms of economic growth and does not have the economic status and means to influence administrative discretion. A systematic dilemma of providing social goods in developing political economies is that decentralization, due to collusive rent-seeking between local political and economic elites, may work to the detriment of weaker segments of the population.[49] Remarkable for an authoritarian polity and clearly influenced by international assistance, since the mid-1990s official experimental programs, aimed at improving the provision of social and public goods, have been complemented by more systematic societal consultation. Developments in the intensely disputed fields of rural health care and land management illustrate this phenonomen.

## *Rural health care*

As a side-effect of rural decollectivization and marketization, the Maoist basic cooperative medical scheme, which had been effective in preventing epidemics and raising life expectancy in the countryside, had almost totally collapsed in the early 1990s. By 2003, about 80 percent of the rural population no longer had any form of health insurance. Beginning in the late 1980s, various local pilot programs in rural health-care reform were endorsed by the central government and carried out with the continuous involvement of international governmental and non-governmental organizations. But none of the pilot efforts became a national reform program.[50] Rural health reform was only pushed to the top of the national policy agenda when the SARS epidemic in 2003 triggered massive public criticism, which resulted in government statements that the official approach to privatize health care in the countryside had been a failure.⁵¹ Public outrage over the outbreak of SARS led to a change in the policy paradigm. Central state co-funding of a "new cooperative medical scheme" became the basis for large-scale experimental programs that were undertaken in 300 of China's more than 2,000 counties beginning in 2003. An innovative feature of several pilot programs made local health providers and administrators accountable and rendered health expenses transparent by giving popular representatives seats on supervisory boards. Though all tested variants of the new medical scheme left many expenses uncovered and therefore only brought about partial solutions, health care was pushed swiftly to the top of the policy-making agenda due to a new intensity of public involvement and societal pressures on policy makers.

*Land management*

In the context of rapid industrial and real-estate development in formerly agricultural areas, since the end of the 1990s abusive requisitions of land and standards of compensation have become an intensely contested policy issue, leading to local protests, petition movements, and public debates about better regulation. After a new law on land management issued in 1998 failed to resolve these massive ongoing conflicts, in 2005 and 2006 the central government sponsored and evaluated several rounds of local experimental programs⁵² and issued a series of trial regulations on the transfer of tenure rights and fair compensation. Continuing public protests were the driving force behind these extensive efforts to revise official policy.

The tensions, conflicts, and abuses inherent in these policy areas have not been settled. But popular voice and peasant interests have been legitimized as an integral part of policy making by the new variant of consultation-based experimentation. Since 2004, new government guidelines for "administration in accordance with the law" have institutionalized the role of public scrutiny as a regular element in drafting legislation.[53] State-sponsored experimentation that seeks societal input has complemented policy making but has not transformed it. Societal input is still ad hoc and selective, and civil society organizations do not play a significant or institutionalized role. Although agenda-setting has become more open to public demands, the overall policy process is still controlled by government decision-makers. Therefore, as officials and foreign advisers involved in years of experimental point work have stated: In China, "efforts to effect change must focus on mobilizing powerful officials ... to allow experimentation to proceed. A major challenge for scaling up program reform in China is to build innovation from within the government, which remains the main actor in service delivery and policy formulation."[54]

Herein is a core dilemma of policy experimentation in China's current political system: experimental programs that do not immediately benefit the interests of local elites have a very slim chance of success. Negligence in dealing with rural health care prior to the SARS crisis makes this clear. Only when public outrage pushed reform of the health system to the top of the national agenda and societal consultation became an integral element in the policy process did experimentation begin to generate more viable reform schemes.

The crucial importance of bottom-up initiative to policy experimentation is also manifest in the economic reforms. Experimentation resulted in transformative change only in those areas in which new social actors, in particular private entrepreneurs and transnational investors, were most actively involved and worked to redefine the entrenched rules of the game and power configurations. The emergence of new profit-seeking entrepreneurs was promoted by political-administrative actors who found many new opportunities for dividend-collecting (a variant of rent-seeking that is compatible with economic growth)⁵⁵ in the rapidly growing private and transnational economic activities. The interplay between profit-seeking and dividend-collecting behavior made policy experimentation and institutional innovation in terms of private business and foreign economic relations so powerful. In policy areas that remained under the control of vested state interests and in which state actors tended to lock in partial reforms, as in SOE management (from 1978 to the mid-1990s) or stock market regulation (1990–2005), extensive experimentation produced only incremental innovation at best.

## Policy learning and rent-seeking

China's economic reforms and the policy processes that facilitated them clearly cannot be reduced to being a rational response by policy makers to inefficiencies in the economic system.⁵⁶ For policy makers who wanted to change how the economy was run, experimentation turned out to be a good way to deal with uncertainties (the inability to predict the precise impact of specific reforms in a rapidly changing economic context) and ambiguities (the ambivalence, vagueness, or even confusion in policy makers' thinking about their policy priorities). From setting policy objectives to selecting model experiments and identifying generalizable policy options, experimentation has always been an intensely politicized process driven by tactical opportunism, personal rivalries, clashes of interests and ideologies, ad hoc crisis management, or strategic consensus-building.

In the political logic of economic reform, policy experimentation minimized political resistance and political risks. In cases of success, it maximized political support and political gains.⁵⁷ Forceful policy makers, such as Zhu Rongji (China's preeminent economic leader from 1992 to 2002), utilized experimental point programs to ultimately prepare for radical policy shifts in the guise of incremental measures, thereby reducing reform risks while increasing the "controllability" of reforms.[58] Zhu applied experimental schemes to smuggle in changes to the system and to achieve objectives that would have been politically obstructed if they had been revealed more explicitly beforehand.[59] Policy experimentation thus reduced the frictions and delays characteristic of top-level consensus-building and interagency accommodations, and helped to avoid protracted policy deadlocks.

In general, decentralized experimentation minimized the risks and the costs to central policy makers by placing the burden on local governments and providing welcome scapegoats in cases of failure. Locally-produced policy innovations were taken up by reformist policy makers eager to bolster their political standing and to keep their rivals at bay by godfathering local models that could demonstrate the success and superiority of their policy preferences. Local reform efforts that did not fulfil these highly contextual and tactical political exigencies did not reach the national policy agenda, as the example of experimental-point work in rural health care up to 2003 illustrates. However, active godfathering of individual reform exemplars by central policy makers could produce fake models that yielded wasteful policies and that were propagated for years until they were revealed to be unsustainable.[60] Since those involved in local experimentation tended to do everything possible to overstate the positive results of the pilot projects within their jurisdictions, ill-conceived and impracticable experiments often were detected only when they were spread "from point to surface." Experiments that got stuck at this stage were rarely publicly terminated in a clear-cut way. More often they were merely silently abandoned after having already created considerable social or budgetary costs (e.g., experiments to transform the structure and functions of local governments in the 1980s, to decentralize pension funds in the 1990s, or more recently to reconstruct the myriads of public-service institutions). Failed local experiments could be costly, but they were certainly much less costly than a failed national policy. Since 1978, "proceeding from point to surface," i.e., testing local experimental findings in more jurisdictions before entering national policy formulation, has been effective as a practical litmus test for novel reform approaches and has prevented the national disasters that were characteristic of several major economic policy initiatives during the 1957–78 period.[61]

Significantly, reform-era experimentation did not stop with the search for individual models and policy solutions. In society at large and among policy makers in particular, the experiments with rural markets, private business, and foreign investment stimulated comprehensive collective learning processes that resulted in serial, and cumulatively radical, redefinitions of policy parameters for economic activity. Experimentation prepared the ground for major policy breakthroughs by unspectacularly furthering dispersed institutional and policy changes, initiating learning processes and ideological reorientation among policy makers, undermining entrenched interests, and providing test runs for innovative administrative and business practices. Experimentation over time fundamentally transformed the economic-policy context for central and local decision-makers. In combination with transnational push factors, such as the Asian Financial Crisis and the WTO negotiations, experimentation also provided policy planks for reform departures in 1997 (SOE reform) and 2001 (foreign-trade liberalization) that included drastic reorganizations of China's economic administration. Protracted policy learning was helped immensely by the massive growth of private and transnational economic activity, which reduced pressures for immediate structural reforms of the public sector and thereby provided policy makers with an unusually opportune environment for long-term adaptation.

One of the most controversial aspects of policy experimentation is how much it promotes rent-seeking. Beyond a doubt, generating new sources of income for local elites has been a key driving force behind experimentation. However, this cannot be simply equated with wasteful or predatory rent-seeking since the material and career interests of local officials became an effective catalyst for entrepreneurship and innovation in many policy areas. In accordance with the logic of dividend-collecting, experimental programs that were seen as conducive to economic growth and generating income within a particular jurisdiction were vigorously pursued by local officials. This incentive structure facilitated the emergence of new profit-seeking entrepreneurship, new administrative practices, and new types of economic organization that frequently turned out to be highly productive in the rapidly changing context of China's political economy. From this perspective, experiments in economic policy generated diffuse benefits that unleashed the energies of local-level institutional and policy entrepreneurs and facilitated a broad realignment of interests among China's administrators in accordance with the economic growth imperative set by the national leadership.

China's record of policy experimentation is key to understanding how it was possible to create a series of transitional institutions that were generally not optimal by market-economy standards but often had efficiency-enhancing and Pareto-improving effects (predominantly during the 1978–94 period of reforms) or Kaldor-improving effects (predominantly since about 1994 and particularly in the state sector), and therefore were politically acceptable even to those who were initially opposed to reform.[62] Neoclassically-oriented Chinese economists tend to reject the use of experimental points in generating policy as an anachronistic instrument of an administrative state, which is incompatible with creating a "level playing field" for competition in a market economy and which blocks market-driven creation of reform solutions.⁶³ However, such a critique appears to be detached from the realities of China's political economy. The omnipresence of state agencies in the Chinese economy cannot be theorized away and render administrative involvement, guidance, and accommodation inevitable in the process of economic restructuring. For China's policy makers, the economic inefficiencies that are seen as inherent in experimentation by neoclassical economic theory constitute, in practice, a "necessary transaction cost" to maintain political control and social stability under conditions of rapid economic change.⁶⁴

## Conclusion

Compared to the standards of legal consistency and political and administrative accountability, which are part of policy implementation and which constrain open-ended experimentation under democratic rule of law, the Chinese practice of experimentation must be seen as arbitrary and volatile. Yet the unexpected capacity of the Chinese party-state to find innovative solutions to long-standing or newly emerging challenges of economic development rests on the broad-based entrepreneurship, adaptation, and learning facilitated by experimentation under hierarchy. It is the combination of decentralized experimentation with ad hoc central interference, which results in selective integration of local experiences into national policy making, that is key to understanding how a distinctive policy process has contributed to China's economic rise.

The limitations of experimentation are obvious in terms of improving the provision of social and public goods, such as access to basic health care and credible protection of land tenure rights in rural areas or environmental protection. The provision of these goods requires a combination of societal interest articulation and imposition of national policy priorities that contravenes the short-term interests of most local elites and therefore is not easily reconciled with the entrenched mode of economic experimentation.

Can China's experiment-based policy process provide lessons for other political economies to overcome obstacles to institutional change? China's experience strongly points to the potency of tapping local knowledge, mobilizing bottom-up initiative, and embracing decentralized policy generation as a contrasting approach to the imposition of international "best practices" that is regularly proposed by foreign economic advisers.[65] Moreover, it demonstrates that applying static standards of legislative consistency to the utterly fluid context of transitional economies may be detrimental to policy learning and institutional adaptation. It is questionable whether, in a context of rapid economic change, "deftly tailored regulations" really increase certainty for market participants and encourage rational market behavior.[66] Rather, by conducting extensive experimentation in advance of formal legislation, it may be possible to avoid many of the leaps in the dark that are inherent risks in rash national legislation.[67]

In addition, the Chinese case explains the complexity of the relationship between policy entrepreneurship and rent-seeking. Policy experimentation was shown to provide effective incentives for administrative and economic actors to embrace new types of both profit-seeking and rent-seeking behavior. Because changing the basic incentives for policy makers and administrators is a precondition for introducing reforms, it is important to allow local officials to derive dividends from entrepreneurial activities and growth in their jurisdictions. However, a symbiotic relationship between officials and entrepreneurs that is conducive to economic growth is likely only in a stable political environment in which actors can afford to take a longer-term perspective, not a grab-and-run view, of their interests in the local economy. The effectiveness of experimentation in China rests on special institutional prerequisites (the Communist Party's unitary, hierarchical organization and the Maoist legacy of cellular economic administration), narrowly defined policy imperatives (growth by any means), particular actor constellations (policy makers who are not subject to electoral cycles or democratic competition and who are unified in their commitment to economic modernization, yet who argue over the priorities, parameters, and methods of reform), and particular actor expectations. Whereas most policy makers, administrators, interest groups, and citizens in advanced political economies tend to view experimental policy departures as risky, destabilizing, and threatening to their stakes in the status quo, political actors in a less advanced, yet rapidly growing economy with a successful reform record, such as China, tend to display more confidence in the benefits of policy change.

Experimentation can innovate policy only as long as the dynamism of growth expectations is intact and newly emerging interest groups feel comfortable in a fluid policy environment. As soon as expectations and interests begin to shift in defense of the status quo or in favor of redistribution, experimentation becomes subject to increasing limitations from both the demand side and the supply side: interest groups and citizens come to ask for universal and irreversible regulation; domestic and transnational economic actors come to demand equal legal protection; and policy makers come to see experiments as a political risk that can be avoided by legislative incrementalism. The result is a hardening of political and legal constraints on policy experiments. In most political economies, this mechanism works against extensive experimentation, despite the many obvious advantages it may entail for institutional adaptation. China's party-state, which, for almost three decades, has demonstrated the potency of experiment-based economic governance but in recent years has begun to narrow the range of experimental activity, will hardly escape this logic.

# 4
# How to Combine Policy Experiments with Long-Term Priorities: Unorthodox Lessons from China*

## The great disillusionment with hegemonic Western paradigms

We are living in a time when many people wonder whether the dominant models that explain market-based political economies may be the product of a blinding ideology that serves only to legitimize unfettered business greed and wealth concentration while unloading the social costs and economic risks onto society at large. Economic paradigms that have enjoyed hegemonic status in the past, such as the much-praised information efficiency of financial markets, are falling apart. In the context of massive state rescue schemes and the nationalization of many financial firms, even the previously hegemonic marketization-cum-privatization paradigm (henceforth, "marcump") is rapidly losing credibility.

The dismantling of the "marcump" paradigm represents a major watershed for the social sciences since this paradigm has

---

\* This is a revised version of "Maximum Tinkering under Uncertainty: Unorthodox Lessons from China," originally published in *Modern China*, Vol. 35, No. 4 (July 2009), pp. 450–462, republished here with permission from SAGE Publications.

defined debates about economic and welfare policy making in advanced and developing political economies as well as in the post-socialist transformation in Eastern Europe and China during the past several decades. Because many standard Western recipes for economic policy are running out of steam, it is imperative to step back from past orthodox explanations and rethink the unusual approaches to managing economic change that we find in China's developmental experience.

The special July 2009 issue of *Modern China* assembles studies by major scholars who open up fresh ways to understand strategies of institutional restructuring,[1] patterns of policy learning,[2] and the pressing challenges of dealing with social equity.[3]

In this chapter, I focus on a critique and refinement of the assumptions, approaches, and normative implications underlying these studies. I criticize the drawbacks of synoptic models of reform-making and instead stress the strengths of processual and open-ended political economy approaches. I argue that the key to understanding the adaptability of China's political economy during the past several decades lies in its unusual combination of extensive policy experimentation with long-term policy prioritization—i.e., foresighted tinkering—that has been practiced under the shadow of a hierarchical authority structure.

As concerns about social equity, inclusion, and stability are gaining urgency both in China and globally, I insert some continental European ideas into the debates on remaking the social contract, drawing mainly on the "ordoliberal" strand of social theory that shaped continental European welfare states but in recent decades has been cast aside by a mainstream market fundamentalism. I conclude with the suggestion that China is an extremely instructive place to look for general lessons on creative management of uncertainty in policy making. Western social scientists and policy makers can learn much from China's distinctive experimentalist approach to structural and policy reform. At the same time, I suggest that in order to promote social inclusion and long-term social stability, Chinese social scientists should turn their attention away from the discredited "marcump" paradigm and contribute to refining those strands of social theory and policy agendas that may help build a more humane society and a robust social contract for tackling the challenges of the twenty-first century.

## The limits to synoptic models of China's reform process

How do we make sense and build models of China's reform process? Fan and Woo's critique of the policy sequencing approach to economic transition is certainly well founded.[4] Yet most of the sequencing models were formulated against the background of early post-socialist transformation (all the works that Fan and Woo cite on sequencing stem from the early 1990s or the 1980s) when issues of fundamental institutional design were at stake. The prescriptive value of "optimal sequencing" models and their usefulness to policy makers who had to navigate and make compromises in an often incalculable environment was subject to early questioning.[5]

More importantly, Fan and Woo's "Parallel Partial Progression" approach appears to share one basic weakness with the sequencing models. Fan and Woo assume that a government can "keep the reforms in different institutions compatible with each other," with the overall aim to "optimize the coherence" of policies and institutional reforms. Such a synoptic view of government as a super-coordinator of extremely complex reform packages is not a robust foundation for building an explanatory or even a prescriptive model. As Braybrooke and Lindblom point out, synoptic, rationalistic-deductive conceptions of policy making are generally untenable because they assume, first, that the entire spectrum of alternative policies is somehow known to the analyst and, second, the ultimate objectives of policy making are well defined and stable.[6] Yet it is precisely the discovery of policy and institutional alternatives in a constantly changing political-economic context that is the most uncertain and demanding part of the policy process.[7] How can we derive the content of the "partial reforms" ("20 percent") that Fan and Woo propose if the ultimate goals (the "100 percent" of "complete" and "required" reforms) remain ambiguous and undefined among both policy makers and social scientists? The underlying assumption that a political economy is transitioning from "status I" to a definable or desirable "status II" is highly problematic due to its teleological or ideological biases: Is it not the now discredited "marcump" paradigm that has served as the benchmark for most economists in assessing China's transitional status? How can we be sure that China is really moving in a "marcump" direction? Furthermore, how do we know whether this paradigm will be working and will be acceptable to a future Chinese society? As a result, the transition paradigm has come under heavy criticism and is no longer widely used in political science.[8]

Lindblom formulates a central proposition for policy studies that has been bolstered by broad empirical evidence from all types of polities over recent decades when he states that policy is "made and re-made endlessly. Policymaking is a process of successive approximation to some desired objectives in which what is desired itself continues to change under reconsideration."[9] Fan and Woo tend to downplay the inherent ambiguity and discontinuity of this search for policy options under uncertainty. In their concluding paragraph, they state that research on an optimal coherence of reform packages may become "more of a science" if intensified. In light of Lindblom's proposition, this represents a "scientistic" misunderstanding of the policy process and ignores the "wicked" character of complex reform agendas. Interlinked institutional and policy reforms represent particularly "wicked problems" or "complex social messes"[10] that are characterized by extensive uncertainties about the feasibility and consequences of interventions, pervasive ambiguities, controversies, and indecision on the part of policy makers, unique and rapidly shifting conditions for intervention and interaction, and multiple unforeseeable feedback as well as unexpected endogenous and exogenous developments or shocks that can transform the entire playing field within a short period of time.

China's concrete experience has rarely been characterized by coordinated reform packages but rather by an unsynchronized, piecemeal process of reform-making whose strength is not its coherence but rather its openness to unexpected and tentative policy solutions that are seized upon when they arise. The tensions between synoptic and piecemeal policy making are illustrated strikingly by the reforms of the urban state sector. Chinese policy makers had already become well aware of the necessity of "comprehensive complementary reform" (*zonghe peitao gaige*) to restructure the urban political economy in the mid-1980s. Hence, they initiated numerous experimental programs to deal with interlinked reform requirements in enterprises, bureaucracies, and welfare provision. Though these efforts at coordinated reform were of modest size, they became "stuck" during their early stages, thereby demonstrating the complexity, costs, and risks of "coherent" reform packages for the urban state sector. Throughout the 1990s we find experimentation with "comprehensive complementary reform" as state-sector debts continued to accumulate. Though many experiments were regarded as failures, they helped policy makers understand the underlying institutional, social, and financial exigencies, to discover the cost and risk structure of state-sector reform, and to try out diverse approaches to problem-solving.

Broad-based tinkering effectively enriched and transformed the economic policy know-how of local and central decision-makers and administrators. Protracted policy learning was helped immensely by the massive growth of private and transnational economic activities that reduced pressures for immediate structural reforms in the public sector and thereby provided policy makers with an opportune environment for adaptation over an extended period. Reform breakthroughs that contained comprehensive packages of interlinked restructuring policies occurred in 1992–93 (the program for market-oriented restructuring), 1997–98 (the state-owned enterprise [SOE] and the financial industry reforms), and 2001–2 (foreign trade and investment liberalization) when external push factors (the collapse of the Soviet Union, the Asian Financial Crisis, and World Trade Organization (WTO) negotiations, respectively, propelled top-level policy decisiveness that could build on the diverse experiences obtained through the years of piecemeal tinkering.

In sum, China's policy makers early on understood that complementary and coherent reform packages were optimal to deal with the administrative and welfare impacts of the SOE reforms. But they could not, and still cannot, build a policy consensus, vision, or agenda about what the state sector should look like at the end of its transformation because sweeping privatization was, and is, neither desirable nor acceptable to most policy makers. Beyond the ultimate policy goals, they were also unsure about the policy instruments. They did not know what types of policies could solve the most pressing deficiencies of the state sector without the loss of control. Instead of settling for a deadlock in economic reform as in Brezhnev's Soviet Union, Chinese policy makers tinkered with incoherent, yet still instructive, piecemeal restructuring. Ultimately, they grasped the opportunity for decisive reform only when they were pushed by exogenous events, felt sufficiently confident about what might work and what should be avoided due to earlier experimentation, and could afford to pursue a proactive fiscal policy that allowed them to placate the losers from the state-sector reforms through ad hoc compensation. In short, the challenges and extent of change in China's political economy were tantamount to "rebuilding the ship at sea" in uncertain waters and winds.[11] The essential fluidity and unpredictability of the policy environment should be taken seriously as a universal constraint for any attempt to design comprehensive reform packages.

## Getting the policy process right: Tinkering, learning, and adapting

In order to deal creatively with uncertainty, political actors must tinker with diverse measures, processes, and institutions and they must adapt them to their specific concrete conditions, thereby determining what works best at acceptable costs. As Dani Rodrik puts it, "getting the policy process right" is the key to a conducive role of governments in developing political economies. Successful policy making is "a process designed to find areas where policy actions are most likely to make a difference."[12] The types of policies that are adopted will critically depend on a country's specific circumstances, and thus the value of standard recipes for economic restructuring is extremely limited. Policy making that is undertaken as an intensive yet open-designed search process and entails positive exposure to accidental discoveries will be the most conducive to problem-solving.

In his contribution to the above-cited issue of *Modern China*, Wang Shaoguang demonstrates how important a particular policy process has been for dealing with the complex challenges posed by rural health care. Wang aptly states that the "resilience of the Chinese system lies in its deep-seated one-size-does-not-fit-all pragmatism.[13] He traces idiosyncratic processes, patterns, and conceptions to their historical origins and explains the reasons for their formation and acceptability in the Chinese context. Wang presents strong evidence for the importance of bottom-up inputs to China's policy process that were facilitated by open-ended experimentation both during and after the Mao era. With surprising continuity, local knowledge and tinkering had the legitimacy and the potential to influence national policy making with respect to rural health care.

Decentralized generation of policy options represents a crucial asset for policy innovation that could never have been realized in the top-heavy, centralized Soviet-type party-states. China's remarkable deviation from the Soviet pattern can best be explained by the particular revolutionary legacies of the Chinese Communists, such as policy generation "from point to surface" (*you dian dao mian*) or policy implementation "in accordance with local conditions" (*yindi zhiyi*), which were key to the Chinese Communists' revolutionary victory and also were extremely conducive to the economic reform and opening.[14]

The problem with policy learning is that it is basically unobservable while it is occurring. Analysts infer that it has happened by looking at the changing debates and contents of policy making or the cognitive and normative shifts in the policy community over time. Whereas policy learning is thus ascertained retrospectively, experiments in the guise of pilot tests, model sites, special zones, or experimental regulations constitute observable "policy making in action," by which we can trace the mechanisms that drive adaptive and learning capacity. Policy learning represents a rather unspecific cognitive *ex post* category that does not tell us what causes Chinese policy makers to be more welcoming to locally-generated policy options than policy makers in other countries. Therefore, China's distinctive strengths in institutional and policy adaptation are much more likely to be grounded in its unusual traditions and mechanisms of experiment-based policy generation than in any cognitive superiority on the part of China's policy makers.

As demonstrated by Wang Shaoguang, a positive advantage of diachronic policy studies is their open and dynamic research design. If new actors, interests, ideologies, or feedbacks enter the game, analyses of the policy process provide an adaptive framework to discover and integrate changes and move beyond the predefined and overstructured models of institutionalist political economy. Researchers who study the policy process are thus sensitive to creeping changes, unorthodox mechanisms, unexpected interactions, and random results. We can step back from stating what the ultimate status of a certain policy or institution must be after reform and thereby avoid the teleological bias ("When and how does China become a 'real' market economy or democracy?") that is so pervasive in social-science debates on China's transformation.[15]

Nassim Taleb suggests that innovative capacity in political economies does not vary according to systemic features (market versus plan, democracy versus authoritarianism) but is determined by the opportunities that political economies provide for "maximum tinkering."[16] Such tinkering can take place in non-democratic political entities if the rulers are willing to give free rein to a decentralized generation of new knowledge. China obviously is very good at such decentralized tinkering. Herein lies a major challenge for Western studies of political economy that tend to cling to the dichotomous categories, rigid assumptions, and so-called rigorous models that are part of the now disintegrating "marcump" paradigm.

One general caveat: Is it plausible to classify entire political systems according to their adaptive capacity, as suggested by Wang Shaoguang? One methodological principle of policy studies is the disaggregation of political systems into policy subsystems, each of which is characterized by very different dynamics.[17] Thus we will find a strong capacity to learn and adapt in certain policy areas, such as China's foreign trade, whereas we will find persistent blockades to learning and problem-solving in other policy realms, such as China's fight against corruption. Due to such crass variations, exercising restraint with respect to generalizing across diverse policy subsystems and jumping to general hypotheses about the entire political system are core lessons for those involved in contemporary policy studies.

The difficult test for systemic adaptive capacity always arrives with disruptive crises in which not only economic and social learning but also political-institutional responsiveness and societal support for the political system and the incumbent government are stretched to their limit. Most political systems are currently facing such difficult tests and it remains to be seen how China's government, beyond the creative policy process that has been so productive in times of normal politics, will deal with crises that simultaneously affect basic social cohesion and several crucial policy areas.

## Why maximum tinkering is not enough: The shadow of hierarchy

Although Wang Shaoguang stresses the importance of bottom-up policy input in rural health care, he makes it clear that local initiative does not help, or at least it does not help much, if higher-level support is not forthcoming. As the peasant quoted by Wang states: "With no push from the top and no action in the middle, the base simply falls apart."[18] Thus it is certainly wise not to underestimate the weight of higher-level attention to decentralized tinkering. Senior patronage and advocacy is decisive to defend and scale up local initiative. Top-level policy makers establish broad policy goals and priorities that often provide legitimacy and leeway for local tinkering. Unapproved experimentation is justified as a search for policy tools that meet the priorities signaled in the speeches, documents, or development plans of the higher levels. Senior leaders have the power to protect or to stop local policy innovators depending on how useful they deem the results of local tinkering to be. Most importantly, higher-level policy makers serve as gatekeepers and advocates in the dissemination of locally generated innovations.

Thus China's adaptive capacity in policy making is not only based on maximum local tinkering. It is better understood as foresighted tinkering under the shadow of hierarchy, serving policy agendas that are constantly set and re-set by the higher levels. Even for the most courageous or self-serving local policy makers, the shadow of hierarchy never completely disappears.

It is clearly worthwhile to re-think the intriguingly ambiguous effects of China's hierarchical authority structure. According to one influential interpretation, China's authority structure is split between "political centralization" and "economic decentralization."[19] The political/economic dichotomy built into this model has led to an unceasing controversy about how to understand or model the dynamics of central-local relations in China's political economy. Instead of diluting the confusing puzzle of hierarchy in China by applying tame Western models of federalism, it may be much more helpful to take a more fine-grained look at the varying effects of hierarchical structures.[20]

In his studies of hierarchical coordination, Fritz Scharpf distinguishes between two very different variants and effects of hierarchical structures, both of which are applicable to China. Hierarchical coordination (as in the Soviet type of central planning or in Communist Party top-down cadre appointments and removals) is characterized by direct, imperative intervention and control overriding the decision preferences of lower-level actors. Yet this type of strict hierarchical control is rarely enforceable and it is usually confined to a few policy areas and to periods of political campaigns and repression. More frequently, and this also appears to be the prevailing variant in the Chinese polity, we find a less coercive hierarchical authority structure that exerts an indirect and patchy effect on lower-level actors, though the shadow of hierarchy (i.e., the threat of sanctions if something were to go wrong) is permanently felt. Unilateral actions, self-interested bargaining, infringement of laws and regulations, or outright corruption on the part of lower-level administrators may be common. Yet local officials remain embedded in the overall authority structure and thus they are vulnerable to ad hoc hierarchical intervention. They are "not freestanding," as Scharpf puts it.[21] Even if the hierarchical authority does not achieve effective control, it still affects the calculations, behavior (be it evasive or loyal), and interactions of lower levels and across levels of state administration. I would suggest that the shadow of hierarchy continues to play a crucial role in the ambiguous, oscillating interplay between China's policy makers and administrators across the various administrative levels, regardless of the decentralization of economic administration or of the disloyalty of local policy makers.

In sum, though locally generated policy innovations have shaped important elements and junctures in China's reform trajectory, decentralized policy tinkering is not equivalent to free-wheeling trial and error or spontaneous policy diffusion in the context of the Chinese polity. Rather, it is a purposeful activity geared to producing novel policy options that are injected into official policy making and then replicated on a larger scale, or even formally incorporated into national law. It is precisely the dialectical interplay between dispersed local initiative and central policy making—maximum tinkering under the shadow of hierarchy—that rendered China's economic governance so adaptive and innovative after 1978.

## Remaking the social contract: Ordoliberal alternatives

It is a strength of many Chinese and Chinese-American social scientists that they not only want to provide data, analyses, and hypotheses, but also they are determined to contribute to resolving pressing economic, social, and political problems through their policy advice. In order to find inspiration about how to deal with these issues in China, it is useful to think about the social contract and those ideas that underlie the European welfare states. Social thinkers and theories that established the foundation for the European welfare state were cast aside during the high tide of the "marcump" paradigm. Yet they represent the viable alternative source of thinking about market-state dynamics that is called for by Philip C. C. Huang. Keynesianism has already been broadly rediscovered in the context of the huge government interventions into markets and companies due to the current financial and economic downturns.[22] Beyond the Keynesians, we find a distinct school of "ordoliberalism" (also called the "Freiburg School"), mainly in Germany and Switzerland, that strives to recombine market and state activity in order to safeguard social equity, economic stability, and political liberty for the long term.[23]

As opposed to the "marcump" paradigm, ordoliberals hold that a functioning market economy is essentially a political creation and a result of human design that must be instituted and protected by an authoritative, yet limited state. Ordoliberals suggest erecting unshakable fences around both governments and markets by way of constitutional and institutional precommitments so as to make them as effective as possible in terms of their respective functions, while preventing them from impairing one another's integrity. Regarding normative objectives, neither governments nor markets are understood as self-serving mechanisms or ends in themselves. Their ultimate, essential function lies in safeguarding human dignity and liberty, which is based on material well-being, civic rights, social inclusion, and a collectively supported social safety net. In the ordoliberal view, markets fulfill an indispensable role in economic coordination. However, in contrast to the "marcump" paradigm, markets are not supposed to define the direction or even the goals of social development.

That markets cannot and do not integrate society is a major ordoliberal argument that is confirmed in Philip Huang's alarming study of China's informal economy.[24] Thus far, neither government policy nor official statistics have made credible or consistent efforts for social inclusion of the huge number of disadvantaged laborers in China's informal economy. This is not only a conspicuous policy omission on the part of the government. It also makes clear how blinded policy makers, with their advisers and statisticians, can become over long periods if their constricted models of economic, political, and social realities merely define away or ignore important social groups and human misery.

Because ordoliberalism is the product of the devastating experiences with economic, social, and political collapse in central Europe, it explicitly integrates the risks of market failure, government disintegration, and human misery into its perspective on political economy. During protracted economic downturns and in the face of disruptive economic shocks, a welfare state that has supported disadvantaged social groups over decades, and thereby has promoted social equity and social inclusion, may be the most effective buffer against social unrest and disintegration. During severe crises, past growth rates do not help to preserve stability. Short-term government rescue schemes cannot compensate for social inequality and social tensions that have accumulated over decades. From the ordoliberal perspective, a welfare state is a crucial device for the long-term upholding of social justice, human dignity, and political-economic stability. It is built to safeguard the legitimacy of the political system even in times of severe stress. In this regard, the Central and Northern European experiences with issues of social equity and inclusion may offer immediate lessons to China.

A reconstituted social contract will have to balance material well-being and economic growth with social inclusiveness and ecological sustainability. State coordination will be essential for dealing with major long-term challenges, such as social inclusion, environmental degradation, and demographic change. Of their own accord, markets will not contain the impacts of these mega-challenges. Yet, with respect to resource allocations, governments will never be as efficient as markets. Therefore, to move beyond both market fundamentalism and big government interventionism, it is time to carefully revisit those strands of social theory, including ordoliberalism, that offer an alternative foundation for rebuilding political economies and establishing a robust social contract for the twenty-first century.

Overall, China's unorthodox approach to policy making that is characterized in this chapter as "foresighted tinkering"—pursuing broad long-term policy priorities while constantly searching for and experimenting with novel policy instruments—may become a huge processual advantage in years to come, if this variant of steady, yet flexible governance is maintained and adapted in creative ways. It is time for Western social scientists to take those aspects of China's developmental experience, such as China's policy process, that deviate from constricted standard models much more seriously to gain general insights into alternative mechanisms that may be conducive to managing large-scale social change. Getting the policy process right so as to allow maximum tinkering in a highly uncertain environment without evoking social disintegration continues to pose a major challenge to both advanced and developing political economies.

# 5
# Making Plans for Markets: Policy for the Long Term in China*

Political efforts at comprehensive development planning—that is, anticipatory public-policy coordination for the long term and across policy sectors—have either come under criticism, declined, or been tacitly abandoned or scaled down in most political economies since the 1980s.[1] Yet, we find one major case that challenges the verdict about a universal collapse of planning: while dismantling many typical features of socialist industrial administration, China, the most dynamic large economy during the past thirty years, from the mid-1990s through the 2000s re-invigorated its ambitions in long-term, cross-sectoral coordination of economic, social, technological, and environmental development.

The Chinese government continues to draft long-term policy agendas that are designed to anticipate, utilize, and shape domestic and global market trends. We find multi-year programs with binding and indicative targets in virtually every sector, from space programs and infrastructural construction to human resources and education

---

\* This is a revised version of an analysis that was originally published in *Harvard Asia Quarterly*, Vol. 13, No. 2 (2011), pp. 33–40, republished here with permission from the editors of *Harvard Asia Quarterly*.

and to health care, cultural life, and tourism. To improve formulation and implementation, Chinese planners attempt to combine the multi-year plans with a multitude of consultative and corrective mechanisms that are intended to make planning more responsive to unanticipated contextual changes, more open to operative adjustments, and more conducive to producing and using new policy instruments.

With respect to the comprehensiveness and intended domestic and global impacts of long-term policy programs, China thus constitutes the most ambitious planning polity of our times.

## New-style development planning

Beginning in 1993, development planning was fundamentally reorganized in terms of content, processes, and methods to give room to market coordination, while also preserving overall state control. It was geared to identify and support the growth potential offered by markets and thereby to move farther away from Soviet-style administrative resource management. Yet the very essence of state development planning has been preserved in China as a government effort for:

- *strategic policy coordination* (prioritizing and coordinating state policies from an anticipatory, long-term, cross-sectoral perspective);
- *resource mobilization* (mobilizing and pooling limited resources to bring about structural changes identified as necessary by policy makers to achieve sustained economic and social development);
- *macroeconomic control* (controlling the level and growth of principal economic variables to achieve a predetermined set of development objectives, prevent severe cyclical fluctuations, and contain the effects of external shocks).

To understand the emergence of the new-style development planning in China, it is especially important to examine the initial years when a "socialist market economy" was introduced. With the fall 1993 Central Committee decision, a radical reorientation and reorganization of the planning system was launched. Whereas planning had previously been used as a substitute for markets, Chinese administrators were now charged to "take markets as the foundation," that is, to plan with and for markets and to absorb major trends in domestic and global markets into multi-year government programs.

## Macro-control and balancing

Instead of completely abolishing plans and planning bodies, planning was redefined as one of three key mechanisms of "macro-control," together with fiscal and monetary policies that were intended to facilitate the "comprehensive coordination" and "aggregate balancing" of economic activities. Instead of fixing a huge number of quantitative targets and control figures, planners were ordered to focus on macro, strategic, and policy issues and to refrain from issuing orders to departments and regions. "*Ex ante* coordination" through plans was supposed to be compatible with "*ex post* coordination" through markets.[2]

In preparing the 10th Five-year Plan for the 2001–5 period, the Zhu Rongji government defined new strategic norms for plan formulation by stating that the government is "no longer the main force in resource allocation" and growth should be driven by competitive allocation through markets. Therefore, the focus of planning was intended to shift from setting narrow, quantitative growth targets to guiding and coordinating structural and qualitative changes in economic and social development, such as promoting the services sector, domestic demand, environmental sustainability, rural urbanization, and western development. Moreover, the 10th Five-year Plan identified science and technology as well as human resources as decisive for China's catch-up with the most advanced societies.[3] Leading planners emphasized that it was the shift from a socialist shortage economy to a surplus economy achieved during the mid-1990s that necessitated a basic reorientation of the planning system from material production and physical growth to a much broader human development–centered approach.[4]

In contrast to Premier Zhu Rongji who held a sceptical attitude about the effectiveness of comprehensive planning in general, and about the reorganized planning bodies in particular, Premier Wen Jiabao and his government that came to power in 2003 emphasized the need for national, long-term coordination of economic, social, technological, and environmental development and placed a renewed trust in planners. During a Central Committee plenum in November 2003, Wen Jiabao introduced the programmatic slogan of the "Five Comprehensive Coordinations" (*wuge tongchou*) to outline the Communist Party's priorities for coordinated and controlled "harmonious" and "scientific" development: the mitigation of urban-rural, interregional, social-economic, human-environmental, and domestic-international imbalances and contradictions that should not be left to a free-wheeling evolutionary process.

As a result of an internal (unpublicized) mid-term evaluation of the 10th Five-year Plan in 2003, important innovations were included in the drafting of the 11th Five-year Plan that actually constituted a major revision of the functions and means of planning that had been established in the mid-1990s. A terminological change from "plan" (*jihua*) to "program" (*guihua*) was undertaken to mark the difference with the previous administrative resource allocations through plans. Most importantly, along with anticipatory "indicative targets" (*yuce zhibiao*), a new category of "binding targets" (*yueshuxing zhibiao*) was introduced. As opposed to the imperative socialist plan targets and quotas of earlier times, these binding targets were now specifically directed at government bodies and they were seen as "government promises," especially in the area of environmental and land-use policies and thus were not aimed at steering company decisions. Leading planners increasingly reached a consensus that plans would have no credibility or effectiveness if they were limited to the post-1993 decision of only serving as "strategic, macro, and policy" guidelines.

Table 5.1   Redirecting Plan Functions in China since the 1980s

| Planning Practices, 1980s–92 | Post-1993 Innovations | Post-2000 Innovations |
|---|---|---|
| ***paramount planning goals*** | | |
| growth of physical output ("material planning"); "comprehensive balancing" | "macro-controls"; transition to intensive growth; rise of productivity and living standards; "sustainable growth" | sectoral restructuring; urban-rural and regional redistribution; environmental protection; technological innovations; human resources ("people-based" planning) |
| ***planning methods*** | | |
| gradual reduction of mandatory targets and administrative resource allocations; "guidance" planning in incipient consumer markets; partial price liberalization | shift to market-oriented "macro" planning; drastic reduction of quantitative targets and administrative resource allocations; price liberalization | new binding targets for government bodies in environmental and land management; functional spatial planning through "development priority zones" |
| ***sectoral industrial policies*** | | |
| sectoral resource management by Soviet-type branch ministries | dismantling of most branch ministries; initial industrial policy programs | proliferation of multi-year sectoral programs and industrial policies |

Although the re-introduction of binding targets initially met with strong criticism from market-oriented policy makers and advisers, planners succeeded in convincing top-level leaders, and even market-oriented economists on the five-year plan advisory committee, that binding targets for regulating government behavior (not for controlling company decisions), especially with respect to environmental protection and land-use policies, were justified and timely.

As it turned out, the nationwide reorientation of administrative behavior in the fields of emission reductions and energy conservation was judged to be the most important, and for many central officials apparently somewhat surprising, success of the 11th Five-year Plan that was implemented for the 2006–10 period. Therefore, for the following 12th Five-year Plan, planners suggested expanding the use of binding targets to make further progress in those fields in which administrative behavior had to be restricted to nationwide standards so as to end the irresponsible and unsustainable use of environmental and land resources.

## East Asian reference models

Chinese planning reforms that took place after the turn to a "socialist market economy" reveal certain commonalities with the Japanese postwar experience with respect to the ideational framework and the priorities of government intervention. Governments in both postwar Japan and post–Cold War China were obsessed with industrial catch-up and international competitiveness, while they also tried to defend national "economic security" and to guard against foreign domination.

As Daniel Okimoto argues in the case of Japan, at the heart of East Asian industrial planning there were deep-seated doubts that unfettered markets on their own could yield an "industrial structure that meets national needs, not simply one that emerges passively out of the global division of labor." Thus markets had to be structured and stabilized through anticipatory government intervention.

Furthermore, social overhead investments had to be accumulated and channeled into priority industrial sectors to achieve strategic goals and needs that were politically determined but that rested on widely shared social aspirations to promote national wealth and status.[5]

With respect to the basic goals of national planning, China's post-1993 approach largely conforms to the reprioritization trends observed across East Asia during earlier periods,[6] including the progressive emphasis on infrastructure, social (including redistribution, income disparities, and rural-urban migration), technological, environmental, human resource, and spatial (urban-rural and metropolitan) developments that gained weight in Chinese national planning since the mid-1990s and assume centerstage today.

Yet the Chinese state-heavy planning process never relied on the subtle public-private sector interactions that facilitated "social bargaining through the bureaucratic system" in Japan.[7] In certain respects, post-1993 Chinese planning appears to be more similar to the earlier South Korean planning practices during the 1960s through the 1980s that employed a mix of policy tools, ranging from binding to incentive-based instruments and differentiating between different needs in various sectors. In South Korea, as in China today, the process of regular planning consultations helped economic administrators learn about new trends across businesses and bureaucracies, adjust their administrative interventions to the changing economic environment, and move beyond narrow "agency points of view" and ministerial jurisdictions.[8]

Apart from such commonalities, we find rather fundamental differences between the Chinese and other East Asian planning experiences. The legacy of a cadre-based command economy that shaped the evolution of China's efforts to coordinate strategic policy entails basic differences with the market-oriented planning undertaken in Japan or South Korea until the early 1990s. The Japanese economy was never centrally planned. Furthermore, Japanese multi-year indicative plans were not binding on local governments, serving only as general forecasts and orientation guidelines for economic and bureaucratic actors. Whereas Japanese plans emerged from largely non-hierarchical and informal network-based communications and exchanges across the public and private sectors,[9] top-down priority-setting, including today, has been much more prevalent in the Chinese planning process. Moreover, due to the predominance of large state-controlled corporations, China's private sector has much less influence in national plan-making, as compared with Japanese or South Korean practices in earlier decades.

Nevertheless, Japanese and South Korean planning approaches have served as reference models for Chinese planners and industrial policy makers from the 1980s to the present. During the last decade, Chinese planners have become more selective and specialized in their solicitation of advice. For instance, today's planning officials turn to Japanese models and specialists for metropolitan infrastructure planning, to German expertise for functional spatial and environmental planning, to Singapore and South Korea for human resource and technology planning, and even to small Scandinavian countries for social welfare planning. Strikingly, the Indian planning experience with its highly sophisticated models and techniques[10] has been repeatedly examined by Chinese planners but never judged to be a practical reference for planning reform in China.

## Corrective mechanisms

After 1993, Chinese planners became much more modest in terms of formal modeling, accepting the vagaries of market dynamics and policy implementation and stressing the need to combine comprehensive planning and national priorities with creative problem-solving and mixed governance modes on the ground. It can be argued that the post-1993 new style of development planning was conducive to, or certainly did not impede, China's economic take-off because it made use of effective corrective mechanisms.

Some of these corrective mechanisms that counter the rigidity and centralization inherent in traditional planning appeared familiar because they had already been observed in other East Asian countries:

- the limitations of imperative planning to a few tightly controlled sectors;
- the expansion and refinement of contractual and indicative (incentive-based, non-hierarchical) planning;
- the opening of diverse channels to absorb foreign expertise and to adapt it to local conditions;
- the exposure to world markets, with the resultant competitive and innovative pressures.

Other core governance mechanisms that have shaped China's recent planning experience and have facilitated continuous or ad hoc adjustments are unusual and distinctive, even in the East Asian context:[11]

- the encouragement of extensive and sustained decentralized policy experimentation across a large spectrum of sectors;
- reliance on transitional, hybrid, and informal institutions ("institutional layering") over extended periods;
- under-institutionalized, oscillating patterns of centralized and decentralized coordination;
- imposition of top-level policy initiatives through the Communist Party hierarchy ("red-letterhead" documents, party meetings, and campaign-style mobilization) in cases of crisis management;

- reorganization of human resource management through the party-controlled cadre system.

Policy coordination in China is thus pursued through processes and instruments that are oftentimes starkly different from those in most present-day advanced or emerging political economies. China has not invented these processes and instruments, but rather it has re-combined features of imperative, contractual, indicative, and experimentalist coordination that can be traced to China's own political-administrative legacies or to earlier Japanese or South Korean experiences during their take-off phases.

The governance of planning that has taken shape in China since 1993 teaches us to refrain from easy classifications: the policy processes and instruments utilized by the Chinese government go well beyond the established analytical features and standard explanatory models of the socialist command economies, the East Asian developmental states, and the Anglo-American regulatory states. This is a major example of recombined governance based on adaptive policy processes that are reshaped in response to constantly changing economic, technological, and social environments.

## Achievements and limitations

Sustained government intervention and planning in post-1993 China thus far have succeeded in boosting investment- and export-driven growth, the build-up of infrastructure, and industrial diversification, while keeping basic macroeconomic indicators and balances (inflation, fiscal deficits, foreign debt, the capital account, the current account, and foreign exchange) under centralized political control. Since 1993, planned and ad hoc interventions have preserved a remarkable degree of macroeconomic resilience despite the major external shocks in 1997 and 2008. Development planning and administrative interference have been employed as a means to benefit from, and at the same time control, domestic and transnational market dynamics and market participants.

A major strength of post-1993 planning may be its elasticity, as demonstrated during the three readjustment periods (1993–95, 1997–99, 2008–10) when serious macroeconomic challenges necessitated a swift and temporary retreat from the original plan objectives and required emergency government interventions. Overall, the incorporation of experimental programs into macro-plans, newly introduced mid-course plan evaluations, and regular top-level policy reviews have allowed Chinese planners to escape the rigidity traps that negatively affected most planning exercises in socialist and non-socialist planning systems during the twentieth century.

In the face of acute threats, Chinese planners "sacrifice the long-term goals for the short-term ones," as one senior planning official conceded. But as soon as recovery from crisis is on the horizon, they attempt to return to the original long-term goals. During the 2008–9 global economic downturn, Chinese planning officials were at the forefront of mobilizing all available resources to fight the economic crisis. But they were equally determined to return to the "correct" long-term goals, as defined in the five-year plans, as soon as the economy stabilized. Overall, the Chinese approach to planning is remarkably adaptive. It is oriented toward well-defined goals, but it provides ample room to tinker with the means and the sequencing of the steps to achieve these goals.[12]

Despite a comparatively successful macroeconomic record, there are obvious and strict limits to planning ambitions with regard to fundamental economic restructuring and the transition to an efficiency-, innovation- and domestic consumption–driven mode of development. In contrast to the record of extensive growth, thus far government planning and intervention have proven to be largely ineffective in promoting and guiding macro-structural shifts, i.e., "transformation of the growth and development mode" that has been defined as a core mission, despite the changing formulas in all the five-year plans beginning in the mid-1990s. With regard to industrial restructuring and innovation, the record of plan fulfilment is mixed, ranging from unexpected achievements in turning around large SOEs and highly uneven progress in technological innovations to costly and oftentimes failing policies in the promotion of an indigenous automobile industry and complete miscalculations about the dynamics of the real-estate market.

In general, it has been difficult for Chinese national planners to impose guidance and restrictions on local governments and companies if the plan prescriptions run counter to market incentives and business interests. Goals and targets stated in Chinese development plans have been implemented most effectively in those policy fields where government programs managed to align the career incentives of political cadres (and therefore take administrative actions) with domestic and transnational market opportunities. The paramount drive of the post-1993 planning-system reforms, i.e., shifting from planning against markets (or planning as a substitute for markets) to planning with and for markets, has been strongly advanced in many Chinese bureaucracies, industries, and regions.

The Chinese mode of planning exposes many well-known drawbacks of sustained government intervention in the economy. State planning creates and sustains groups with vested interests in planning. Consequently, some of the most controversial debates among policy makers and advisers in China revolve around how the government should curtail monopolistic and oligopolistic structures in strategic economic sectors through targeted, multi-year programs of competition policy.

One key issue remains completely unresolved: limiting administrative interference and defining thresholds for "government exit" in those sectors that can be left to market competition or societal self-organization. Presently, many sectors of China's economy and society may still be at a stage whereby private initiative must be embedded "in a framework of public action that encourages restructuring, diversification, and technological dynamism beyond what market forces on their own would generate.[13] But, as other East Asian late industrializers have experienced, economic and social diversification cannot be guided top-down in an increasingly complex and sophisticated economy and society that require decentralized information flows and bottom-up innovations for further development. The politically difficult task for all East Asian governments has been to organize this unavoidable retreat in a phased and timely manner.

Based on the recent record of reinforced administrative interference in China, the prospects for achieving gradual government retreat from economic and social life are not promising.

## Planning as administrative integration

Beyond its significant, yet uneven, role in economic coordination, development planning serves crucial integrating functions in China's polity that are regularly overlooked. The formulation of comprehensive multi-year plans provides top policy makers with an extraordinary opportunity to demonstrate their authority by setting the agenda, defining new priorities, and coining new slogans for communication and coordination across all levels of the Chinese administration.

Lower-level administrators may prefer to ignore the novel policy priorities and high-minded goals defined by the central leadership. But they are still compelled to follow national policy conceptions and to regularly spend a considerable amount of time formulating and justifying local development policies that do not contradict nationally defined priorities.

Central and provincial officials interviewed for this study stressed the importance of having an authoritative, encompassing plan that serves as a central point of reference for all specialized policy documents. High-level policy advisers emphasized the importance of a regular rethinking, justifying, and adjusting of development strategies as well as including the scientific and scholarly communities in plan consultations as a major strength of the planning process. Across administrative levels and functional units, plan-making is thus a strategic exercise in administrative communications that includes a formal demonstration of compliance with the national leadership and helps to identify, and possibly bridge, disagreements about policy priorities and approaches among decision-makers and bureaucracies.

Development planning thus fulfills important, and possibly indispensable, functions to integrate China's vast and fragmented administrative apparatus and to legitimate the central leadership. Therefore, the role of post-1993 development programs in terms of political-administrative integration may be even more important than the allocative, redistributive, and regulatory roles of many planning exercises.

## Critique of short-cycle policy making

Chinese plan-making fundamentally aims to impose political priorities on economic markets. Along with the recent global financial and economic crises, such planning ambitions have been bolstered by a growing distrust and critique of the policy making in Western democracies. According to Chinese planners, policy making in democratic systems is limited to compensatory ad hoc interventions, and it leaves control over the direction of development of human societies to "blind" market forces, even though comprehensive and long-term strategies are obviously required to cope with fundamental challenges, such as capital market dysfunctions, environmental degradation, or demographic change. In brief, Chinese national planning ambitions focus on long-term policy making, as opposed to short-cycle policy making that is characterized by the frequent and ad hoc changes in priorities that occur in most political economies.

Despite their continued planning ambitions, Chinese policy makers have come to accept that future economies and societies will be characterized by many unknowns and uncertainties that cannot be anticipated through planning. One top-level planner interviewed for this study stated that even the most careful planning cannot prevent disastrous events, economic downturns, or external shocks, since far too many variables are outside the control of the planners. In his view, foresighted planning can nevertheless provide a strong foundation to deal with the impact of such events in a swift and coordinated manner, thereby greatly helping to contain societal damage. Consequently, shielding China from the cyclical crises of financial markets has recently been strengthened as a central mission of macroeconomic control.

China's unorthodox approach to development planning—pursuing broad long-term policy priorities while constantly searching for and experimenting with novel policy instruments—may become a processual advantage in years to come if this variant of adaptive governance is sustained under the current challenging conditions and the policy makers' constant search for broadly acceptable development goals and novel policy instruments continues.

Against the background of the post-2008 secular trend toward expanding government interference in markets, the Chinese experience with planning and its corrective mechanisms hold valuable lessons for policy coordination efforts that go beyond ad hoc fixes and emergency measures. At the very least, the Chinese post-1993 planning experience challenges conventional wisdom about an inherent infeasibility or an unescapable collapse of development planning under the conditions of a globalized economy. Yet, as a product of a very special political and economic context and trajectory, the Chinese approach to planning is clearly not a replicable "model" for elsewhere.

Chinese policy makers attempt to keep key variables that they identify to be crucial to China's current and future development trajectory—Communist Party rule and executive continuity; political control over economic sectors and corporations identified as strategic; macroeconomic variables such as growth, inflation, fiscal deficits, the volume of credit, the current and capital accounts, and currency exchange rates—under tight control and as steady as possible. Controlling such a wide range of political and economic factors through authoritarian or bureaucratic-legal means is impossible for almost any political system, and likewise it will be difficult to sustain such control in China as well. As soon as the Chinese government loses control over one or more of these key variables, the ambitions of the new style of development planning may come to an abrupt end.

# 6
# The Reinvention of Development Planning in China*

## Introduction

In Western studies of China's economic rise and political system, the uses and impact of planning processes in policy coordination are widely ignored. The "demise of the plan" and the "transition from plan to market" are taken for granted as the determining trajectory of China's transformation. Recent comprehensive treatises on China's economic rise refer to state planning only in passing, if at all.[1] Chinese multi-year programs tend to be played down as futile efforts to rein in a complex and dynamic economy, or as outright symbolic gestures without any potential for meaningful implementation. Consequently, academic debates have concentrated on

---

\* This is a revised version of an analysis that was co-authored with Oliver K. Melton and originally published as "The Reinvention of Development Planning in China, 1993–2012," in *Modern China*, Vol. 39, No. 6 (2013), pp. 580–628, republished here with permission from SAGE Publications and Oliver Melton. Much of the information on the planning process contained in this chapter has been produced or confirmed from several waves of interviews with senior and mid-ranking officials in central- and provincial-level planning bodies between 2007 and 2015.

market liberalization, regulatory reform, privatization of state-controlled enterprises, private entrepreneurship, and ownership rights. Contrary to this widely shared focus, we will argue that the "demise of the plan" has not taken place in China. Beginning in 1993, development planning was fundamentally transformed in terms of function, content, process, and methods.  It provides room for market forces and the decentralization of decision-making authority, while also preserving the ability of the state bureaucracy to influence the economy and ensuring that the party retains political control even though it has abandoned many of its former powers.

China's planning system evolved along with the economic transition and remains central to almost all domains of public policy making and to the political institutions that have fostered China's high-speed growth and economic stability. Moreover, the planning system adds a new dimension to studies of China's political system by emphasizing the oscillating nature of central-local interactions and the complexity of institutional authority and autonomy. Rather than a vestige of the planned economy that operates in the background of political and economic life, the planning system remains one of the driving forces behind the priorities of the policy makers, adjusting the parameters and mandates of institutional authorities and shaping political relationships at all levels of the government. More specifically, as our case study will show, the planning system has been at the center of efforts to tackle persistent problems of governance, such as China's serious environmental challenges.

## Growing out of the plan: 1978–93

Despite the pervasiveness of mid- and long-term, and cross-sectoral and sectoral programs, in Chinese policy making, detailed studies of post-Mao development planning are extremely rare.² Only individual non-mainstream (i.e., not widely read and quoted) studies point to the significance of remolded planning approaches to the pace and pattern of China's development, but they generally do not examine primary research.[3]

A widely accepted explanation of plan-market dynamics in post-Mao China is provided by Barry Naughton in his book *Growing Out of the Plan*. He argues that the rapid growth of the non-planned economy in the 1980s and early 1990s, along with the simultaneous stagnation or decline of the state-dominated planned sector, reduced the importance and range of state planning and facilitated the emergence of an increasingly market-dominated economy. However, this "growing out of the plan" framework focuses on explaining the atrophy or reduction of certain core features of old-style socialist planning, such as innumerable mandatory targets, material supply balances, direct state allocations of resources, and state controls over investment, credit, prices, and foreign trade.

This narrative is not incorrect, but it is incomplete. During this period, the central government curtailed its commanding role, delegated many powers over economic administration to local governments, and emphasized the decision-making autonomy of enterprises. As the non-command segments of the economy grew, Soviet-style planning became less relevant and was effectively abandoned in the mid-1990s.

The "growing out of the plan" narrative should thus be viewed mainly in terms of the role of market forces within the economy; it does not help to explain the resilience of multi-year planning in China's political economy and the administrative efforts that have been undertaken since 1993 to re-model and re-orient China's planning system to deal with novel tasks and circumstances. Nor does it explain why the five-year plan remains central to a wide range of public-policy initiatives, such as environmental protection or education policy as well as China's industrial policy initiatives.

Importantly, during the 2000s the role of planning was actively re-invigorated and institutionalized as it reemerged as a central component of economic and public-policy coordination and oversight. A new type of binding targets was introduced in the 11th and 12th Five-year Plans (2006–10 and 2011–15) to reinforce party influence over administrative actions, especially in non-economic spheres such as environmental protection and land management.[5] Its renewed importance in economic policy was highlighted when Premier Wen Jiabao stated at a State Council meeting that no investment project would be approved if it was not incorporated in a multi-year program (*meiyou guihua jiu bu pi xiangmu*).[6]

China's post-1993 "new-style development planning system" (*xinxing fazhan jihua tizhi*) has been geared to identify and support the growth potential offered by domestic and global markets and thereby it has moved farther away from Soviet-style administrative resource management.[7] Yet, in response to the macroeconomic stability challenges of the early 1990s and the political concerns that arose from the economic and political decentralization, the party leadership under Jiang Zemin and Zhu Rongji launched a series of reforms aimed at increasing central authority while preserving the flexibility of a market-oriented system. The decentralization of economic decision-making and policy implementation in the 1980s served to mobilize local knowledge and to promote policy innovation. But it also threatened Beijing's control over macroeconomic policy. The new-style planning tackled this problem by creating a dynamic, nested hierarchy of policy authority.

Despite the transformation to a market-oriented economic system, the very essence of state development planning has been preserved in China as a government effort to coordinate strategic policy (prioritizing and coordinating state policies from an anticipatory, long-term, cross-sectoral perspective); resource mobilization (mobilizing and pooling limited resources to bring about structural changes identified by policy makers as necessary to achieve sustained economic and social development); and macroeconomic control (controlling the level and growth of principal economic variables to achieve a predetermined set of development objectives, prevent severe cyclical fluctuations, and contain the effects of external shocks.[8] In addition, as our section on the "plan-cadre nexus" will show, policy targets established through the planning system have become crucial to the party's management of cadre incentives as a way to improve policy compliance and quality of local governance in accordance with the goals set by the national leadership.

## Redirecting plan functions

As a result of explorative reorganizations of planning institutions and controversial debates in the early 1980s, central ministerial resource allocations were drastically reduced beginning in 1984.[9] Though imperative planning was not abandoned in those sectors that political leaders identified as the "commanding heights" or "lifelines" (*mingmai*) of China's political economy, it was combined with more decentralized and enterprise-based forms of "guidance planning" (*zhidao jihua*), a transitional institutional arrangement that strengthened enterprise decision-making while upholding administrative control over aggregate resource flows in light industry sectors and increasingly supported market-driven allocations in the rapidly growing realm of consumer goods.[10] Although long-term planning was identified as a major goal in the reform documents of the 1980s, the dominance of operative annual planning over programmatic five-year plans that were a legacy of the Mao era continued between 1984 and 1992, even as the role of the market slowly assumed many of the former functions of the planning apparatus.[11]

To understand the emergence of the new-style development planning system that was established in China in the early to mid-1990s and consolidated in the 2000s, the initial years of introducing a "socialist market economy" after 1992 are particularly important. A radical reorientation and reorganization of the planning system was launched after the fall 1993 Central Committee decision. Whereas planning had previously been used as a substitute for markets, Chinese administrators were now charged with the task of "tak[ing] markets as the foundation" (*yi shichang wei jichu*), that is, to plan with and for markets and to absorb major trends in domestic and global markets into multi-year government programs. Yet, instead of completely abolishing plans and planning bodies, planning was redefined as one of three key mechanisms of "macro-control" (*hongguan tiaokong*), along with fiscal and monetary policies that were supposed to facilitate the "comprehensive coordination" (*zonghe tietiao*) and "aggregate balancing" (*zongliang pingheng*) of economic activity. Instead of fixing a huge number of quantitative targets and control figures, planners were ordered to focus on macro-, strategic, and policy issues and to refrain from giving orders to departments and regions. Plan functions were curtailed and redirected to provide "overall guidance" for the transformation of the economic structure and to implement market-oriented industrial policies.[12]

In an elaborate report on the implementation of plan reform, reformers within the State Planning Commission stated that the "basic function of plan coordination" rested with "maintaining an overall balance of supply and demand in society and general coordination of the major proportional relationships (*zhongda bili guanxi*) in the national economy, providing a good environment for fair market competition" and "complementing the deficiencies of market coordination."[13]

In preparing the 9th Five-year Plan for the 1996–2000 period, policy makers and planners made a serious effort to put the "new method of plan-making" (*zuo jihua de xin fangfa*) into practice.[14] The plan had to explicate the new approaches and policies for economic restructuring and transformation. Plan targets were given as aggregates and communicated as prognostic-indicative, rather than imperative as they had been in the past. Except for a small number of particularly large national investment projects, individual projects were no longer written into the five-year plans. By the late 1990s, the traditional Soviet-style attachment to the plan that listed all major investment projects to be undertaken within the five-year period was completely missing from the reformed plan. Instead, government-sponsored projects were dealt with on a year-by-year basis through annual plans and budgets.[15] Near the end of the 9th Five-year Plan and amid the fallout of the 1997–99 Asian Financial Crisis and the rapidly shifting economic environment, newly installed Premier Zhu Rongji finally completely eliminated the practice of setting imperative economic targets.[16]

In preparing the 10th Five-year Plan for the 2001–5 period, Zhu Rongji's government defined new strategic norms for plan formulation, stating that the government is "no longer the main force in resource allocations." Instead, growth was to be stimulated through market signals and competition. The focus of planning would therefore shift from setting narrow, quantitative growth targets to guiding and coordinating structural and qualitative changes in economic and social development, such as promoting the services sector, domestic demand, environmental sustainability, rural urbanization, and western development. Moreover, the 10th Five-year Plan identified science and technology and human resources as decisive for China's catch-up with the most advanced societies.[17]

China's 2002–3 leadership transition came as the government began to shift its attention from fundamental economic restructuring to improvements in administrative functions and the provision of basic public services, such as social welfare and environmental regulation. In contrast to Premier Zhu Rongji who held a skeptical attitude about the effectiveness of comprehensive planning and especially about the reorganized planning bodies,[18] the Wen Jiabao government found the planning system useful to coordinate long-term economic, social, technological, and environmental development programs, and he put renewed trust in the planners. During the November 2003 Central Committee plenum, Wen introduced the programmatic slogan of the "Five Comprehensive Coordinations" that served to outline the Communist Party's priorities of coordinated and controlled, "harmonious" and "scientific" development: the mitigation of urban-rural, interregional, social-economic, human-environmental, and domestic-international imbalances and contradictions that the party was unwilling to leave to a free-wheeling evolutionary process.[19]

In addition to the shifting emphasis in the 11th Five-year Plan, there were important structural reforms and changes in the relationship between central and local plans as well as among the different types of plans (discussed in detail below). As a result of the internal (unpublicized) mid-term evaluation of the 10th Five-year Plan in 2003, important innovations were included in the drafting of the 11th Five-year Plan that actually constituted a major revision of the functions and means of planning that had been established in the mid-1990s.[20] A terminological change from the traditional "imperative plan" (*jihua*) to a more flexible "coordinative plan" (*guihua*) was undertaken to mark the difference from the previous administrative resource allocations through plans, though this terminological change had actually been proposed by the National Development and Reform Commission (NDRC) planners in preparation for the 10th Five-year Plan to indicate the earlier break from socialist planning. The top leaders eventually approved the new term in the run-up to the 11th Five-year Plan.[21]

More importantly, along with anticipatory indicative targets, a new category of binding targets was introduced in the 11th Five-year Plan and then was expanded in the 12th Five-year Plan (see Table 6.1 below). As opposed to the socialist imperative plan targets and the quotas of earlier times, these binding targets were now specifically directed at government bodies and seen as "government promises" (*chengnuo*), increasingly in areas of public-service provision and environmental and land policies rather than direct intervention in the economy.[22] This final step, discussed in detail below, led to a direct link between China's top policy priorities and the party's control over the leaders of major institutions and state-owned enterprises, that is, the plan-cadre nexus.

## Hierarchy and process

The five-year plan begins with brief, fairly general guidelines (*jianyi*) approved by the Communist Party Central Committee in the fall of the year prior to the start of the plan period, and with a more detailed—but still fairly broad—outline (*gangyao*) approved by the National People's Congress in the following March. Collectively, they establish national priorities and outline the ways in which the priorities will be met, but these documents—which are commonly referred to as the five-year plan—are only executed through a network of thousands of subplans that evolve into detailed execution instructions for all levels of government. This web of plans evolves over the entire five-year period and is better thought of as a planning coordination and evaluation cycle rather than as a cohesive, unified blueprint. The planning system's layered and nested programs can be found in almost every Chinese policy area and across the three core levels of government: the center, provincial-level jurisdictions, and the counties and county-level cities (*shixian ji*).

The relationships among the multiple planning efforts were formalized by the State Council in 2005. In addition to the most prominent five-year plan outlines for national and local governments, there are three distinct types of subplans that are released in successive waves throughout the planning period. This triple structure of comprehensive plans (*zonghe guihua*), special plans (*zhuanxiang guihua*), and macro-regional plans (*quyu guihua*) is then replicated in a complex, interlocking web of development programs at the provincial, municipal, and county levels.[23] Additionally, they play a coordinating role among the central bureaucracies and their local counterparts and also frequently serve as the foundation for similar plans at lower levels of government. Cross-provincial macro-regional plans, which are also replicated inside provinces and among cities and regions, play a major role in coordinating regional development objectives among the diverse regions. The three types of plans collectively form a complex framework that shapes the priorities of the policy makers throughout the government.[24] These plans contain policy prescriptions, but they are only implemented based on detailed follow-up instructions, fiscal outlays, and individual policy decisions. Though often overlooked, they represent the core link between the macro-level aspirations of the plan outline and the policy actions of the Chinese bureaucracies.

Table 6.1  Binding and Indicative Targets of the 11th and 12th Five-year Plans

|  | 11th Five-year Plan (2006–10) |  | 12th Five-year Plan (2011–15) |  |
| --- | --- | --- | --- | --- |
| **Economic Growth** | | | | |
| GDP | 7.5% annual growth | Indicative | 7% annual growth | Indicative |
| Per Capital GDP | 6.6% annual growth | Indicative | N/A | |
| **Economic Structure** | | | | |
| Service Industry / GDP | 3 percentage point (pp) cumulative growth | Indicative | 4 pp cumulatitve growth | Indicative |

|  | 11th Five-year Plan (2006–10) | | 12th Five-year Plan (2011–15) | |
| --- | --- | --- | --- | --- |
| **Economic Structure** | | | | |
| Employment in Service Industries / Total Employment | 4 pp cumulative growth | Indicative | N/A | |
| R&D Spending / GDP | 0.7 pp cumulative growth | Indicative | 0.45 pp cumulative growth | Indicative |
| Patents / 10,000 People | | | 16.000 pieces cumulative growth | Indicative |
| Urbanization Rate | 4 pp cumulative growth | Indicative | 4 pp cumulative growth | Indicative |
| **Population, Resources, and the Environment** | | | | |
| Population | < 0.8% cumulative growth* | Binding | <0.72% cumulative growth | Binding |
| Energy Consumption Per GDP Unit | 20% cumulative reduction | Binding | 16% cumulative reduction | Binding |
| $CO_2$ Emissions Per GDP Unit | N/A | | 17% cumulative reduction | Binding |
| Non-Petro Chemical Energy / Non-Renewable Energy | N/A | | 3.1% cumulative increase | Binding |
| Water Consumption Per Unit of Industrial Value Added | 30 pp cumulative reduction | Binding | 30 pp cumulative reduction | Binding |
| Effective Irrigation (Utilization Coefficient) | 0.05 pp cumulative increase | Indicative | 0.03 pp cumulative increase | Indicative |
| Rate of Comprehensive Use of Solid Industrial Waste | 4.2 pp cumulative increase | Indicative | N/A | |
| Total Acreage of Cultivated Land | 0.3% cumulative reduction | Binding | No cumulative change | Binding |
| Major Pollutants | 10 pp cumulative reduction | Binding | | |
| Sulfur Dioxide | Not initially specified | | 8 pp cumulative reduction | Binding |
| Chemical Oxygen Demand | Not initially specified | | 8 pp cumulative reduction | Binding |

|  | 11th Five-year Plan (2006–10) | | 12th Five-year Plan (2011–15) | |
| --- | --- | --- | --- | --- |
| **Population, Resources, and the Environment** | | | | |
| Ammonium Nitrate | N/A | | 10 pp cumulative reduction | Binding |
| Nitrogen Oxide | N/A | | 10 pp cumulative reduction | Binding |
| Forest Cover | 1.8 pp cumulative increase | Binding | 1.3 pp cumulative increase | Binding |
| Total Stock of Forests | N/A | | 600 billion sqm increase | Binding |
| **Public Services, People's Livelihood** | | | | |
| Average Years of Education | 0.5 year (to 9 years) | Indicative | N/A | |
| Enrollment in Higher Education | N/A | | 4.5 pp (to 87%) | Indicative |
| Rate of Completion of Compulsory Education (9 years) | N/A | | 3.3 pp (to 93%) | Binding |
| Coverage of Urban Basic Old-Age Pension | 49 million increase in coverage | Binding | 100 million increase in coverage | Binding |
| Coverage of the Three-Point Rural Medical Care System | 56.5 pp increase in coverage rate | Binding | 3 pp increase in coverage rate | Binding |
| New Social Housing | N/A | | 36 million units | Binding |
| New Jobs Created for Urban Residents | 45 million jobs created | Indicative | 45 million jobs created | Indicative |
| Rural Laborers Transferred to Non-agricultural Sectors | 45 million people | Indicative | N/A | |
| Urban Unemployment Rate | | Indicative | <5% | Indicative |
| Per Capita Urban Disposable Income | 5% annual growth | Indicative | >7% annual growth | Indicative |
| Per Capita Rural Net Income | 5% annual growth | Indicative | >7% annual growth | Indicative |

Sources: State Council, "Zhonghua renmin gongheguo jingji he shehui fazhan di shiyige wunian guihua gangyao" [China's 11th Five-year Plan for National Economic and Social Development], 2006, at http://www.gov.cn/ztzl/2006-03/16/content_228841.htm, accessed January 6, 2013; State Council, "Guomin jingji he shehui fazhan di shierge wunian guihua gangyao" [The 12th Five-year Plan for National Economic and Social Development], 2011, at http://news.xinhuanet.com/politics/2011-03/16/c_121193916.htm, accessed January 7, 2013.

## Regional planning

One of the most important and tangible aspects of China's planning system is its effort to coordinate regional economic growth, with an emphasis on spreading the gains of economic development to the poorer parts of the country as well as within the wealthier coastal provinces, and to guide China's massive urbanization drive and investment in infrastructure.

In a process that typifies the system of nested authority and "planning and experimentation under hierarchy," these structures are parallel at each stage: the center actively coordinates macro-regional planning, but it also must approve and authorize intra-provincial planning, with city and multi-city regional planning approved by the State Council. Efforts to align regional interests with national objectives through particularistic contracting (most visibly in the authorization of special development and technology zones, or more recently in the central government–sponsored macro-regional development plans) have been a common practice in China's political economy since the 1980s.[25] In the 2000s, new forms of contractual planning, especially in technology policy, were established between the central ministries and the provincial-level governments.[26] But a much more comprehensive initiative to align central and regional development policies through joint programs was introduced by launching a series of macro-regional cross-provincial plans.[27]

A new wave of ambitious, centrally-sponsored macro-regional plans was introduced with the Western Development Program that was launched at the end of the 1990s and they were supported by massive central investments in infrastructure and in other development bottlenecks in the western regions of China (see Table 6.2). Whereas the programs for the western and central regions were directed at balancing disparities between China's interior and coastal areas, other macro-regional programs launched during the past decade have been aimed either at comprehensive industrial restructuring (the Northeastern Revitalization Program), at promoting world-class industrial and service-sector clusters (the Yangzi Delta Program), or at more effective cross-border collaborations and a division of labor among the economic powerhouses of the Cantonese economic area (the Pearl River Delta Program, including Hong Kong and Macau). The Western Development Program and the Northeastern Revitalization Program were given the elevated status of a national-priority task by the establishment of a top-level leadership small group with administrative offices under the NDRC. Moreover, the various programs can be differentiated based on their projected duration, principal goals, and funding channels. Many missions and goals defined in the programs transcend provincial boundaries and thereby necessitate coordination by the central government.[28]

Macro-regional development plans can be characterized as implicit contracts because the central government decides the functions of the macro-regions within the national development strategy and at the same time authorizes the regional governments to try out novel ways and means to achieve the goals as defined in the plan. For plan implementation, central funding and investment play a supportive (in northeast and central China) or even a paramount (in western China) role. For the economically advanced Yangzi and Pearl River Delta regions, the macro-regional programs do not imply central funding but they are invaluable as an "imperial sword" (*shangfang baojian*), that is, as official authorization of local development ambitions and discretionary policy-making powers.[29] Local initiatives are often supported by national projects, such as the large-scale investment in infrastructure linking Chongqing and Chengdu to the coast, or regulatory coordination, such as the limits on new financial centers that are meant to focus resources and clustering in Guangdong and Shanghai (and, to a lesser extent, Tianjin).

Table 6.2 Macro-regional Plans and Experimental Schemes

| Programs | Decentralized Experimental Schemes Explicitly Authorized (selection) |
|---|---|
| Western Development Program for the "11th Five-year Plan period" *xibu dakaifa "shiyiwu guihua"* (adopted March 2007) | • Circulatory (recycling-based) economy<br>• Agricultural technology dissemination<br>• Urban-rural integrated economic administration<br>• Human resources |
| Northeast Revitalization Program *dongbei diqu zhenxing guihua* (adopted August 2007) | • Organizational and technological transformation of local industrial structures<br>• Economic restructuring in natural resource–based cities<br>• Circulatory (recycling-oriented) companies and districts<br>• Small and medium enterprise (SME) credit issuance |
| Pearl River Delta Program (2008–20) *Zhujiang sanjiaozhou diqu gaige fazhan guihua gangyao* (2008–20) (adopted January 2009) | Authorization of twenty-four experimental schemes, e.g.:<br>• Administrative reorganization and reform of government investment<br>• Financial market reforms<br>• Technological innovations through integrated R&D production bases<br>• Urban-rural integrated administration and land-use management<br>• Reform of public hospitals |
| Yangzi River Delta Program *changjiang sanjiaozhou diqu quyu guihua* (adopted May 2010) | Authorization of twenty-five experimental schemes, e.g.:<br>• Information industry<br>• Urban-rural integrated administration and land-use management<br>• Property (real estate) and environmental taxes<br>• Funding of cross-provincial infrastructural and environmental projects<br>• Comprehensive management of lakes and rivers; local low-carbon economies<br>• Promotion of the private sector |
| Central Regions Program *(cujin zhongbu diqu jueqi guihua)* (adopted August 2010) | Authorization of fourteen experimental schemes, e.g.:<br>• Land-use management<br>• Environmental support funds for priority river management<br>• Public hospitals and old-age insurance<br>• Sustainable development for coal industry regions<br>• Cross-provincial collaboration projects |

Sources: Macro-regional development plans as given on the NDRC homepage. The plan documents include specifically authorized experimental points, policy experiments, and demonstration models.

Interviews with planning officials in Chongqing and Guangdong made it very clear that from the perspective of provincial-level administrators, such centrally authorized, regional development programs can provide significantly augmented policy capital and flexibility relative to the broader national five-year plans or even the national laws and regulations because these plans are understood as "red-letterhead documents that govern other red-letterhead documents" (*guan hongtou wenjian de hongtou wenjian*), thereby providing both policy safeguards (*zhengce baozhang*) and policy discretion to "go ahead of the rest and try out new things" (*xianxing xianshi*).[30]

Although Chongqing municipality was designated by the central government to serve as a multi-functional "dragonhead" for development in western China (as a hub for transport, education, science and technology, etc.), it also benefited from extensive central government policy authorizations and fund allocations for the transformation of the Three Gorges Dam area and as one of only two National Experimental Zones for Integrated Urban-Rural Development (since June 2007) that are supposed to experiment with the thorny issue of residence permit (*hukou*) reforms (urban-rural household registration) and to inform national policy making in this area.[31] The Pearl River Delta Program resulted from a cross-jurisdictional initiative that involved core locations in China's export economy and nine extremely diverse, both economically and administratively, jurisdictions (including Shenzhen, Hong Kong, and Macau).

A remarkable feature of both the Chongqing and Pearl River Development Programs is that the central government, in the guise of large NDRC-led State Council delegations sent out from Beijing, monopolized the plan-drafting process. Regional governments were asked to submit proposals, statistics, research, and they were consulted during several drafting stages. But the formulation of cross-provincial or, in the case of the Pearl River Delta, cross-border development strategies was ultimately treated as a central government affair that transcended regional competencies. Whereas the local authorities focused on their own interests, NDRC planners emphasized that the Pearl River Delta Program was designed to devise a productive division of labor among the competing jurisdictions in the area and to promote future administrative and regulatory convergence.[32]

Under the leadership of the State Council, the NDRC's Division for Regional Economies, in collaboration with provincial-level governments, has made an effort to systematically combine macro-regional development programs with decentralized experimentation by establishing a "multi-level pattern of experimental points."[33] Based on these NDRC-coordinated efforts, national planning and regional experimental zones have become closely linked initiatives. Although "the simultaneous push for multiple schemes of regional development may actually dilute much of the focused effort and policy attention as the center has only limited resources," the macro-regional programs can be seen as a governance mechanism through the implicit contracts between the central and regional governments: granting policy authorization to regional governments in exchange for their compliance with national development priorities and a claim to strategic coordination by the central government.[34]

Whereas experimental schemes are seen by Beijing planners as an instrument for correcting and optimizing the planning process, regional policy makers tend to see them as a way to expand their leeway to make policy adjustments and simultaneously to raise their profiles with the central government. The establishment of experimental zones thus constitutes a contractual mechanism within the planning framework that serves different purposes for the national NDRC technocrats and for the local policy makers. Beijing intentionally grants this leeway, with clear core objectives and parameters, and it encourages experimentation as well as competition among the localities to resolve difficult policy problems. Combining planning with experimentation was officially proposed in the 1993 Central Committee decision to establish a "socialist market economy." The third article of the decision states that government plans should allow room for "bold experiments" and some plans "should be tried out first in selected localities or areas and then extended after experience has been gained."[35]

China's regional plans thus serve multiple functions. Most basically, they create a framework for medium- and long-term regional development strategies, which allows local and national policy makers to coordinate infrastructure investments and industrial policies. The regional plans also carve out a policy space for local officials to creatively address problems, either to adapt to local conditions and resource constraints or to experiment with solutions to broader challenges that, if successful, can be applied nationally. They therefore provide both an assurance of stable policy objectives as well as flexibility to adapt and innovate.

## Special plans and comprehensive plans

Special and comprehensive plans are designed to coordinate investments, regulations, and administrative actions among numerous agencies and levels of government.[36] Importantly, these plans are thematic, not agency-specific, so an individual bureaucracy may play a role in multiple plans. These plans, which can span more than one planning period, also play a role in establishing high-level support for individual projects, which can be important for obtaining resources and expediting regulatory approvals. The tiered implementation system also encourages experimentation in policy making, with considerable autonomy delegated to both local governments and central ministries to design the implementation programs.

According to the 2005 State Council document that clarifies the roles and responsibilities in national planning, the comprehensive plans set major strategic responsibilities and oversee major projects as well as the legal and administrative rules and regulations required by the State Council.[37] National-level special plans are, in principle, limited to those issues that affect the overall development of the national economy and society, large programs that need State Council authorization and approval, and those projects that require large-scale investments. This primarily includes basic infrastructure, such as agriculture, water, energy, transportation, and communications; the development and use of land, water, oceans, coal, oil, gas, and other important resources; and the provision of public goods and public services, such as ecological development, environmental protection, disaster prevention and mitigation, development of science and technology, education, culture, sanitation, social security, and national defense, as well as industries that require government assistance or adjustments.

In practice, however, there is significant diversity in the scope and character of the national and local-level plans. There were roughly 160 national-level special plans during the 11th Five-year Plan period, many of which were issued late into the plan period, as well as dozens of special plans issued by every provincial and county-level government.[38] Nationally, this included five-year plans for individual industries, such as pharmaceuticals, food processing, chemicals, cement, and textiles, as well as slightly broader medium- and long-term industrial development plans, including shipping, oil refining, and cement. Even more general thematic plans guide government policy to support the economy, as in science and technology, energy efficiency, and renewable energy sources, or to coordinate long-term policies, such as plans for railway and highway networks and the regional power infrastructure or to improve the quality of government services, such as for disaster mitigation, education, and preservation of cultural relics. These plans are sometimes replicated by provincial and city governments in a second wave of special plans authorized by the corresponding level of government. They then culminate in several waves of implementation guidelines, divisions of responsibility, and tailored targets and spending plans for one or more bureaucracies.

Western analysts of the Chinese policy-making processes often observe the initial high-level statement of intent and the eventual implementation of only loosely coordinated or deviating policies on the ground. The dynamics of the planning processes in bridging this gap is generally overlooked. The diversity of the special and comprehensive plans makes any broad statements exceedingly difficult.

Yet the energy-efficiency initiative in the 11th Five-year Plan, as detailed in the following section, provides an instructive case study on how planning processes and documents are interrelated. It highlights how policy incentives, political decentralization, and the plan-updating process work in practice. Energy efficiency is particularly relevant, because it will be sustained in the future (as it is in the 12th Five-year Plan) and it typifies efforts to improve governance and the provision of public services that go beyond a mere focus on economic growth. It is also an interesting case because it is one in which policy objectives ran counter to (and successfully overcame) other incentives for local leaders (i.e., economic growth and revenue), and therefore it was a more challenging policy to implement in China's political economy. One prominent subcomponent of the energy-efficiency drive, the 1,000 Enterprise Initiative, is given particular attention to illustrate the way in which national objectives are translated into concrete action via the special plan system. Although the energy-efficiency drive was problematic in certain respects, it was assessed, by both government and external evaluators, as broadly successful against the benchmarks of the very ambitious original targets.[39]

## Case study: The energy-efficiency drive under the 11th Five-year Plan[40]

Following an alarming jump in China's energy consumption between 2002 and 2005, China's leadership formulated an ambitious energy-efficiency drive.[41] A 20 percent reduction in energy intensity (energy consumption per unit of GDP) was one of eight newly introduced "binding" targets of the 11th Five-year Plan, and one of three "binding targets" that received particular attention during plan implementation.[42] This commitment was sustained through the 12th Five-year Plan, which aims for a reduction of 16 percent.[43]

The first iteration of the energy-efficiency drive was actually revealed in 2004, with the Medium- and Long-Term Energy Conservation Plan.[44] This plan became a cornerstone for the energy-efficiency component of the 11th Five-year Plan outline, which was released fifteen months later.[45] The outline set out specific, mandatory energy-efficiency targets and specified ten major projects to achieve these targets, such as energy-savings building standards and improved efficiencies in coal plants.[46] But the implementation programs to manage these projects, design new standards, and coordinate policy took shape gradually over several years, and in some cases (notably the 1,000 Enterprise Initiative described below) the central programs were replicated at the provincial levels. A crucial point is that although the five-year plan outline focused on the energy-efficiency targets, it marked neither the start of an energy-efficiency drive (which began at least a year earlier with the long-term plan) nor a full plan to achieve the targets (since many specific policies did not emerge until two or three years later). Therefore, the proposal and targets in the plan outline in early 2006 were little more than markers—albeit very important ones—in a gradually unfolding policy process.

One of the many policy programs to help execute the goals in the five-year plan was the 1,000 Enterprise Initiative, which had its roots in a 2003 Shandong province experiment to upgrade energy efficiency through individual, firm-level contracts, subsidies, and evaluations.[47] Following this successful experiment, the idea of mandating company-level targets for energy conservation was incorporated first in the Medium- and Long-Term Energy-Conservation Plan, and later in the 11th Five-year Plan outline.[48] A detailed implementation plan for mandated energy reductions for the nation's 1,000 largest energy consumers was released the following month, introducing the initiative as one of many policy tactics to help local and national officials achieve their plan goals. The 1,000 Enterprise Initiative was explicitly linked to the five-year plan, but in many other cases, similar sets of policies were only loosely tied to the plan or they were completely ignored, even when they emanated directly from the plan's requirements and instructions.

In a process repeated hundreds of times throughout the country for different issues, this implementation document was coordinated by a lead agency (in this case the Department of Resource Conservation and Environmental Protection of the NDRC) and then jointly published by the cooperating agencies—the Office of the National Leading Small Group for Energy, the National Bureau of Statistics (NBS), the State-owned Assets Supervision and Administration Commission (SASAC), and the General Administration of Quality Supervision, Inspection and Quarantine (AQSIQ).[49] This was a crucial first step in interagency coordination because such instructions generally flow down through a defined chain of command, and a joint document is necessary to provide coordinated instructions to all subordinate offices.

This implementation plan divided responsibilities among agencies and listed the 1,000 enterprises and their energy-conservation targets. Each agency had a clear role: NBS was instructed to begin building a comprehensive statistical reporting system, the provinces and directly-administered cities were to establish monitoring and oversight procedures, SASAC was told to introduce an oversight and evaluation system for central government state-owned enterprises (SOEs) in the program, and so on.[50] In August 2006 the State Council issued a decision on energy conservation that further clarified responsibilities.[51] In September it released yet another document specifying individual provincial-level energy-efficiency targets, which had been the subject of lengthy negotiations with the provincial governments.[52] To address previous failures due to under-enforcement or poor implementation of conservation goals, energy-intensity targets and monitoring systems were incorporated into the performance evaluations of local officials.[53]

Meanwhile, provincial governments were busy creating their own plans for meeting their assigned targets. Guangdong, for instance, in November 2006 released both a general policy to meet its mandated 16 percent energy-intensity reduction target and an implementation plan for its share of the 1,000 Enterprise Initiative.[54] The latter comprised two elements. Guangdong had partial responsibility for supervising twenty-seven enterprises in the national 1,000 Enterprise Initiative. But it also created a provincial-level 1,000 Enterprise Initiative under which the most energy-intensive enterprises within the province—originally only 625, actually—were assigned energy-savings quotas, in a process that replicated the delegation of targets, cadre evaluations, and administrative responsibilities in the national program; 159 enterprises were ultimately assigned to large prefectural-level cities, and supervision of the energy targets for the remaining enterprises, which grew to 914 by 2008, were delegated to city and county governments.[55] In December 2006, Guangdong published the division of labor, including the revised energy-conservation quotas for each city and district and the performance criteria for local officials.[56]

Thus, by early 2007, a year after the national energy-efficiency target was announced, thousands of enterprises throughout the country had received energy-conservation targets; responsibility for assuring accountability for meeting these targets was divided among a range of government agencies at the central, provincial, and city levels, and officials at all levels were put on notice that they would be rated on their success in meeting these targets. But many of the specifics were yet to come. Energy standards for new investment projects, for example, were gradually published during 2007.[57] Procedures for reporting and monitoring energy consumption were not established until 2007 and 2008, and financial incentives and punishments to ensure enterprise compliance with the energy targets continued to evolve with varying degrees of formality.

It was only toward the end of 2008, just as the five-year plan was passing the half-way mark and the mid-term evaluation process was beginning, that national, provincial, and city governments had the necessary basic tools to administer a major component of an energy-efficiency plan—and many of these were still in the pipeline or had to be tweaked in 2009 and 2010. Even so, the efficiency drive in general, and the 1,000 Enterprise Initiative in particular, scored notable successes, which have been validated by outside experts. A detailed study of China's energy-efficiency drive by the Lawrence Berkeley National Laboratory found that overall by the end of 2008 China had achieved about one-third of the energy savings targeted in the 11th Five-year Plan. Energy savings accelerated sharply in 2007 and 2008 as the programs took root, reflecting the long process of policy development, and they appear to have continued well enough through 2009–10 to nearly meet the 20 percent target. Among the various initiatives, the 1,000 Enterprise Initiative was a particular success, achieving 95 percent of its five-year energy-savings target during the first three years of the plan.[58]

Although the energy-conservation initiative in the 11th Five-year Plan appears to have been a success, there were initial problems and some energy-savings initiatives severely underperformed. Its success can largely be attributed to two key features. First, it was an extremely high priority for the leadership and within the plan's hierarchy of targets. Wen Jiabao took a direct interest in the plan's success and, in addition to ensuring that the initiative remained a top policy priority even during the economic crisis of 2008–9, he repeatedly emphasized the importance of the plan as a national policy goal and a factor in cadre evaluations. This political backing ensured that under-performance would hurt the career prospects of ambitious officials, thus providing a counter-weight to the contradictory incentive to promote economic growth at the expense of other priorities.

Second, the energy-efficiency plan was comprehensive, well-coordinated, and adaptive. When programs succeeded, they were expanded and replicated; when they failed, there were attempts to improve or to redesign them. The plan even contained efforts to build the government's capacity to collect information so as to better analyze and evaluate policy and to improve the political incentives for compliance. The plan was good at the latter—adaptation and refinement of tactics were built into the system—but top-level policy makers could only intervene in a limited number of issues. A plan with a lower priority might have been allowed to whither.

One final feature of China's planning system, which is illustrated by the energy initiative, is that the process of learning by doing is messy even when it is effective. The initial experimental stages of implementation were launched before coordination and evaluation mechanisms were in place. Many energy-savings programs, such as closures of outdated factories, were strongly resisted by local officials and produced limited results. Negotiations over plan responsibilities and burden-sharing were followed by renewed—and highly public—pressures from Beijing to meet performance targets. This led to many skeptical assessments of the plan's likely impact, even though it now appears to have succeeded in meeting its objectives, and ultimately it evolved into a relatively effective policy program during the latter half of the plan period.

## Plan formulation

As opposed to most other aspects of China's planning process, the steps involved in plan formulation are treated quite extensively in the existing literature, both in China and in the West.[59] Top party leaders and the State Council, as well as their affiliated research arms, sit at the apex of the planning process, but the various offices of the NDRC are the locus of many drafting and planning functions: they approve and oversee regional strategic plans down to the city level, manage major regional investment projects, and are deeply involved in virtually every macroeconomic issue. The same is true at the local levels, where province- and city-level Development and Reform Commissions (DRCs) enjoy an analogous leadership role in the drafting, implementation, and evaluation stages of the local plans. Provincial commissions supervise city-level planning in the same way that the NDRC oversees the provincial commissions, although more important issues, including long-term plans, are subsequently sent to the NDRC in Beijing for review and, in some cases, approval by the State Council.

As the planning and implementation processes unfold, targets and responsibilities are assigned to lower-level governments and to individual ministries, which then draft and execute detailed implementation plans. Leading small groups—interagency panels that aim to coordinate the work of multiple government bodies on particular issues—also play an important role. At the central level, leading small groups are generally chaired by a state councilor, but the Secretariat for the leading small group is usually an office within the NDRC, which effectively gives the NDRC agenda-setting authority.

The same organizational structure is repeated at the provincial and city levels: vice-governors and vice-mayors chair leading groups or project committees, but their staff frequently comes from the local commissions. Additionally, many key national and local special plans are ultimately led by the commissions, even after the plans are finalized. For example, after Guangdong began its 11th Five-year Plan in 2006, the provincial government named the provincial Develoment and Reform Commissions as the lead agency for implementing fifteen of fifty-one special plans, and it was also granted a supporting role for implementing many others. These relationships endow the local and NDRCs with varying degrees of authority over their partner ministries, particularly in designing policy and monitoring and evaluating progress. Responsibility for policy execution, however, is shared or controlled by the dozens of ministries or bureaus that receive a number of assignments to support the multitude of plans above them.

## The planning cycle

The planning process is a continuous cycle of information gathering, analysis, policy formulation, policy implementation, evaluation, and revision. It is better thought of as a five-year policy cycle rather than as a unitary plan. Preparatory work begins as early as two years before the formal five-year plan period begins and it culminates when the Central Committee approves the new guidelines at a plenary session that is held in the final months of the current plan. Local governments and ministerial offices collect and organize information to feed the successive higher levels of political authority whereas senior officials coordinate the drafting process.[60]

In the months following the approval of the national outline, ministries, provinces, and cities release dozens of thematic special plans that provide the first level of practical details on how the main objectives of the new five-year plan outline are to be realized. But even these plans are rarely sufficiently detailed to begin executing policy. Government offices, Develoment and Reform Commissions, and ministries at all levels start issuing a flurry of documents—decisions (*jueding*), opinions (*yijian*), programs (*fang'an*), explanations (*shuoming*), and methods (*fangfa*)—to guide policy execution and coordinate the different types and levels of plans. These documents name the lead agencies for further coordination, execution, supervision, and evaluation of individual plans and projects. They also provide individualized targets tailored to regional conditions and resources, and they set initial guidance for how progress will be measured and evaluated. After the division of responsibilities and targets is set, government offices develop a series of "work programs" (*gongzuo fang'an*) and "implementation programs" (*shishi fang'an*), with increasing levels of detail and specificity as to how the plan goals will be achieved and how they will be evaluated. These documents may not emerge for one or two years, and they may build upon either existing experiments or independent initiatives.

In the middle of the third year of the plan period, all levels of government initiate a formal mid-course review and adjustment process. The review may continue throughout the remainder of the plan period: the 11th Five-year Plan review began in mid-2008, but policy revisions and adjustments continued through 2010. Therefore, the review process blends with the preliminary work for the subsequent plan, and the cycle begins anew.

In addition to collecting information and providing a mechanism for policy revision and improved coordination, the review plays an important political role. Ministries and local governments that have a high degree of autonomy to oversee their own programs and to experiment with policy ideas are evaluated by both outside experts and superior levels of government, who can reassert policy authority directly through policy revisions or indirectly through the performance evaluations that play an important role in shaping the leaders' priorities. The system thereby produces dynamic institutional authority relationships, with levels of independence enjoyed by lower-level policy makers varying over time. It also produces distinct phases of policy making and implementation, with early plan initiatives experimenting with new tactics or launched without the coordinated support and institutional resources that will come later. Then, in the latter half of the plan, as the mid-term reviews are completed, leaders in Beijing and local capitals will reassert their authority as needed, thus producing yet another cycle of center-local negotiations and, at times, expressions of political authority (see Table 6.3).

Table 6.3   Plan Formulation in China: The Example of the 11th Five-year Plan

|      | Decision-Making | Administrative Planning |
| --- | --- | --- |
| 2002 | From October: New party and government leadership established; work priorities continue to be defined by the 10th Five-year Plan (2001–5) | |
| 2003 | July: State Council orders the NDRC to begin drafting the next five-year plan for the 2006–10 period | September: The NDRC asks for public and research input to define the agenda for the next plan |
| 2004 | Politburo/CFELSG identifies core challenges and tasks for the next plan period | Year-end: CFELSG office and the NDRC request research reports on twenty-two core tasks for the next plan period |
| 2005 | February: Drafting group for the "11th Five-year Plan guidelines" is formed, headed by the premier, with a total of over fifty members: departmental and regional policy makers and economic experts; February–June: Drafting group meets eight times | February–June: CFELSG Office/NDRC task force formulates the "11th Five-year Plan guidelines" based on the meetings of the drafting group |

|  | Decision-Making | Administrative Planning |
|---|---|---|
| 2005 | June/July: The Party Core Group of the State Council discusses and approves the draft guidelines | |
| | July: The General Office of the Party Center sends the "11th Five-year Plan guidelines" to more than one hundred party and non-party units for consultation | |
| | July: The general secretary of the CCP holds consultation meetings with non-party groups and individuals | |
| | August: Top party leaders go on regional investigation tours to solicit opinions about the plan proposal | July–October: CFELSG Office/NDRC task force integrates new suggestions and new input into the plan guidelines |
| | October: Central Committee plenum approves the five-year plan guidelines (*jianyi*); document is made public | End of October: State Council issues order to transform CCP plan guidelines into a more detailed government document; NDRC establishes a thirty-seven-member expert group |
| | | October–December: The NDRC asks for public input on the new plan; central government departments provide additional input |
| 2006 | February: State Council holds four days of meetings on the final revisions of the new five-year plan; listens to opinions of representatives from state/private/rural sectors | |
| | March: NPC plenum approves the new five-year plan outline (*gangyao*) for the 2006–10 period | July: The NDRC holds a national conference to sum up the work on the 11th Five-year Plan, to arrange implementation, and to prepare special-program plans and macro-regional plans |
| 2007 | Beginning in November: Reshuffling of the Party Center and the State Council; top leaders remain in place | |
| 2008 | | Year-end: The NDRC announces the results of the mid-term evaluation of the five-year plan |
| | The NDRC receives an order to prepare the next five-year plan but it slows down the drafting of the document because of global economic uncertainties | |

Abbreviations: NDRC: National Development and Reform (Planning) Commission; CFELSG: Central Financial and Economic Leadership Small Group; CCP: Chinese Communist Party; NPC: national People's Congress.

## Embedded autonomy in the planning process

The national-level planners' network that crafts the initial plan guidelines (Communist Party document) and the ensuing plan outline (State Council document) includes top policy makers, including the premier and vice-premier(s) responsible for economic affairs. They are supported by policy advisers active in the staff office of the Central Finance and Economics Leadership Small Group (CFELSG), diverse departments of the NDRC, a small number of affiliated research bodies, and a select group of high-level economists and economic advisers. This group retains a technocratic insulation from sectoral, regional, and bureaucratic vested interests, yet it is close enough to the policy process to be able to absorb information through regularized policy consultations and debates. As such, the core plan drafting process fits the standards of "embedded autonomy."[61]

Beginning from the drafting of the 7th Five-year Plan in the mid-1980s and increasing during the 1990s, China's planning process has become much more inclusive and consultative (beyond mere stakeholders, it also engages domestic and foreign experts). The drafting process for the 11th Five-year Plan was characterized by several planning officials in a thoroughly innovative approach because ministerial and provincial proposals that traditionally determined core components and objectives of the national plan were then juxtaposed with pluralistic research input that was commissioned through public tenders from major Chinese think-tanks and international advisers from the World Bank and the Asian Development Bank (ADB). Moreover, in preparing the 11th Five-year Plan, the NDRC convened a commission of thirty-seven experts (mostly academics representing a broad spectrum of approaches to development coordination, from more state guidance–oriented academics (e.g., Hu Angang) to more market-oriented economists (e.g., Wu Jinglian). This commission was consulted during several drafting stages and, according to officials in the NDRC's Division of Planning, managed to reach a consensus on the core objectives and reorientations contained in the plan document.[62]

Interviews conducted at central- and provincial-level planning bodies revealed that frequent communications and a unifying "agency point of view" provide a certain degree of coherence to the planning system across administrative levels (Develoment and Reform Commissions at both the central and local levels regard themselves as "policy pivots" whose mission is to hold together the universe of China's government bureaucracies). In addition to the high-profile year-end planning conferences, there are frequent central, provincial, or joint work meetings attended by officials from different administrative levels. Moreover, the daily administrative routines include communications through phone calls and personal visits between provincial-level and central-planning officials to deal with ad hoc policy or investment adjustments. Overall, quite typically in China's administration, central, provincial, and municipal planning officials are often personally familiar with their counterparts at other administrative levels and they attempt to cultivate good relations.

One high-powered, though not much publicized, mechanism of regional government input into central-plan drafting is the so-called "four slices meetings" (*sige pian hui*) held for the northeast, northwest, southeast, and southwest macro-regions (*dongbei pian, xibei pian*, etc.) respectively, during the early stages of the drafting. During these meetings, governors and other provincial-level economic decision-makers meet with central policy makers and planners to identify and debate the most pressing development issues to be addressed in the next five-year plan.[63] Information on informal exchanges and ad hoc meetings between central and provincial policy makers is incomplete and non-transparent because many consultations and bargaining meetings are not reported in the official media. The diary of ex-premier Li Peng contains many entries from the mid-1990s that document frequent economy-related meetings of provincial party and government leaders that were not publicized at the time.[64]

During preparation for regional development plans and strategies, central-planning officials go on extended fact-finding provincial tours (*diaoyan*) and provide advice and guidelines to provincial planners. Moreover, in recent years provincial-level governments have increasingly hired policy researchers from central government institutes (such as the NDRC's Academy of Macroeconomic Research [AMR]) to advise them on crafting regional development strategies and individual policies. This new trend in policy consultancy serves to strengthen coherence, or at least to limit contradictions, in concurrent central and local policy programs.

The process helps separate the policy makers responsible for plan implementation from those involved in the evaluation and monitoring processes.[65] Similarly, the structure of the plans—with the guidelines and outline written by technocrats in Beijing and the policy details set by implementing agencies in subsequent subplans—helps insulate the core objectives and policy goals from industrial and bureaucratic interest groups. The planning process thereby helps preserve a degree of embedded autonomy in its overarching goals and strategies.

## Negotiations, harmonization, and plan lock-in

Overall, China's macro-level five-year planning moved from the early reform era mode of centralized, closed, intra-state bargaining, and coordination to controlled multiple advocacy that is based on carefully orchestrated consultations of state, non-state, and even foreign inputs and on much more regularized administrative procedures that are intended to support "scientific" policy making. Because the post-1996 five-year plans no longer include long lists of priority investment projects, the drafting of the comprehensive five-year programs is much less exposed to intra-state lobbying by sectoral vested interests.

However, this has not eliminated the problem of intra-state bargaining and coordination, and the plan outline does not translate into action without extensive coordination, bargaining, and negotiations over individual responsibilities and targets. Key policy details and special plans are usually written by local governments or ministries that are directly engaged in implementation. Although the outline and the regional and comprehensive plans provide an important framework, there can be significant latitude during execution when bureaucratic, regional, and private interest groups have a voice in the way the plan details are crafted.

Central drafters must coordinate actively with the agents of policy implementation when targets, resources, and responsibilities are allocated. A challenge in the drafting of the plans is the harmonization (*xianjie*) of plan agendas and plan targets across various administrative levels. During Mao-era plan coordination, central planners adjusted and aggregated the indicators and quotas submitted from the ministerial and regional planning bodies in the national plan, and then subdivided the aggregate national plan targets into regional quotas to be adopted and implemented by provincial-level governments (*guojia fenjie zhibiao dao ge sheng*). In the post-1993 development planning system, target harmonization has depended less on top-down orders and more on intensive communications between the central and provincial levels in the planning system.

The harmonization of the top priority binding targets spelled out in the 11th Five-year Plan is a striking illustration of the complexity of administrative harmonization. In 2006, four overworked officials in the NDRC's twenty-seven-person planning department (*guihua si*) were charged with checking on the provincial-level plans, and the provincial plan documents were submitted to the NDRC only after the respective provincial people's congresses had approved them. The NDRC officials then focused on checking the inclusion of national binding targets in the regional plan documents, especially the targets of 20 percent energy conservation and 20 percent emissions reductions for the 2006–10 period. Yet the five-year program that Shanghai submitted to the NDRC set the energy-conservation target at only 15 percent, justifying this lower target by pointing to Shanghai's already technologically advanced economy that would make a 20 percent reduction target impractical. The NDRC planners raised objections and asked the Shanghai government to revise the target upwards. The Shanghai government responded by establishing an experts' committee to reassess the potential for energy improvements. As a result, the Shanghai plan target was raised to 20 percent. Fiscal allocations for promoting energy-savings and environmental technology had to be revised upward. The NDRC's unwelcome interference in Shanghai's plan targets therefore directly impacted the municipal budget.[66]

A similar conflict over national-regional target harmonization occurred with the Guangdong provincial government. Guangdong province set its energy-intensity reduction target at 13 percent in its provincial plan outline, which was approved in early March 2006, even though the national plan, which was released one week later, set a national goal of 20 percent.[67] Provincial planners argued that environmental technologies in Guangdong's economy had already been upgraded to a level whereby further emissions reductions could only be achieved at a slower pace and at much higher costs. An expert commission installed to reassess Guangdong's potential for rapid emissions reductions confirmed the objections raised by the provincial government, but the NDRC and the State Council mandated that Guangdong accept a slightly higher target of 16 percent.[68]

Officials at the NDRC saw these interactions and compromises as substantial progress in regularizing central-local plan-making and they accepted the need for more variation in plan targets across regions and sectors, thereby moving away from an "unscientific" imposition of uniform targets (*yi dao qie*) at different administrative levels. However, once completed, the targets are incorporated into the performance criteria and contracts (discussed below) and are effectively locked-in for the plan period (although some renegotiations are possible if conditions change or problems are identified).

It is one of the most remarkable features of the current Chinese planning system that the regular five-year planning periods are not synchronized with the turnovers in party and state leaders. Incoming new leaders remain bound to the previous plan for three full years and thus cannot openly discard the policy goals that were established by their predecessors. Plan mandates are thus overlapping, and we find a "plan lock-in" and a continuity of comprehensive policy programs across leadership changes and different administrations. The non-synchronicity between government turnover (e.g., 1998, 2003, 2008, and 2013) and the launch of a new five-year plan (1996, 2001, 2006, and 2011) helps to safeguard basic policy continuity across leaderships and institutional changes in the executive and the legislature. The drafting process of a new five-year plan must begin in the middle of a government's term of office and cannot immediately be revised by a new government.

Thus the CCP's guidelines for a new five-year plan are prepared after a new CCP leadership has been established (e.g., 2003–5, with the official plan document adopted in 2006) or after the CCP leadership has reviewed the economic situation during its year-end central economic work conference. Therefore, the "CCP rhythm," not the rhythm of State Council turnovers, governs plan-making. This is crucial for understanding how the plan is administered and how it shapes the priorities and interests of individual policy makers. The link between plan goals and cadre evaluations means that the career prospects of policy makers throughout the government depend on how well they meet objectives that are often set by their predecessors.

## The plan-cadre nexus

Authority, policy preferences, and many individual interests in China are controlled through the party's extensive nomenklatura system. Traditionally, plan implementation has also been driven by personalized, cadre-based mechanisms of ideological and career controls.[69] The economic administration is held together by a Communist Party cadre hierarchy that facilitates a coarse and inconsistent, yet in the eyes of the central leaders mostly "satisficing" kind of control (non-optimum but enough to hold together formal hierarchies and informal networks). In effect, only those parts of the plan that are reconfirmed and emphasized through party documents have the binding authority of commands that can define the priorities and interests of subordinate levels of government.

The linkages between plan targets and cadre assessments were loose and unsystematic until the early 1990s. Thereafter, as a result of a thorough overhaul of the party's personnel system, cadre evaluations became more systematic, and they included more economic and social indicators rather than only GDP growth or unemployment in each jurisdiction.[70] A breakthrough in systematically linking a more complex set of economic and non-economic plan targets with cadre appraisals resulted from the re-institution of a "binding target" category in national-, provincial- and local-level planning beginning in 2006. As a lesson derived from ill-defined (and therefore poorly enforced) environmental targets contained in the 10th Five-year Plan, NDRC drafters took care to establish clearly defined and easy to understand indicators so as to facilitate scrutiny of the quality of implementation for both the planning bodies and the CCP organization departments. In effect, the top-priority binding targets defined in the 11th Five-year Plan and scrutinized during the mid-course evaluations of plan implementation were included in the cadre performance appraisals throughout the country. According to NDRC officials, these measures gave a big boost to the enforcement of key plan targets during the 2006–10 period.[71]

Although binding targets are transmitted by national planners to provincial-level governments, the crucial implementation link is between the provincial and municipal/county levels. In 2006, the Chongqing municipal government passed down six binding targets (that were partially identical with those in the national five-year plan and partially locally specific; the national plan referred to eight binding targets) to county-level governments—not only at the beginning of the five-year planning period but during every annual planning exercise. Environmental, land-use, birth control, and health-care targets were among the binding targets emphasized by the municipal government and they were directly included in the local plan-cum-cadre evaluation system to check on annual administrative performance. Cadre evaluations were thus designed to make use of not only the binding plan targets (as benchmarks for cadre performance) but also the evaluations undertaken by planning and statistical bodies.[72]

The 11th Five-year Plan ultimately contained twenty-two targets, of which eight were binding; the 12th Five-year Plan contained twenty-three targets, of which thirteen were binding (see Table 6.1 above). The eight binding targets in the 11th Five-year Plan were included in the metrics for the local cadre performance evaluations, and three—preservation of arable land, increases in energy-efficiency, and pollution reductions—received renewed, high-level attention from Beijing throughout the plan period.[73] Beijing therefore made it clear which targets it really cared about through the performance contracts it signed with local officials and, in some cases, even with enterprises, effectively creating a veto (*yi piao foujue*) over career advancement and other benefits for leading cadres who did not meet their goals.[74] This process was replicated at lower levels of government and integrated into the plan evaluation system. Through this system, Beijing is able to establish a small number of very high-priority policy objectives far beyond the formal administrative structures.

One side-effect of the plan-cadre nexus is that these procedures effectively raise the political status of national and regional DRCs and increase the political weight of their plan prescriptions and evaluations beyond economic administration to the cadre system, which is a core pillar of the political hierarchies. In recent planning documents drafted by NDRC departments, a tendency toward strengthening central policy authority and control is evident. (Even terminology stemming from socialist planning that had been discarded in the late 1990s [e.g., the "level-by-level subdivision of plan targets" (*zhu ji fenjie*)] made a comeback in NDRC documents.) This effect is replicated within local-level governments, where DRCs play a similar role in coordination, plan approval, and evaluations on behalf of provincial, city, and county governments.

Plan targets and cadre evaluations have thus become complementary policy tools. This linkage points to the persistence of the distinctive features of China's political economy that are radically different from other government-guided political economies. The plan-cadre nexus is a mechanism stemming from both the command economy and Leninist party organization. The plan-cadre nexus establishes person-based policy accountability instead of law-based and bureaucracy-based accountability for implementation.

## The recombined governance of planning

Looking closely at specific typologies of planning, it is possible to discover a system of authority relationships, delegations of responsibility, and experimentation parameters that produces typical patterns and ways to deal with difficult policy problems.

Table 6.4  Recombined Governance in Chinese Development Planning

|  | I<br>Mandatory<br>(administrative and SOE-based provision of public/social goods) | II<br>Contractual<br>(central-regional and government-enterprise cooperation) | III<br>Indicative<br>(government-induced market activities) |
|---|---|---|---|
| *Allocative-Promotional* | railway construction | technology policy | "going global" program for outbound investments |
| *Redistributive* | anti-poverty programs | rural health services | rural income generation |
| **Regulatory** | land-use management | energy industry restructuring | private/SME sector restructuring |

Typology based on the range of special plans (*zhuanxiang guihua / jihua*) during the 11th Five-year Plan period (2006–10). Adapted from Sebastian Heilmann, "Economic Governance: Authoritarian Upgrading and Innovative Potential," in Joseph Fewsmith, ed., *China Today, China Tomorrow: Domestic Politics, Economy, and Society* (Lanham, MD: Rowman & Littlefield, 2010), pp. 109–126.

By examining the practice of planning in specific policy sectors, we can provide a matrix of governance modes that are all based on formal planning, yet that reveal strong variation in effectiveness and implementation characteristics. We find policy sectors in which public and social goods (such as railroad infrastructure, anti-poverty programs, land-use management) are supposed to be provided through mandatory planning that includes direct allocations of funding and administrative oversight (see Table 6.4, column I). In addition, Chinese planners have increasingly employed non-standardized forms of contract-based planning to ensure and to provide incentives for implementation of their policy goals by lower-level agents (see Table 6.4, column II). Targets and funding arrangements are written into the formal contracts that are concluded between, for instance, a central ministry and a provincial government, or between a provincial government department and major enterprises that take part in implementing state plans. Plan implementation through contractual targets is most visible in road construction, technology zones, energy production, hospital reforms, and marketing reforms (e.g., for rural or cultural products), for which the central government needs the collaboration and bottom-up initiative of local governments and market participants. Such informal arrangements help supplement the incentives in the formal plan and refine the parameters for central oversight and lower-level autonomy within the planning cycle and in cases where complex and competing incentives create challenging principal-agent problems.

In addition to mandatory and contractual planning, we find a plethora of less binding forms of indicative planning, which is based on government forecasting (e.g., statements that estimate the growth potential in certain industries), signaling (e.g., announcements about substantial, step-by-step cuts in rural taxes or about preferential policies for SMEs), and indirect incentives (e.g., improved access to bank credits and domestic/overseas markets) to stimulate market activities and resource mobilization in sectors that are identified by the government as having development potential (see Table 6.4, column III).

## Experimentation and adaptive planning

One of the greatest strengths of the five-year plan implementation is that it includes purposive action to give room to decentralized experimentation and discovery of new policy instruments. A careful examination of the macro-regional plans, comprehensive plans, and special plans issued by China's central and regional governments provides ample evidence that decentralized experimental programs have actually become a standard technique for providing policy leeway to local administrations and improving the ability to adapt policy implementation (see above, Table 6.2).

Since experimentation under hierarchy is a purposeful and controlled process (not merely trial and error), it is regarded as compatible with the planning objectives in the Chinese context. The interplay between processes of economic planning and economic experimentation in China's governance thus constitutes a particular mechanism of policy correction during implementation that is both institutional, through the tiered hierarchy of plan authority, and cyclical, through the changing levels of involvement by top officials. Local knowledge about practical policy instruments thereby can be fed back into the planning process. In effect, experimental zones and projects serve to connect national and local policy processes and help align local policy incentives with central goals.[75]

Chinese plan-makers set goals and priorities while providing legitimacy and leeway for local tinkering during implementation. This distinctive Chinese approach to bottom-up program adjustments is very different from both the Soviet-style command economies and Western legislation-driven policy making. The decentralized generation of policy options represents a crucial asset for innovation that was never realized in the top-heavy, centralized Soviet-type party-states. At the same time, constant tensions between centralized "synoptic" and decentralized "experimentalist" policy making are built into China's policy process.

It can be argued that the post-1993 new style of development planning was conducive to, or certainly did not impede, China's economic take-off and stability because it made use of effective corrective mechanisms. Some of these corrective mechanisms that counter the rigidity and centralization that are inherent in traditional planning governance appear familiar since they were already observed in other East Asian countries: the limitation of imperative planning to a few tightly controlled sectors; the expansion and refinement of contractual and indicative (incentive-based, non-hierarchical) planning; the opening of diverse channels for absorbing foreign expertise and adapting it to local conditions; and exposure to world markets, with the resulting competitive and innovative pressures.

Other core governance mechanisms that have shaped China's recent planning experience and facilitated its continuous or ad hoc adjustments appear unusual and distinctive even in the East Asian context: the encouragement of extensive and sustained decentralized policy experimentation across a large range of sectors; reliance on transitional, hybrid, and informal institutions ("institutional layering") over an extended period; under-institutionalized, oscillating patterns of centralized and decentralized coordination; imposition of top-level policy initiatives through the Communist Party hierarchy ("red letterheads," party meetings, campaign-style mobilization) in the case of emergency measures; and human resource management through the party-controlled cadre system.

Policy coordination in China is thus pursued through processes and instruments that are oftentimes starkly different from those in most present-day advanced or emerging political economies. The Chinese government has not invented these processes and instruments anew; rather it has re-combined features of imperative, contractual, and indicative coordination that can be traced to China's legacy of socialist planning or to earlier Japanese or South Korean experiences during their take-off phases. The planning process is central to encouraging and preserving this distinctive policy system that is highly effective at experimenting with new policy prescriptions and adjusting existing programs.

## Weaknesses of the planning system

During the 11th Five-year Plan period (2006–10), striking progress in the implementation of new environmental standards was reported during the mid-term and pre-final NDRC and World Bank evaluations. Whereas during the 9th and 10th Five-year Plan periods (1996–2005), the decoupling of pollution discharge from economic growth made only initial progress and many quantitative indicators of environmental protection were not reached, the evaluation reports on emissions reductions and energy conservation in the 11th Five-year Plan period point to striking successes. Senior NDRC officials in charge of evaluation work attribute these successes to the introduction of a limited number of binding targets that are more easily overseen. The links between the cadre management system and the plan targets have succeeded in influencing policy priorities and the incentives of officials charged with implementation, but there are still limits to this system.

Cadres may receive scores on as many as forty targets, ranging from GDP growth to environmental protection, from rural wages to arable land preservation. With so many targets, the effectiveness of the system may become diluted and policy makers may devise strategies to maximize their performance ratings in ways that diverge from the intentions of the leadership.[76] The party's personnel management system attempts to resolve this by assigning each target a weight, providing the appearance of a scientific hierarchy of policy priorities. But in reality, most officials know that this part of their performance review depends on meeting a handful of "hard targets" and most of the others can be safely ignored. Since economic growth, population control, and social stability have historically been hard targets, officials will be inclined to favor these targets until they receive an overwhelming signal that other things matter more (as was the case with Wen Jiabao's insistence on energy efficiency). Additionally, despite the elaborate scoring methods and the appearance of objectivity, in practice the evaluation system—like employee evaluation systems everywhere—can be highly subjective. There are questions about whether corruption and factional or instrumental relationships play an important role behind the scenes, with "objective" criteria mainly used to justify decisions made for other reasons.

In general, it has been difficult for Chinese national planners to impose guidance and restrictions on local governments and companies if plan prescriptions run counter to market incentives and business interests. Goals and targets stated in Chinese development plans have been implemented most effectively in those policy fields in which government programs manage to align political cadres' career incentives (and therefore administrative actions) with domestic and transnational market opportunities. Although provincial-level plan evaluators shared the basic view that local governments take the binding targets seriously and work toward their fulfillment, they also made it clear that the contradictory incentive structure of local-level administrations is not alleviated by the binding environmental targets.[77] De facto, aggregate economic and revenue growth remain the most important performance criteria for local cadres. If new environmental and energy technology help to boost local growth and income, if the closure of highly visible polluting and economically run-down local companies can bring good publicity without hurting revenue and employment, or if central funds or special loans are available to invest in green technologies, local governments are generally willing to comply with the new plan targets. In such cases, cadre power will be aligned with both local economic incentives and top-down cadre incentives.

However, when agents face multiple competing incentives, including targets in the plan, market forces, and practical constraints such as revenue growth, the delegated authority system can break down. The planning system is dynamic and can adjust the relative value of various objectives—such as reducing the importance of growth in the cadre evaluations or increasing the importance of environmental protection—but it can only do so if the absolute number of priority objectives remains relatively small, or if the objectives do not conflict with the other incentives that the agents face. As Chinese policy makers are emphasizing social welfare and public services and are increasing the priority of objectives that limit economic growth, such as environmental protection and energy efficiency, the planning system's reliance on performance evaluations will face strains.

The planning system also is not effective to eliminate resource constraints. China's development planning efforts so far have displayed a pronounced weakness in pursuing re-distributive goals and improving the development potential of the disadvantaged population groups. Such goals are at the heart of the rural healthcare reforms, social security reforms, and more equitable education that so far, as judged by the plans, have produced extremely uneven or disappointing results.[78]

Detailed implementation measures are supposed to guide provincial governments in fulfilling the goals of macro-regional development plans—this is the core of the reformed planning process—but this too has its limits.[79] Though many central and provincial officials admit that NDRC centralization tendencies have become a source of contention in central-regional communications, the actual effects of strong-handed rhetoric are generally regarded as limited. NDRC officials concede that they do not have the manpower or the means to check on real-life implementation in the provinces.[80]

In China's bureaucratic hierarchies, policy evaluations are dependent on data provided up through the political chain of command. If achievements in a policy area are difficult to measure (or failures are easy to conceal), the basis for the evaluations becomes murky. When environmental and energy targets threaten to affect business, revenue, and employment interests in a jurisdiction, local governments tend to resort to manipulating the environmental data.

Such manipulations are rarely exposed or punished, since both the DRCs and the CCP organization departments at the provincial levels have a strong incentive to report positive evaluation results and to avoid presenting an unpleasant regional record to the higher-level party bodies.[81] Therefore, implementation of official plans and cadre evaluations must be judged with the usual strong caveats regarding any data coming from China's statistical system. It also points to the serious limitations of using the party's personnel system, which flows through party secretaries at the apex of the political units, rather than endowing the legal and regulatory (or statistical) institutions with the necessary political independence to enforce a rule-based system.[82]

Finally, there are also obvious and difficult limits to the planning ambitions with regard to fundamental economic restructuring and a transition toward an efficiency-, innovation-, and domestic consumption-driven mode of development. Government planning and intervention have proven largely ineffective to promote and guide macro-structural shifts, i.e., "transformation of the growth and development mode" that has been defined as a core mission with changing formulas in all five-year plans beginning in the mid-1990s. The least successful element of the 11th Five-year Plan—the energy-intensity campaign—was an effort to move the economy away from energy-intensive industries and toward services. Such a structural shift can be encouraged with better incentives, but without a wholesale revision of priorities (e.g., drastically reducing the importance of growth relative to the development of the service sector), it is best accomplished through a re-pricing of capital and other factor inputs (notably energy), reforms in the financial sector, and simplifying regulations governing the service industries, rather than through the planning system.

Despite these limitations, in addition to the direct economic incentives found in local economic development, the cadre appraisal system has become the core mechanism for promoting plan priorities. The recalibration of cadre performance criteria and the reorganization of cadre evaluations have become subjects of intense efforts by the CCP's organization departments.[83] In the test case of ambitious energy-conservation and environmental targets defined in the 11th Five-year Plan, the plan-cadre nexus conveyed a credible commitment by national policy makers. In combination with large-scale public investments in green technologies, the Party Center forcefully signaled that environmental protection and green technology are a major new field for creating growth and income for local businesses and governments. Yet this requires persistent interventions and emphasis by top policy makers (especially the premier), and such political capital cannot be dispersed widely.

## Conclusion

Chinese planning practices confirm one core lesson of policy studies: political economies should be disaggregated into policy subsystems, each of which is characterized by very different dynamics.[84] Thus, we will find effective plan implementation in certain policy areas, whereas we find persistent blockages or outright failures of plan-based coordination in other policy realms. Due to such stark variations, it is imperative to exercise restraint when generalizing across policy subsystems and to refrain from jumping to sweeping hypotheses (e.g., "China makes planning work" or "Chinese planning is a complete failure and must make way for markets"). By better understanding how the planning cycle influences incentives and resources in successive layers of bureaucracies and jurisdictions, and how it updates itself and adapts to new challenges, it is possible to better understand the Chinese policy-making process, both its successes and its pathologies.

Development planning in contemporary China is driven by an unceasing process of information gathering, consultation, analysis, document drafting, implementation, experimentation, evaluation, and revision. This is better thought of as a recurrent cycle of cross-level, multi-year policy coordination rather than as an integrated, unitary planning system. Considering the mix of coordination mechanisms as well as the variation in the effectiveness and credibility of planning efforts across policy sectors, it is clear that China's planning system is incapable of dealing simultaneously with everything that it claims to address. Yet, at the same time, its evaluation and updating functions are useful even when the system fails because greater priority can be attached to new or different issues as policy makers identify shortcomings.

This chapter adds to the existing literature by moving beyond static authority relationships and incentive structures to illustrate a dynamic process of evolving and sometimes competing priorities, with periods of experimentation and consolidation. The planning process allows for a high degree of adaptability and regional variation in policies and targets, and it strikes an oscillating balance between over-centralized planning and complete regional autonomy. A major strength of post-1993 planning is its elasticity, as demonstrated by the three re-adjustment periods (1993–95, 1997–99, 2008–10) when serious macroeconomic challenges necessitated a swift, temporary retreat from the original plan objectives and emergency government interventions.

Overall, the incorporation of experimental programs into macro-plans, newly introduced mid-course plan evaluations, and regular top-level policy reviews allow Chinese planners to escape the rigidity traps that debased most planning exercises in socialist and non-socialist planning systems during the twentieth century. In the face of serious threats, Chinese planners "sacrifice long-term goals for short-term goals," as one NDRC official put it, but they strive to return to the original long-term goals as soon as stability returns to the economic environment.[85] The Chinese approach to planning is often geared to very ambitious goals. But it provides ample room to tinker with the means and the sequence of the steps to achieve these goals.

The hallmark of Chinese development planning lies in the dynamics of recombined governance based on loosely institutionalized, malleable, and adaptive policy processes. These governance mechanisms exceed the standard explanatory models of the command economy, the East Asian developmental state, or the regulatory state. The variability and recombination of the policy processes require more research focus so as to transcend static institutionalist categories and established normative assumptions that cannot capture the striking fluidity, and often unexpected effectiveness, of China's planning and policy cycles.

# Epilogue

## Changes in China's Policy Process under General Secretary Xi Jinping*

Western assessments of Chinese political development have traditionally tended to focus on a progressive transition to a more liberal political order and the conflicts that arise between state authority and an emerging civil society during this process. From the perspective of the Chinese party-state, however, it is the progressive deterioration of the organizational hold and the internal discipline of the Chinese Communist Party (CCP) since the 1998s that are seen as the decisive change and catalyst for the transformation of the political system of the People's Republic of China (PRC). Economic transformation followed a hesitant, selective, and restricted process of opening, deregulation, and liberalization that continued despite recurring but mostly short-lived efforts by the central party leadership to enforce organizational and political discipline.

---

\* This is an abridged and revised version of analyses that were originally published in Sebastian Heilmann, ed., *China's Political System* (Lanham, MD: Rowman & Littlefield, 2017), pp. 398–427, republished here with permission of Rowman & Littlefield Publishing Group.

Although official political institutions have appeared sclerotic, since the 1980s decision-making powers in many economic and administrative fields have been delegated to lower levels of government. In addition, informal modes of exchange between political and economic players have undermined the formal CCP command structure, resulting in the emergence of a shadow system of endemic corruption that has eluded control by party headquarters. China's political order has changed considerably from the totalitarianism of the Mao era (when CCP functionaries and party organs enjoyed practically limitless control over economic and social life) to a "fragmented authoritarianism" in which centralized intervention by the party only takes place during exceptional periods of crisis governance (see below for this characteristic shift to a "crisis mode"). Toward the end of the Hu Jintao–Wen Jiabao administration (2002–12), China appeared to be entering a "post-socialist" political system—one in which changes in the official political institutions lagged far behind the rapid developments in the economy, society, technology, and, indeed, the global environment (see Figure 7.1).

In 2012 the Xi Jinping–Li Keqiang administration initiated a pronounced change of direction in terms of China's political development: the party leadership revealed an extraordinary determination to combat the previously unstoppable erosion of the party's internal organization by launching an extensive anti-corruption and discipline campaign and it began to reinforce the hierarchies of the party-state by concentrating decision-making powers at party headquarters, even in those policy areas that had previously been delegated to government organs or subnational authorities. General Secretary Xi Jinping made it clear that only the CCP was capable of steering the country through the twenty-first century and that the party would fight vehemently against any attempt to undermine its leadership or to drive the country in the direction of a Western-style democratic system.

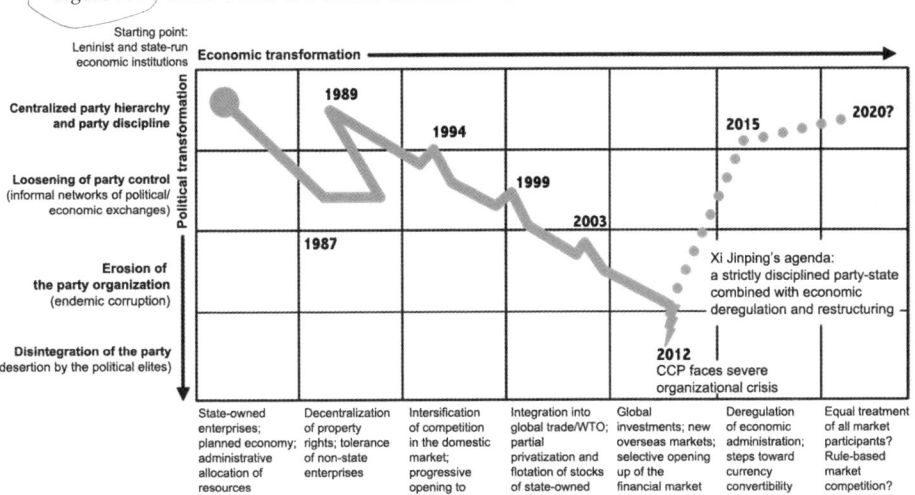

Figure 7.1 China's Path to Political and Economic Transformation

Sources: Based on Tsuyoshi Hasegawa, "The Connection between Political and Economic Reform in Communist Regimes," in Gilbert Rozman, with Seizaburō Satō and Gerald Segal, eds., *Dismantling Communism: Common Causes and Regional Variations* (Washington, DC: Woodrow Wilson Center Press; Baltimore: Johns Hopkins University Press, 1992), pp. 59–117; Sebastian Heilmann, *Die Politik der Wirtschaftsreformen in China und Russland* [The Politics of Economic Reform in China and Russia] (Hamburg: Institut für Asienkunde, 2000).

For the new party leadership, this was a case of reconfiguring the entire party-state in order to achieve a national "China Dream." In order to rapidly increase "comprehensive national strength," there was a need to create the proper political and economic conditions. Hence, in 2013 the party leadership launched a structural-reform program that was designed to avoid the much-feared "middle-income trap" and to transform China into one of the world's most advanced and innovative economic and technological powers. The program promised to allow market forces to play a "decisive role" in the future development of the economy, thus implying deregulation for the private sector, legal security and equal treatment for all types of businesses in the financial system, reorganization and partial privatization of state-owned enterprises, and a drastic reduction in state interference in the economy.

Rigorous application of this reform agenda did indeed have extraordinary political consequences for China's developmental state. A comprehensive program of economic liberalization greatly curtailed the party-state's capacity to intervene and it faced direct conflicts with the interests of the established party- and government-backed economic elite. As it turned out, by 2017 the economic liberalization measures of 2013 were being implemented inconsistently and selectively. Only piecemeal or marginal restructuring was undertaken in crucial yet politically sensitive areas, such as deregulation of state-sector oligopolies, transparency in debt management of the fiscal and banking systems, establishment of a level playing field for non-state market participants, and improved market access for foreign investors.

The strengthening of centralized party control over the political and economic system clearly was the prerogative of Xi Jinping who held the helm of power. The only chance for a boost in economic liberalization was if the party leadership were to feel it was politically safe to loosen controls or if a decline in economic growth posed an immediate threat to CCP rule. During the first several years of Xi Jinping's tenure, political objectives, such as enforcing domestic discipline and pursuing great power diplomacy in combination with military modernization, took precedence over economic restructuring.

## Shifting from a "normal mode" to a "crisis mode" in central decision-making

Observers of contemporary Chinese affairs are continually faced with the conundrum that previously "pragmatic," "moderate," and "reformist" Chinese leaderships suddenly apply drastic measures of repression. For example, Deng Xiaoping—twice named "Person of the Year" by *Time* magazine—according to Western media was transformed into a "dictator" and "butcher" practically overnight, when the pro-democracy protests were violently crushed by the military in June 1989. The leadership under Hu Jintao and Wen Jiabao, both of whom were initially rated favorably by the West for their commitment to social and environmental reforms, experienced a rapid negative swing in public opinion due to their suppression of unrest in Tibet in 2008. When he assumed the position of CCP general secretary in 2012, Xi Jinping took the West by surprise by introducing a combination of decidedly market-oriented reform programs and strong anti-corruption measures, along with a tightening of ideological controls and domestic repression.

In order to understand these apparent contradictions, it is useful to differentiate between a "normal mode" and a "crisis mode" in Chinese politics.[1] Whereas decisions in times of "politics as usual" are reached after protracted processes of compromise, an exceptional mode of decision-making enters into force during acute crisis situations that are perceived as threats to stability. This mode is characterized by centralized ideological decision-making and rule by decree. The highest levels of the party leadership monopolize all decision-making powers during such phases, and intra-party directives have top priority, severely constricting the latitude previously granted to subordinate state agencies and local governments. On the basis of China's contemporary political history, it is possible to identify certain events that are likely to trigger moves to a crisis mode (see Table 7.1).

Table 7.1  Events That May Trigger a Crisis Mode

| | Typical trigger factors | Examples since 1989 |
|---|---|---|
| I | Domestic security crises with nationwide impact | Urban protest movement of 1989; Falun Gong movement in 1999; protests in Tibet in 2008; Xinjiang unrest in 2009; terrorist attacks in Beijing and Kunming, 2013–14 |
| II | Intra-party decision-making and organizational crises | Loss of Politburo decision-making capacity in 1989; fight against intra-party corruption and the formation of cliques since 2012 |
| III | Scandals that have repercussions for the national leadership | Anti-smuggling campaign in 1998; combating the severe acute respiratory syndrome (SARS) epidemic after an initial cover-up in 2003; criminal proceedings against members of the Politburo since 2012 |
| IV | Foreign policy and military tensions | Taiwan Straits crisis in 1996; bombing of the Chinese Embassy in Belgrade in 1999; Sino-Japanese dispute, 2012–13 |
| V | Acute threats to economic stability | Inflation control, 1993–95; centralization of the financial vision, 1997–98; economic stimulus program, 2007–9 |
| VI | Natural disasters | Floods in 1998; earthquake in southwest China in 2008 |
| VII | External shocks | Collapse of the socialist states in Eastern Europe, 1989–91; Asian Financial Crisis of 1997–98; global financial crisis of 2007–9 |

Sources: Sebastian Heilmann, *Das politische System der Volksrepublik China* [The Political System of the PRC] (Wiesbaden: VS Verlag für Sozialwissenschaften, 2nd rvsd. ed., 2004); Sebastian Heilmann, "Das Modell des ostasiatischen Entwicklungsstaates in der Revision" [Revising the Model of the East Asian Developmental State], in Verena Blechinger-Talcott, Christiane Frantz, and Mark R. Thompson, eds., *Politik in Japan: System, Reformprozesse und Aussenpolitik im internationalen Vergleich* [Politics in Japan: System, Reform Processes, and Foreign Policy in International Comparison] (Frankfurt am Main: Campus, 2006), pp. 103–116.

During the normal and routine mode, decision-making at the center of power is characterized by the following:

- Responsibilities and tasks are divided among the members of the Politburo Standing Committee or the members of the inner cabinet of the State Council according to their specific portfolios (such as the financial system, foreign trade, or domestic security).

- Coordinated, interdepartmental programs, with participation by relevant specialists, are implemented; internal and external expertise is enlisted from think-tanks and universities, and ad hoc task forces are set up to research decisions, negotiate compromises, and design a system of documentation.
- Consultative meetings to generate compromises are lengthy processes that require a high degree of coordination; top functionaries must act both as advocates and as mediators among the various state agencies.
- Top party leaders tend to exercise their authority only if they are under pressure to make decisions quickly (e.g., if there are timelines to pass multi-year programs or to implement international treaty obligations, or scandals that have attracted public interest).

Decision-making methods and longer-term political programs in China have changed whenever there has been a transition to a new generation of leaders—be it the veterans, the technocrats, or the cadres with more diversified qualifications who were appointed to the party leadership in 2007 and 2012. Compared to the rule by Mao Zedong or Deng Xiaoping, the decision-making process under party leaders Jiang Zemin and Hu Jintao was considerably less centralized and personalized, at least during periods of routine politics when there was no acute sense of urgency. However, significant changes took place in 2012 under Xi Jinping's leadership, with the general secretary holding an unusual concentration of decision-making authority across a vast number of policy areas.

The changes in the decision mode under Xi Jinping fulfill all of the criteria listed in Table 7.2 for a transition to a crisis mode of governance. Xi Jinping and his colleagues in the party leadership bodies obviously sensed that the decision-making and loyalty crises in the Politburo under General Secretary Hu Jintao (2002–12) and the corruption and organizational crises in the Communist Party had collectively reached a dangerous level that represented a threat to the system. Therefore, the best way to achieve institutional renewal and organizational stability within the party and state apparatuses was through a concentration of political power and centralized decision-making, organizational and ideological discipline, extensive anti-corruption measures, and the prevention of any attempts to form factions or cliques within the party, coupled with a campaign against Western values and concepts.

Table 7.2  Characteristics of the Normal and Crisis Modes in Chinese Politics

| Normal mode | Crisis mode |
| --- | --- |
| • Party and government leaders set general guidelines and objectives for national policies<br>• Government departments negotiate with one another about the drafting of national legislation<br>• Local governments flexibly apply national laws and directives in accordance with local conditions<br>• The Party Center's capacity to enforce national rules vis-à-vis the local governments is limited | • Abrupt centralization of the decision-making processes and central interventions across the party hierarchy<br>• Feelings of urgency; limited willingness on the part of the central party headquarters to hold consultation meetings<br>• Personalization and increased emphasis on ideology for consensus-building<br>• Recourse to the militant rhetoric and mobilization of the Cultural Revolution<br>• Political upgrading of the disciplinary and security organs<br>• If the party executive is united, the elite close ranks leading to a temporary increase in their capacity to enforce policies<br>• If the party executive is divided, then difficulties in implementing decisions and resultant conflicts occur at all levels of the party-state |

Source: Sebastian Heilmann, ed., *China's Political System* (Lanham, MD: Rowman & Littlefield, 2017).

In the crisis mode, decision-making procedures are abruptly centralized and dominated by the personalities of the top individual leaders. The familiar Mao-era ideology and militant rhetoric are reactivated. The central party leadership exerts an extraordinary sense of urgency in isolated policy areas, resorting to techniques that were used during the pre-1978 mobilization and campaign regimes. During such phases, China's political leadership is more assertive than regimes in most other developing countries or emerging economies.

The crisis mode represents the central leadership's ad hoc response to events that are deemed to be a threat to the stability of the national political system or a challenge to the authority and legitimacy of the national leadership. As soon as the acute threat has abated, Chinese politics tends to revert back to a normal mode. But such a swing back to low-pressure, decentralized governance (a cycle of tightening and loosening of top-down control that has been typical of China's domestic political development since 1978) has not occurred under Xi Jinping.

The drastically strengthened concentration of decision-making power at party headquarters under Xi Jinping is intended to enforce the authority of the Party Center with respect to ministerial, regional, and business special interests and to narrow the space for corrupt patronage networks within the political system. Since 1978 such a centralized and personalized decision-making process has been implemented only during very short periods of crisis.

The extent to which the concentration of power at CCP headquarters can be an effective remedy for enforcing a nationwide institutional reorganization during a period of up to ten years under Xi Jinping's leadership remains uncertain. From 2013 to 2016, widespread uncertainty was felt in many party and government bodies below the Party Center (hence in the ministries, regional/

local administrations, and companies) regarding whether decentralized initiatives were desirable and could be pursued without any political risks. This wait-and-see attitude put the brakes on implementation of many reforms that had been announced by party headquarters. As a consequence, party leadership organs resolutely criticized such inactivity by local governments and officials.

From 1978 to 2012 decentralized initiatives were crucial to creating an agile and adaptable political and economic system. Since 2013, however, the drastic measures undertaken by the Party Center to enforce hierarchical discipline and centralized authority have restricted policy initiative and reform agility at the lower levels of China's state administration.

## How the concentration of power at the center reduces adaptive capacities

One analytical model derived from the series of economic and political crises that took place at the beginning of the twenty-first century focuses on the conditions required for the robustness and resilience (i.e., "anti-fragility") of a political system when faced with unexpected internal or external shocks. According to this model, the resilience of a political system is not determined by outwardly stable and powerful institutions; rather, it is derived from its capability to absorb shocks and to avoid functional collapse in the event of an acute crisis and to actually reorganize and strengthen performance during periods of recovery from crises.[2] Based on the criteria of this model, China's political system scores higher under the previous administrations than it does under Xi Jinping's more centralized, personalized, and rigid decision-making system (see Table 7.3).

Table 7.3 A Stable Exterior with Underlying Fragilities: How Resilient is China's Political Order to Unexpected Shocks?

| | Prerequisites for a resilient political system | Jiang Zemin–Zhu Rongji administration (1998–2002) | Hu Jintao–Wen Jiabao administration (2002–12) | Xi Jinping–Li Keqiang administration (2012–present) |
|---|---|---|---|---|
| 1 | Diversified economic structure | + | + | + |
| 2 | Decentralized policy initiatives | + | ~ | ϴ |
| 3 | Moderate levels of state debt | + | ϴ | ϴ |
| 4 | Political variability and diversity | ϴ | ϴ | ϴ |
| 5 | Experience in dealing with systemic crises | + | + | ~ |

Notes: + means "resilient"; ~ means "not very resilient"; ϴ means "fragile."
Source: Modified and applied to the China case based on the general model in Nassim Nicholas Taleb and Gregory F. Treverton, "The Calm Before the Storm: Why Volatility Signals Stability, and Vice Versa," *Foreign Affairs*, Vol. 94, No. 1 (2015), pp. 86–95.

One of China's greatest sources of resilience is its diversified economic structure, especially in comparison to other historically authoritarian states (particularly the Communist party-states). China is not solely dependent on specialized industries or on the export of raw materials—its economy has exhibited a limited, yet arguably growing, innovative capacity and it is able to fall back on its huge domestic market that will allow it to expand further in the future, even if export markets shrink. This economic diversification is also a huge advantage in terms of the resilience of the political system: if drastic contractions occur in some parts of the economy, national social and political stability will not necessarily be disrupted because the other parts of the economy that remain dynamic will help to buffer the shocks and will provide resources to compensate for those individual sectors or regions that have been affected by the crises.

In other areas, however, in comparison to previous decades, the resilience of China's political economy is now in danger of weakening as a result of both structural economic changes and heavy-handed political interventions. This applies in particular to the level of state and corporate debt in relation to GDP and GDP growth, and the resultant negative effects on the fiscal and financial systems. The extremely rapid increase in national debt since the massive post-2007 stimulus package seriously limited the government's ability to act in the event of an acute economic or political crisis. The Xi–Li administration could no longer rely on the rapidly growing and abundant tax revenues that the Chinese government commanded after the turn of the millennium to implement an expansionary fiscal and financial policy over an extended period.

The results in other areas that affect resilience are inconclusive, but the overall trend points toward a weakening. In times of political or economic stress, decentralized policy making by effective local authorities helps to compensate for blockades, political errors, or failed reforms on the part of the central government. Yet Xi Jinping's centralization of policy initiative has weakened this all-important buffer against crises and has limited the Chinese government's adaptive and innovative capacities. In effect, over-centralized decision-making has eliminated the systemic advantages of distributed intelligence and local initiative that Deng Xiaoping had purposively crafted in the 1980s and 1990s.

It remains unclear whether China's historical experiences in dealing with earlier systemic crises are still present in the minds of the Xi–Li administration (particularly the 1989 crisis). All of the current members of the Chinese leadership have experience as political decision-makers in the wake of the 2007–9 global financial and economic crises. However, they do not have any experience in making decisions during large-scale political crises. Judged by the wording of public speeches and internal communiqués, Xi Jinping and the party headquarters are fixated on the "lessons" learned from the downfall of the former Soviet Union and the "failure" of the political regime under Gorbachev. But external analyses cannot determine the extent to which such lessons have resulted in a more repressive political program instead of any sort of willingness on the part of the Chinese leadership to respond flexibly and creatively when confronted with political destabilization.

The greatest systemic weakness in terms of the resilience of the Chinese government system is its lack of political variability and diversity. Open and legitimate political competition is not possible in China's political system—neither within the ruling party nor between the ruling party and the opposition forces. Open debates on the underlying shortcomings of the political system are rare and they are only permitted within strict confines. Critical political views, and those who spell them out, are much less likely to be tolerated in the inner policy-making circle of the Xi–Li administration than they were during previous governments. These restrictions make it more difficult to notice any early signs of impending crises that might threaten the system or to be able to respond to them in a timely manner with measures to reinforce stability.

## The systemic risks of a top-down policy process

The political "top-level design" introduced with great fanfare under Xi Jinping contains systemic risks that cannot even be discussed in domestic policy circles. The new system involves a substantial hardening and narrowing of the previous much more flexible and exploratory policy processes. In effect, decision-making powers with respect to the institutional restructuring of the state and the economy are concentrated in Central Leading Small Groups located in the party headquarters. Xi Jinping has acquired a considerable amount of personal power within a short period. A personality cult around him, unlike that enjoyed by any other party leader since Mao, has been created by the media.

As a result, political decision-making under Xi Jinping is much more top-down. Experiences and initiatives put forward by various regions tend to be ignored by the centralized, personality-based decision-making system. This leads to typical policy failures. During the 2014–16 period, centrally imposed policies on fiscal reform, stock market regulation, and IT security faced immediate heavy criticism from regional governments and market participants respectively, resulting in their eventual withdrawal and revision. The decision-makers and their advisers at party and government headquarters apparently were unable to realistically assess and anticipate the consequences of the new regulations.

Xi Jinping prefers centralized decision-making by a small circle of top leaders and his trusted advisory staff. Such (top-down) decision-making contrasts strikingly with the type of (bottom-up) policy making promoted by Deng Xiaoping and later continued by Jiang Zemin. For decades, China's reform policy had been the result of exploratory leadership based on decentralized reform experiments and the specific lessons learned from implementation of such experiments. Xi Jinping does not actively curtail or prohibit local experimentation. In high profile statements, he has even referred favorably to local experimental zones and pilot initiatives. But under conditions of a concentration of power at the top levels and in combination with sustained and intense campaigns to enforce intra-party discipline, there are no longer any credible or powerful incentives to permit local policy makers to embrace the political risks inherent in bottom-up policy experimentation.

The CCP leadership styles shaped by Deng Xiaoping and Jiang Zemin, which explicitly included initiatives and innovations by local authorities on how best to implement policies, are very different from the "top-level design" preferred by Xi Jinping. As a self-assured political leader with a mission to achieve a national "China Dream," Xi relies much less than his predecessors on consultation, exploration, and reflection in making decisions. This more impulsive or even aggressive style of decision-making has become apparent in China's foreign and security policies, for example with respect to the territorial disputes in the South China Sea.

It is an open question whether the changes in the decision-making system under Xi Jinping will endure. In a case of a series of policy failures or deepening economic problems, it may well turn out to be merely a temporary centralization and rigidity. A return to a more exploratory leadership may take on an urgency if implementation of the 2013–20 structural-reform program should reach a deadlock.

However, if China moves further in the direction of top-down policy making, the fragility of the political system will increase and its ability to learn from and to correct policy mistakes will decrease, rendering the system both rigid and inflexible. Should there be irrefutable failures of central policy or should Xi Jinping for some reason become incapacitated, there will no longer be any reserve government legitimacy in the provinces because in such a rigidly centralized system regional authorities will not be able to compensate for the failing authority and actions of the central government.

## Can China be a developmental model for other countries?

The rapid global economic rise of the PRC has resulted in extensive debates as to whether a "Chinese model" is evolving that can be followed by other developing nations and emerging markets that combine market-based economic development with authoritarian leadership. The controversy centers around very different ideas about the different characteristics of an East Asian "developmental state,"[3] the emergence of an authoritarian economic "Beijing consensus," in contrast to the liberal "Washington consensus,"[4] novel "state capitalist" systems,[5] an economically and technology-driven output boost in certain authoritarian systems of government ("authoritarian upgrading"),[6] historically-based, self-reliant, ideological beliefs and legitimacy,[7] or the benefits of a meritocratic form of government when recruiting political leaders and legitimizing power in the twenty-first century.[8] Table 7.4 summarizes the most important characteristics and methods that are attributed to a potential "Chinese development model."

Table 7.4 Characteristics and Methods Attributed to a "Chinese Development Model"

| | |
|---|---|
| Domestic and legal policies | Authoritarian, developmental, economically agile, and adaptive government; prohibition against political competition; suppression of political opposition; recruitment of local political and administrative leaders according to their experience, qualifications, and performance ("meritocracy"); compartmentalized administrative reforms in reaction to economic pressures; neither constitutional reform nor political liberalization; legitimization based on economic performance and nationalism; consultations with important lobbies ("consultative authoritarianism"); an extensive system of laws and regulations; lack of an independent judiciary |
| Social and welfare policies | Suppression of political self-organization in NGOs and instead promotion of state-controlled, government-organized non-governmental organizations (GONGOs); prevention of unrest through preventive "social management" (surveillance, complaints offices, social services, the possibility of police repression); strict residence and birth controls; high investment in the education system, with a focus on mathematics, informatics, natural and technical sciences; extension of social security; official aim is "prosperity for all" |
| Labor relations | State-guided official unions; prohibition against strikes and collective bargaining across companies; close alliances between government and big business |
| Domestic economy | Long-term development planning; strong willingness to learn from international experience; strictly pragmatic (aimed at specific problem-solving) non-ideological economic policy and a willingness to try out new options; growth at any price; massive state investments in industry and infrastructure; protection of government-linked companies; state control of the banking system |

| Financial markets | State financial repression (low interest rates on deposit accounts with limited alternatives for savings and investments); channeling of private savings into investments for state-approved industries and infrastructure; state-controlled sovereign wealth funds invested internationally; capital controls; active currency management and limited currency convertibility |
|---|---|
| Foreign policy | Global diplomatic presence; blend of diplomacy with foreign-trade policy and financial diplomacy ("checkbook diplomacy"); strict defense of national sovereignty and territorial claims; insistence on national sovereignty in all political issues (including human rights) as well as in cyberspace; massive military build-up |
| Foreign trade | Orientation toward global markets and exports; government-sponsored programs aimed at import substitution; selective protectionism for domestic infant industries; targeted promotion and control of foreign investments; preference for global market share over short-term revenue; special funding for overseas involvement by Chinese companies; support for geopolitical goals via foreign-trade policy |
| Industrial policy | Targeted state promotion of "strategic emerging industries"; state interference in sectoral industrial structure; maintenance of state control in "strategic" industries |
| Energy/ environmental policies | Extensive use of resources with serious environmental consequences; technology-driven efforts to move to a more resource-conserving energy and environmental policy |
| Technology policy | Acquisition of advanced foreign technology through targeted regulations and incentives; access to the market in exchange for investment and technology; long-term programs for building a globally competitive national innovation system |
| Media and general public | Active steering of media and shaping of public opinion; commercialization and de-politicization of the media sector; enlargement of electronic surveillance systems on the Internet |
| Domestic security | Expansion of the security apparatus (including in cyberspace); comprehensive IT surveillance systems |

Even within China there have been lively debates regarding the main features of a high-performance "Chinese model" (*Zhongguo moshi*)[9] or even a "new type of superpower" (*xinxing chaoji daguo*).[10] Such discussions have been popularized in a series of publications written mainly by prominent social scientists (many of whom come from party or government backgrounds), with some contributions also from retired party cadres.[11] However, arguments in favor of a distinct "Chinese model" have encountered strong criticism within China.[12]

It is noteworthy that the Chinese government has never attempted to portray its political and economic systems as an exemplary model for other states to follow. In fact, Chinese diplomats are insistent that their partner countries in Asia, Africa, and Latin America should follow independent national development strategies in accordance with their local circumstances. Chinese diplomats and commentators criticize cooperative Western development programs for imposing conditions on the beneficiaries and offering one-size-fits-all solutions. In contrast, they hold that China avoids setting any standardized conditions that do not match the specific national and regional contexts.

International discussions of the "Chinese model" did not attract much attention until the global financial and economic crisis of 2007–9. In the West, public and social-science discussions were dominated by the logic of the "interdependence of orders" that maintains that political and economic freedoms and competition are mutually dependent, and that wealth and growth can only be guaranteed over the long term in a democracy with a market-based economy. However, this explanatory model does not offer any plausible explanation for the economic and political developments in China after 1989. The contrasts with the experiences of the Eastern European Communist party-states with regard to economic and institutional flexibility as well as to competitiveness within the global economy are obvious.

Investors and companies operating in China believe that one of the greatest strengths of the Chinese political system is that the government places much greater emphasis on long-term development priorities and large-scale projects than do governments operating in short-winded, reactive, and seemingly volatile democratic

EPILOGUE

systems. Leading proponents of the "Chinese model" view China as one of the few remaining systems that is capable of implementing strategic, long-term policies. The chances of pursuing long-term priorities in China, ranging from infrastructure and education to technology planning, are, however, inseparable from authoritarian rule and executive continuity—including the absence of democratic elections and checks on executive power.

Does China really offer a model for an efficient, technocratic state characterized by cooperation among political, economic, and technological players and resources, long-term development goals, and greater assertiveness against lobbies and vested interests?

When discussing these issues, nothing is as plausible or sustainable as it first appears if one is to examine beyond the simplified descriptions. Remarkably, even the traditional hierarchical foundations of state power in China tend to crumble when scrutinized under a microscope. In addition, state capacity to actively shape and control key development issues (such as the financial system, income distribution, the environment, and demography) also appears to be rather limited, and the push toward greater centralization under Xi Jinping has not done much to change that. All in all, the widespread perception of China as a centralized autocracy explains only a small part of the overall political and social dynamics. These dynamics are driven much more by decentralized, uncontrollable forces than all-or-none thinking in terms of different types of systems (autocracy versus democracy) suggests.

With regard to the influence that Chinese experiences and practices may have on other developing nations and emerging markets, there is no suggestion that they should be directly implemented in the same way in other countries. In fact, China's economic approach is seen as a more flexible, more selective, alternative frame of reference that may provide productive ideas, methodologies, justifications, and legitimization beyond the so far predominant Western models and influences. In particular, authoritarian or "illiberal" polities, and the political elite within them, can refer to China's success story as providing legitimacy for authoritarian methods of leadership and national development under a "strong state."

The Chinese government has not approached its own foreign economic, financial, and development policies with missionary zeal: rather than publicizing its development experience as a self-contained model, it is promoted as a suggestion about how to advance independent, national "catch-up" development. However, even without active propagation, the combination of an authoritarian state and rapid economic development has obvious demonstration effects and strong appeal for authoritarian and illiberal governments, such as those in Russia, Hungary, Venezuela, Ecuador, Iran, Ethiopia, Zimbabwe, Thailand, and Cambodia. Even if the political elite and societies in countries with diplomatic and economic links to China are suspicious of Chinese influence, the Chinese approach to politics and economic development is still hugely attractive to their ruling classes. China's global economic and investment activities encourage the spread of Chinese approaches to governance and the legitimation of a "strong state."

Is a form of modern Chinese statehood that might challenge or even reject the Western model of a market-based democracy currently in the making? The leading Western democracies and market economies of the United States, Europe, and Japan have experienced a significant loss of reputation and credibility among the developing nations and emerging markets, particularly since the global financial and economic crisis of 2007–9—something that China has seized upon to promote its own global agenda. Current Chinese geopolitical initiatives are based on the assumption that the United States and Europe are in a state of decline and that China is the only nation currently capable of filling the gap. This weakening of the established market-based democracies that formerly held strong appeal as a model has become a key to understanding China's improved prestige and attraction.

Under certain circumstances, this new configuration may result in veritable competition between the two different models: should Xi Jinping's agenda (increased political discipline and centralization combined with economic deregulation and restructuring) be successful before the year 2020—and without the revival of the respective economic and technological performance and ability to take political action in the United States and the European Union—the much stronger authoritarian Chinese party-state will doubtlessly represent formidable systemic competition and a permanent yardstick for comparison with the market-based democracies. In the crisis-prone twenty-first century, discussions will focus on whether China has succeeded in developing a more efficient, flexible system of government with a more stable core. The greater global presence and activities of Chinese diplomats and investors are bound to foster methods of rule in partner and target countries that tend to correspond with Chinese practices. One of the leading fields for this type of convergence will be the continued rollout of comprehensive and effective state surveillance systems based on new IT and communications technologies. Commercial interests will drive this development globally, as China exports its increasingly powerful security and surveillance technologies.

In the context of a volatile, crisis-ridden twenty-first century, one specific feature of China's approach to governance might substantially challenge the Western democracies: its capability to react and adapt in a flexible and agile manner to recurrent acute crises and to novel demands on government activities. This important quality of political systems has been downplayed and neglected for decades in both Western Europe and the United States, based on the simplified argument that democratic competition automatically results in the development of an adaptive and innovative political system.

However, as a result of the recent failings of democratic systems to correct serious structural and regulatory shortcomings, both before and even after the global financial crisis and the euro crisis, such assumptions are risky and no longer tenable. Complacency and psychological barriers with regard to renovating traditional political institutions and approaches to governance may ultimately result in their downfall. Today's political systems must respond to novel requirements for managing recurrent economic and security crises, reducing risks in capital markets, regulating cyberspace, countering growing social inequities, and incorporating social media–driven public opinion in the policy process. Traditional political and legal systems are lagging in terms of being able to deal with these urgent contemporary challenges. Use of the organizational and administrative models of the nineteenth and twentieth centuries, persistent institutional and political inertia, and the resultant lack of drive to renew approaches to governance are among the central weaknesses of many governmental systems. Inevitably, all political and legal systems will be required to undertake huge adjustments in the radically changing economic, technological, and communications environment of the twenty-first century while at the same time avoiding breakdowns of their political systems and economic depressions.

China's authoritarian party-state is unacceptable and unsuitable as a model for democratic societies. Rule of law, limited state power, and guaranteed individual civil liberties remain the most attractive form of government, not least for large sections of Chinese society. A very visible indication of this is the many people among China's political and economic elite who send their children and assets abroad so as to prepare an exit option and to have access to an alternative lifestyle. China's "system insiders" do not appear to have much confidence in the sustainability of the current regime, thereby undermining the public façade of self-confidence and loyalty that is cultivated by official government statements.

Despite these profound weaknesses, the apparent recent success of the Chinese system of government has resulted in debates on the international stage that have cast doubt on the decades of undisputed institutional and economic superiority of the market-based democracies. The era when the West was the obvious, or the only, model to follow is most definitely over. Competition in terms of economic and technological efficiencies as well as in terms of state capacity and credibility is intensifying. In the face of a rising China, liberal Western models of governance currently face growing pressures to perform better and to reassert their legitimacy.

# NOTES

## Introduction

1. Nassim Nicholas Taleb, *The Black Swan: The Impact of the Highly Improbable* (London: Penguin, 2008).
2. Jennifer Gandhi, *Political Institutions under Dictatorship* (New York: Cambridge University Press, 2010); Jan Teorell, *Determinants of Democratization: Explaining Regime Change in the World, 1972–2006* (New York: Cambridge University Press, 2010); Milan W. Smolik, *The Politics of Authoritarian Rule* (New York: Cambridge University Press, 2012).
3. Steven Levitsky and Lucan A. Way, *Competitive Authoritarianism: Hybrid Regimes after the Cold War* (New York: Cambridge University Press, 2011); Larry Diamond, "Thinking About Hybrid Regimes," *Journal of Democracy*, Vol. 13, No. 2 (2002), pp. 21–35; Wim Naudé, Amelia U. Santos-Pauline, and Mark McGillivray, eds., *Fragile States: Causes, Costs, and Responses* (Oxford: Oxford University Press, 2011).
4. Valerie Bunce, *Subversive Institutions: The Design and the Destruction of Socialism and the State* (New York: Cambridge University Press, 1999); Archie Brown, *The Rise and Fall of Communism* (London: Bodley Head, 2009).
5. Michael Howlett, M. Ramesh, and Anthony Perl, *Studying Public Policy: Policy Cycles and Policy Subsystems* (Toronto: Oxford University Press, 3rd ed., 2009).
6. Dani Rodrik, *One Economics, Many Recipes* (Princeton, NJ: Princeton University Press, 2007).
7. Sebastian Heilmann and Elizabeth J. Perry, eds., *Mao's Invisible Hand: The Political Foundations of Adaptive Governance in China* (Cambridge, MA: Harvard University Asia Center, 2011).

## Chapter 1

1. Roderick MacFarquhar, "The Anatomy of Collapse," *New York Review of Books*, Vol. 38, No. 15 (1991), pp. 5–9; Jack A. Goldstone, "The Coming Chinese Collapse," *Foreign Policy*, No. 99 (1995), pp. 35–52.
2. Gordon G. Chang, *The Coming Collapse of China* (New York: Random House, 2001); Minxin Pei, *China's Trapped Transition: The Limits of Developmental Autocracy* (Cambridge, MA: Harvard University Press, 2006); Susan L. Shirk, *China: Fragile Superpower* (New York: Oxford University Press, 2007); Bruce Gilley, *China's Democratic Future: How it Will Happen and Where it Will Lead* (New York: Columbia University Press, 2004).
3. The concept of a "mechanism" (policy, administrative, and so forth) as used in this volume follows Jon Elster's definition as "frequently occurring and easily recognizable causal patterns that are triggered under generally unknown conditions or with indeterminate consequences." Cf. Jon Elster, *Explaining Social Behavior: More Nuts and Bolts for the Social Sciences* (New York: Cambridge University Press, 2007), p. 36.
4. Valerie Bunce, *Subversive Institutions: The Design and the Destruction of Socialism and the State* (New York: Cambridge University Press, 1999); Archie Brown, *The Rise and Fall of Communism* (London: Bodley Head, 2009).
5. The proliferation of "hybrid regime" types is also of limited utility to understand the Chinese case. See Larry Jay Diamond, "Thinking About Hybrid Regimes," *Journal of Democracy*, Vol. 13, No. 2 (2002), pp. 21–35; Steven Levitsky and Lucan A. Way, *Competitive Authoritarianism: The Origins and Evolution of Hybrid Regime Change in the Post-Cold War Era* (New York: Cambridge University Press, 2011).
6. Cf. Andrew G. Walder, *Communist Neo-Traditionalism: Work and Authority in Chinese Industry* (Berkeley: University of California Press, 1986).
7. Cf. Mark Beeson, "Developmental States in East Asia: A Comparison of the Japanese and Chinese Experiences," *Asian Perspective*, Vol. 33, No. 2 (2009), pp. 5–39.
8. On the limits of such comparisons, see Elizabeth J. Perry, "Studying Chinese Politics: Farewell to Revolution?" *The China Journal*, No. 57 (2007), pp. 2–5.
9. For the analogous "Black Swan" concept and its significance for social-science epistemology and methodology, see Nassim Nicholas Taleb, *The Black Swan: The Impact of the Highly Improbable* (New York: Random House, 2007).
10. Cf. John Gerring, *Case Study Research: Principles and Practices* (New York: Cambridge University Press, 2007), p. 101.

11. We are well aware that the term Maoism is not officially used in China. But because "Mao Zedong Thought" has been defined as representing the Communist leadership's "collective wisdom" derived from the socialist revolution and socialist construction, we take the liberty to call the pre-1976 official political ideology and leadership doctrine by the popular Western term "Maoist."
12. Andrew J. Nathan, "Authoritarian Resilience," *Journal of Democracy*, Vol. 14, No. 1 (2003), pp. 6, 13–15.
13. David Shambaugh, *China's Communist Party: Atrophy and Adaptation* (Washington, DC: Woodrow Wilson Center Press; Berkeley: University of California Press, 2008), pp. 2, 176.
14. Barry J. Naughton and Dali L. Yang, eds., *Holding China Together: Diversity and National Integration in the Post-Deng Era* (New York: Cambridge University Press, 2004), p. 9.
15. Andrew G. Walder, "The Party Elite and China's Trajectory of Change," *China: An International Journal*, Vol. 2, No. 2 (2004), pp. 189–209.
16. Kellee S. Tsai, *Capitalism Without Democracy: The Private Sector in Contemporary China* (Ithaca, NY: Cornell University Press, 2007).
17. Lily L. Tsai, *Accountability Without Democracy: Solidary Groups and Public Goods Provision in Rural China* (New York: Cambridge University Press, 2007).
18. See, for example, Ping-ti Ho and Tang Tsou, eds., *China in Crisis*, 2 vols. (Chicago: University of Chicago Press, 1968, 1969); Michel Oksenberg, ed., *China's Developmental Experience* (New York: Praeger, 1973).
19. On the catastrophic famine of the 1959–62 period and its political ramifications, see Dali L. Yang, *Calamity and Reform in China: State, Rural Society, and Institutional Change since the Great Leap Famine* (Stanford, CA: Stanford University Press, 1996); and Jasper Becker, *Hungry Ghosts: Mao's Secret Famine* (New York: The Free Press, 1996). On the serious environmental destruction produced by the Maoist campaigns, see Judith Shapiro, *Mao's War against Nature: Politics and the Environment in Revolutionary China* (New York: Cambridge University Press, 2001). On progress in basic educational skills and public-health standards from the 1950s to the 1970s, and the stark contrast with India, see Jean Drèze and Amartya Sen, *India: Economic Development and Social Opportunity* (Oxford: Oxford University Press, 1995).
20. Li Zehou and Liu Zaifu, *Gaobie geming: Ershi shiji duitan lu* [Farewell to Revolution: A Twentieth-century Dialogue] (Taipei: Maitian chuban gufen youxian gongsi, 1999).
21. This term was employed by Roderick MacFarquhar in his comments on post-Mao policy experimentation at a July 2008 conference held at Harvard University.

22. The definitions in this paragraph are based on Brian Walker et al., "A Handful of Heuristics and Some Propositions for Understanding Resilience in Social-Ecological Systems," *Ecology and Society*, Vol. 11, No. 1 (2006), pp. 2–3, 8–9.
23. Douglass C. North, *Institutions, Institutional Change and Economic Performance* (New York: Cambridge University Press, 1990), pp. 80–81; Douglass C. North, *Understanding the Process of Economic Change* (Princeton, NJ: Princeton University Press, 2005), p. 154.
24. Taleb, *The Black Swan*, p. xxi; Sebastian Heilmann, "Maximum Tinkering under Uncertainty: Unorthodox Lessons from China," *Modern China*, Vol. 35, No. 4 (2009), pp. 450–462.
25. For a sophisticated conception of development as a large-scale process of self-discovery, see Dani Rodrik, *One Economics, Many Recipes: Globalization, Institutions, and Economic Growth* (Princeton, NJ: Princeton University Press, 2007).
26. For a critique of the notion of "path dependence" in the social sciences, see Wolfgang Streeck and Kathleen Thelen, "Introduction," in Kathleen Thelen and Wolfgang Streeck, eds., *Beyond Continuity: Institutional Change in Advanced Political Economies* (Oxford: Oxford University Press, 2005), pp. 4–9.
27. For detailed documentation of recurrent and comprehensive government restructurings throughout PRC history, see Guojia xingzheng xueyuan, ed., *Zhonghua renmin gongheguo zhengfu jigou wushinian, 1949–1999* [Fifty Years of Government Structure in the People's Republic of China, 1949–1999] (Beijing: Dangjian duwu chubanshe, 2000).
28. Harry Harding, *Organizing China: The Problem of Bureaucracy, 1949–1976* (Stanford, CA: Stanford University Press, 1981).
29. Cf. Jeremy Richardson, Gunnel Gustafsson, and Grant Jordan, "The Concept of Policy Style," in Jeremy Richardson, ed., *Policy Styles in Western Europe* (London: Allen and Unwin, 1982), p. 13; Michael Howlett and M. Ramesh, *Studying Public Policy* (Oxford: Oxford University Press, 1995), pp. 228–233.
30. In numerous interviews conducted in China's economic bureaucracies in recent years, the term *zuofeng* was repeatedly raised to explain governmental practices that deviate from Western or Soviet concepts that are rooted in historically grounded administrative routines. The impact of national and sectoral "administrative styles" on policy outcomes has become a subject of serious research and debate in European political science; cf. Christoph Knill, "European Policies: The Impact of National Administrative Traditions," *Journal of Public Policy*, Vol. 18, No. 1 (1998), pp. 1–28.
31. See Roderick MacFarquhar, *The Origins of the Cultural Revolution*, 3 vols. (New York: Columbia University Press, 1974, 1983, 1997); Frederick C. Teiwes, *Leadership, Legitimacy, and Conflict in China:*

*From a Charismatic Mao to the Politics of Succession* (Armonk, NY: M.E. Sharpe, 1984); Parris H. Chang, *Power and Policy in China* (University Park: Pennsylvania State University Press, 1975); Jürgen Domes, *The Internal Politics of China, 1949–1972* (New York: Praeger, 1973).
32. On a discussion of such shared understandings from an institutionalist perspective, see Kathleen Thelen, "How Institutions Evolve: Insights from Comparative Historical Analysis," in James Mahoney and Dietrich Rueschemeyer, eds., *Comparative Historical Analysis in the Social Sciences* (New York: Cambridge University Press, 2003), pp. 216–217; see also Paul Pierson, *Politics in Time: History, Institutions, and Social Analysis* (Princeton, NJ: Princeton University Press, 2004), pp. 38–39.
33. Quoted in Michel Oksenberg, "The Political Leader," in Dick Wilson, ed., *Mao Tse-tung in the Scales of History: A Preliminary Assessment* (New York: Cambridge University Press, 1977), p. 78.
34. Among the most instructive studies on how guerrilla tactics shaped Maoist politics and policy making are Samuel B. Griffith, trans., *Mao Tse-tung on Guerrilla War* (Champaign: University of Illinois Press, 2000; originally published in 1961); Oksenberg, "The Political Leader," pp. 70–116; MacFarquhar, *The Origins of the Cultural Revolution*, Vol. 3, pp. 326–330.
35. A particularly instructive and straightforward source on the Chinese Communists' guerrilla tactics, with special emphasis on operating under uncertainty and threat, the limits to central command, and the necessity of local operative autonomy is Mao Zedong, *Kang Ri youji zhanzheng de yiban wenti* [General Questions about anti-Japanese Guerrilla Warfare] (Yan'an: Jiefangshe, 1938). This publication (parts of which serve as the basis of Griffith's study on Chinese guerrilla tactics) gives a vivid impression of the extreme tactical flexibility, organizational plasticity, and opportunistic ruthlessness that were at the heart of the Communists' approach to war and politics. Strikingly, the straightforward wording and unprincipled tactics contained in this and other wartime pamphlets were significantly toned down and polished away in the collections of Mao's works that were published after the founding of the PRC. A useful sourcebook on the formative pre-1949 experiences of combining unconventional military and political approaches during the revolutionary war is Gene Z. Hanrahan, comp., *Chinese Communist Guerrilla Tactics: A Source Book* (New York: Columbia University, 1952).
36. That is how Mao characterized his concept of "permanent revolution" in 1958; see the quote in Stuart Schram, "The Marxist," in Wilson, ed., *Mao Tse-tung in the Scales of History*, pp. 68–69.
37. Cf. Oksenberg, "The Political Leader," pp. 76–77.

38. See, for example, C. Kenneth Allard, *Business as War: Battling for Competitive Advantage* (Hoboken, NJ: John Wiley, 2004); Jack Welch, *Winning* (New York: HarperBusiness, 2005).
39. Oksenberg, "The Political Leader," pp. 86–87.
40. For classic studies on the role of the bureaucracy in Chinese policy making, see Kenneth Lieberthal and Michel Oksenberg, *Policy Making in China: Leaders, Structures, and Processes* (Princeton, NJ: Princeton University Press, 1988); Kenneth G. Lieberthal and David M. Lampton, eds., *Bureaucracy, Politics and Decision Making in Post-Mao China* (Berkeley: University of California Press, 1992); David M. Lampton, ed., *Policy Implementation in Post-Mao China* (Berkeley: University of California Press, 1987).
41. Cf. Guojia xingzheng xueyuan, ed., *Zhonghua renmin gongheguo zhengfu jigou wushinian* and Wang Yukai et al., *Zhongguo xingzheng tizhi gaige 30 nian huigu yu zhanwang (1978–2008)* [Prospects and Reflections on Thirty Years of Chinese Political Reform (1978–2008)] (Beijing: Renmin chubanshe, 2008).
42. This term was coined by Lily Tsai in her comments at a July 2008 conference at Harvard University.
43. For instructive studies that elaborate on these distinctive features in traditional and contemporary Chinese strategic thinking, see François Jullien, *A Treatise on Efficacy: Between Western and Chinese Thinking* (Honolulu: University of Hawai'i Press, 2004); Ralph D. Sawyer, *The Essence of War: Leadership and Strategy from the Chinese Military Classics* (Boulder, CO: Westview Press, 2004).
44. Alastair Iain Johnston, *Cultural Realism: Strategic Culture and Grand Strategy in Chinese History* (Princeton, NJ: Princeton University Press, 1995).
45. Jae Ho Chung, "Central-Local Dynamics: Historical Continuities and Institutional Resilience," in Heilmann and Perry, eds., *Mao's Invisible Hand*, pp. 297–320.
46. Patricia M. Thornton, "Retrofitting the Steel Frame: From Mobilizing the Masses to Surveying the Public,"in Heilmann and Perry, eds., *Mao's Invisible Hand*, pp. 237–268.
47. We concur with Bo Rothstein's warning about the risks of conceptual overstretch in institutionalist explanations: "If 'institution' means everything, it means nothing." Variable policy processes should be treated as distinct from durable and structured institutional arrangements. Cf. Bo Rothstein, "Political Institutions: An Overview," in Robert E. Goodlin and Hans-Dieter Klingemann, eds., *A New Handbook of Political Science* (Oxford: Oxford University Press, 1996), pp. 133–166, at p. 145. For a critique of the static and linear assumptions that characterize most explanations of institutional change, see Kurt Weyland, "Toward a New Theory of Institutional Change," *World Politics*, Vol. 60, No. 2 (2008), pp. 281–314.

48. Cf. Peter Rutland, *The Politics of Economic Stagnation in the Soviet Union: The Role of Local Party Organs in Economic Management* (New York: Cambridge University Press, 1993).
49. On the general challenge of linking and balancing structure and agency in social-science analyses of large-scale change, see Ira Katznelson, "Periodization and Preferences: Reflections on Purposive Action in Comparative Historical Social Science," in Mahoney and Ruschemeyer, eds., *Comparative Historical Analysis in the Social Sciences*, pp. 270–301, especially p. 282.
50. For this argumentation, see Pierson, *Politics in Time*, pp. 30–31, 40–41.
51. Andrew J. Nathan, "Authoritarian Impermanence," *Journal of Democracy*, Vol. 20, No. 3 (2009), p. 40.

## Chapter 2

1. Thomas G. Rawski, "Implications of China's Reform Experience," *The China Quarterly*, No. 144 (1995), pp. 1150–1173; Gérard Roland, *Transition and Economics: Politics, Markets, and Firms* (Cambridge, MA: MIT Press, 2000), pp. 63–65; Justin Yifu Lin, Fang Cai, and Zhou Li, *The China Miracle: Development Strategy and Economic Reform* (Hong Kong: Chinese University Press, 2003), pp. 321–325; Sharun W. Mukand and Dani Rodrik, "In Search of the Holy Grail: Policy Convergence, Experimentation, and Economic Performance," *American Economic Review*, Vol. 95, No. 1 (2005), pp. 374–383.
2. Sebastian Heilmann, "Policy Experimentation in China's Economic Rise," *Studies in Comparative International Development (SCID)*, Vol. 43, No. 1 (2008), pp. 1–26.
3. Background interviews conducted for this study revealed that even senior officials in charge of designing and supervising "experimental point works" during the last three decades (cadres up to the rank of vice-minister were among the interviewees) apparently are unaware of a historical trajectory behind reform-era experimentation; instead, they ascribe the emergence of the "experimental point method" to Deng Xiaoping and the pursuit of administrative pragmatism.
4. Jiang Boying, *Deng Zihui yu Zhongguo nongcun bianqe* [Deng Zihui and the Transformation of China's Countryside] (Fuzhou: Fujian renmin chubanshe, 2004), pp. 44–64, 210–225; Li Jianzhen, "Deng Zihui tongzhi yu tugai shiyan" [Comrade Deng Zihui and Land Reform Experiments], in *Huiyi Deng Zihui* [Remembering Deng Zihui] (Beijing: Renmin chubanshe, 1996), pp. 233–238.
5. The 1943 report was published as Zhang Dingcheng, *Zhongguo gongchandang chuangjian Minxi geming genjudi* [The Founding of the Minxi Revolutionary Base Area by the CCP] (Beijing: Renmin chubanshe, 1982); cf. Yu Boliu and Ling Buji, *Zhongyang Suqu shi* [The

History of the Jiangxi Soviet] (Nanchang: Jiangxi renmin chubanshe, 2001), p. 246.
6. See Dong Ping, "Wang Guanlan: Guanzhu 'sannong' diyi ren" [Wang Guanlan: A Pioneer in Paying Attention to the 'Agriculture-Village-Farmer' Issue], *Dangshi zongheng* [Party History], No. 9 (2006), pp. 15–20.
7. See *Taihang dangshi ziliao huibian, di san juan, 1940.1–1940.12* [Compilation of Materials on Party History in Taihang, Vol. 3, January 1940–December 1940] (Taiyuan: Shanxi renmin chubanshe, 1994), pp. 260–281, 513–515 and *Li Xuefeng huiyilu (shang): Taihang shinian* [The Memoirs of Li Xuefeng (Vol. 1): The Ten Taihang Years] (Beijing: Zhonggong dangshi chubanshe, 1998), pp. 105–108.
8. This argument is put forward by David Goodman who points to "interesting similarities [of policies tried out in Taihang] with the economic policies of the post–Cultural Revolution period." Cf. David S.G. Goodman, *Deng Xiaoping and the Chinese Revolution: A Political Biography* (London: Routledge, 1994), pp. 41–45.
9. Mao Zedong, "Guanyu lingdao fangfa ruogan wenti" [Some Questions Concerning Methods of Leadership], in *Mao Zedong xuanji* [Selected Works of Mao Zedong] (Beijing: Renmin chubanshe, 1966), Vol. 3, p. 855.
10. See a selection of Mao statements on the function of "models" in *Mao Zedong zhuzuo zhuanti zhaibian* [Thematic Excerpts from Mao Zedong's Works] (Beijing: Zhongyang wenxian chubanshe, 2003), pp. 238–239, 325–336. CCP propaganda brochures introducing local cases of a "model experience" were widely distributed after 1945; see, for example, *Laodong huzhu de dianxing lizi he jingyan* [Typical Examples and Experiences of Mutual-Aid Labor] (N.p., 1945). See also the Politburo decision of February 28, 1951, personally drafted by Mao, in *Mao Zedong xuanji* [Selected Works of Mao Zedong] (Beijing: Renmin chubanshe, 1977), Vol. 5, pp. 34–38.
11. Mao Zedong, "Zhengce he jingyan de guanxi" [On the Relation between Policy and Experience], March 6, 1948, in *Mao Zedong wenji* [Collected Works of Mao Zedong] (Beijing: Renmin chubanshe, 1993), Vol. 5, p. 74.
12. Mao's comments were first published in *Renmin ribao* (cited hereafter as *RMRB*), March 24, 1948. A reprint of his comments is contained in a widely disseminated CCP brochure: Liu Shaoqi et al., *Tugai zhengdang dianxing jingyan* [Typical Experiences in Land Reform and Party Rectification] (Hong Kong: Zhongguo chubanshe, 1948).
13. See the central party directive personally drafted by Mao: "Xin jiefangqu tudi gaige yaodian" [Essential Points in Land Reform in the New Liberated Areas], February 15, 1948, in *Mao Zedong xuanji* [Selected Works of Mao Zedong] (Beijing: Renmin chubanshe, 1991), Vol. 4, pp. 1283–1284.

14. Vivienne Shue, *Peasant China in Transition: The Dynamics of Development toward Socialism, 1949–1956* (Berkeley: University of California Press, 1980), p. 69 and pp. 322–323, respectively.
15. Based on Zhou Enlai's report to the Chinese People's Political Consultative Conference as reported in *RMRB*, November 3,1951, p. 1.
16. See Wang Ruoshui, "Qunzhong luxian he renshilun" [Mass Line and Epistemology], *RMRB*, September 20, 1959, p. 11.
17. Sebastian Heilmann: "From Local Experiments to National Policy," *The China Journal*, No. 59 (2008), p. 11.
18. Despite an intensive search, Chinese and Russian sources do not provide explicit clues on how the term "experimental point" made its way into China. Based on an electronic search of the digital archive of *RMRB* from 1946 to 1953, from 1946 to 1948 the term *shidian* was not mentioned at all; from 1949 to 1950 it was used in twenty-one articles, with a clear geographical concentration in the Northeast region (the center of activities by Soviet advisers in the early PRC) that was designated by the Party Center to carry out experiments, especially in industrial reorganization. It is likely that the Russian term was transferred to China by the Soviet advisers. From 1951 to 1953, after Zhou Enlai used the term in several speeches, it became fashionable and was used in more than 1,000 articles dealing with all sorts of subjects, ranging from land reform to education and marriage regulations. Mao used the term *shidian* only late in life, and even then very rarely. For prominent use of the term *shidian* by Mao, see "Dui Hubei shengwei guanyu zhubu shixian nongye jixiehua shexiang piyu" [Comments on the Hubei Provincial Party Committee's Tentative Plan of Step-by-Step Implementation of Agricultural Mechanization], February 19, 1966, *Jianguo yilai Mao Zedong wengao* [Manuscripts by Mao Zedong Since the Founding of the State] (Beijing: Zhongyang wenxian chubanshe, 1998), Vol. 12 (January 1966–December 1968), pp. 12–14.
19. The term "experimental point" is not contained in any major Soviet works on social experimentation that were published in the 1960s. For an influential example, see B. Ionas, "Ob ekonomicheskikh eksperimentakh" [On Economic Experiments], *Kommunist*, No. 9 (1962), pp. 51–59. From the Brezhnev era, "ekonomicheskii eksperiment," "eksperimentiro¬vanie" [experimentation], and "opytnaia proverka" [experimental/empirical examination] became standard terms denoting official experimentation. Cf. Darell Lee Slider, "Social Experiments and Soviet Policy-Making," PhD diss., Yale University, 1981.
20. Peter Rutland, *The Politics of Economic Stagnation in the Soviet Union* (Cambridge: Cambridge University Press, 1993) argues that local experiments became a widespread feature of administrative practice under Brezhnev. However, because they met with bureaucratic

obstruction and legal criticism, they were rarely rolled out and they did not help to break up the ossified planned economy.
21. Liu Zijiu, "Lun 'shidian'" [About "Experimental Points"], *Xuexi* [Learning], No. 10 (October 1953), pp. 10–11.
22. Yang Luo, "Lun shidian fangfa de renshilun yiyi" [On the Epistemological Significance of the Experimental Point Method], *Zhexue yanjiu* [Philosophical Research], No. 1 (1984), pp. 1–2.
23. Donald J. Munro, *The Concept of Man in Early China* (Ann Arbor: University of Michigan Press, 2001), pp. 149–150.
24. Yang Luo, in "Lun shidian fangfa," puts much effort into finding references in the Chinese translations of the Marxist-Leninist classics that might point to the usefulness of policy experiments. However, Yang comes to the conclusion that experimentation as an instrument for revolutionary transformation or policy making is not raised in the works of Marx, Engels, Lenin, or Stalin and that the experimental point method really is "a creation of Comrade Mao Zedong."
25. To my knowledge, the political use of experimentation is mentioned in Chinese translations of Lenin's works only in the context of transforming capitalist economic and technical expertise into a resource that serves the proletariat. See *Liening quanji* [Complete Works of Lenin] (Beijing: Renmin chubanshe, 1958), Vol. 27, p. 386.
26. Cf. Robert Himmer, "The Transition from War Communism to the New Economic Policy: An Analysis of Stalin's Views," *Russian Review*, Vol. 53, No. 4 (1994), pp. 515–529.
27. Qu Qiubai, as quoted by Yuan Jingyu, "Qu Qiubai bixia de xin jingji zhengce" [The New Economic Policy as Depicted by Qu Qiubai], *Shenyang jiaoyu xueyuan xuebao* [Journal of Shenyang College of Education], Vol. 4, No. 4 (2002), pp. 8–10.
28. On Lenin's conception of the NEP as a "transitional mixed system," see Maurice Dobb, *Soviet Economic Development Since 1917* (London: Routledge, 6th ed., 1966), pp.144–148.
29. John Dewey, *Lectures in China, 1919–1920*, trans. and ed. R.W. Clopton and T.C. Ou (Honolulu: University Press of Hawai'i, 1973), pp. 248, 58, 247, respectively.
30. Hu Shi states that Dewey preferred the terms "experimentalism" and "instrumentalism" to "pragmatism" to characterize his school of thinking. See Kang Degang, comp., *Hu Shi koushu zizhuan* [Hu Shi's Oral Autobiography] (Guilin: Guangxi shifan daxue chubanshe, 2005), pp. 112–113. See also Gu Hongliang, *Shiyong zhuyi de wudu: Duwei zhexue dui Zhongguo jinxiandai zhexue zhi yingxiang* [The Misreading of Pragmatism: The Influence of Dewey's Philosophy on Modern Chinese Philosophy] (Shanghai: Huadong shifan daxue chubanshe, 2000), p. 105.

31. Yu Yingshi, *Xiandai weiji yu sixiang renwu* [Modern Crises and Thinkers] (Shanghai: Sanlian shudian, 2005), pp. 160–165.
32. Sun Youzhong, "Cong gailiang zhuyizhe dao Makesi zhuyizhe: Mao Zedong zaoqi sixiang de zhuanbian" [From Reformist to Marxist in Mao Zedong's Early Thought], *Tansuo* [Exploration], No. 2 (2002), pp. 7–9.
33. Quoted in Stuart R. Schram, "Mao Studies: Retrospect and Prospect," *The China Quarterly*, No. 97 (1984), pp. 105–106. Analogies between Dewey's and Mao's epistemologies are also referred to in John Bryan Starr, *Continuing the Revolution: The Political Thought of Mao* (Princeton, NJ: Princeton University Press, 1979), pp. 70–71.
34. Di Xu, *A Comparison of the Educational Ideas and Practices of John Dewey and Mao Zedong in China* (San Francisco: Mellen Research University Press, 1992), p. 73.
35. Ibid., p. 111, states that Mao attended a talk by Dewey in Shanghai in spring 1920; Li Rui, *Sanshisui yiqian de Mao Zedong* [Mao Zedong Before He Was Thirty Years Old] (Guangzhou: Guangdong renmin chubanshe, 1994), p.322 (quoted in Sun Youzhong, "Cong gailiang zhuyizhe dao Makesi zhuyizhe," p. 7) claims that Mao was present during a talk by Dewey in Changsha in late October 1920.
36. *Duwei wu da jiangyan* [Dewey's Five Major Lectures] (Beijing: Chenbaoshe, 1920), pp. 125, 137–138, quoted in Gu Hongliang, *Shiyong zhuyi de wudu*, p. 102.
37. "Gongzuo fangfa liushitiao (caoan)" [Sixty Articles on Work Methods (Draft)], drafted by Mao in January 1958, in *Jianguo yilai Mao Zedong wengao* [Manuscripts by Mao Zedong since the Founding of the State] (Beijing: Zhongyang wenxian chubanshe, 1992), Vol. 7 (1958), pp. 45–65; method No. 13 states: "Unleash and mobilize the masses. Everything through experimentation."
38. Chow Tse-tsung, *The May Fourth Movement* (Cambridge. MA: Harvard University Press, 1960), p. 176. Sun Youzhong, "Cong gailiang zhuyizhe dao Makesi zhuyizhe," pp.7–9, presents evidence indicating that Mao was a Dewey-style "reformist" up to 1920 and he did not become a committed radical until 1921.
39. John Dewey, "Introduction by the Editors" in *Lectures in China, 1919–1920*, p. 13.
40. Liu Haixi, "30 niandai guomin zhengfu tuixing xianzheng jianshe yuanyin tanxi" [Some Findings on Why the Nationalist Government Carried out County Administrative Reconstruction in the 1930s], *Minguo dang'an* [Republican Archives], No. 1 (2001), p. 80.
41. In a truly global diffusion of institutional innovation, the American system was inspired by the organization of German agricultural research that later also served as a model for Soviet experimental stations; cf. Mark R. Finlay, "The German Agricultural Experimental Stations

and the Beginnings of American Agricultural Research," *Agricultural History*, Vol. 62, No. 2 (1988), pp. 41–50.
42. Randall E. Stross, *The Stubborn Earth: American Agriculturalists on Chinese Soil, 1898–1937* (Berkeley: University of California Press, 1986), pp. 123–124, 145, 185.
43. These terms were used, for example, in a May 1924 article published in the national journal *Nongxue* [Agricultural Studies]; cf. Stross, *Stubborn Earth*, p. 258.
44. James Y.C. Yen, *The Mass Education Movement in China* (Shanghai: The Commercial Press, 1925), pp. 17–18.
45. Cf. Guy S. Alitto, "Rural Reconstruction during the Nanking Decade: Confucian Collectivism in Shantung," *The China Quarterly*, No. 66 (1976), pp. 213–246.
46. See Tan Zhongwei, "Xiangcun jianshe shiyanjia Qu Junong" [Qu Junong, an Experimenter in Rural Reconstruction], *Yanhuang chunqiu* [Annals of Chinese Descendants], No. 8 (1998), pp. 36–39.
47. For official CCP policy, see Liu Shaoqi, "Guanyu baiqu de dang yu qunzhong gongzuo" [On Party and Mass Work in the White Areas], May 1937, in *Liu Shaoqi xuanji* [Selected Works of Liu Shaoqi] (Beijing: Renmin chubanshe, 1981), Vol. 1, pp. 61–64. For reports on CCP and NGO "double activists," or close personal interactions between NGO leaders, non-Communist experimental county heads, and CCP cadres (sometimes based on old alumni connections), see "Zhang Donghui zai Dingzhou de suiyue" [Zhang Donghui's Time in Ding District], *Dangshi bocai* [Party History], No. 12 (2002), pp. 42–43; "Jinian Sun Fuyuan xiansheng" [Commemorating Mr. Sun Fuyuan], *RMRB*, September 18, 1987, p. 8; Li Guozhong, "Suweiai yundong, xiangcun jianshe yundong yu Zhongguo nongcun de shehui bianqian bijiao" [A Comparison of the Soviet Movement and the RRM in China's Rural Social Transformation], *Gannan shifan xueyuan xuebao* [Journal of Gannan Teachers College], No. 5 (2002), p. 30.
48. Li Guozhong, "Suweiai yundong," pp. 28–32.
49. On Mao's talks with Liang Shuming in Yan'an, see Guy S. Alitto, *The Last Confucian: Liang Shu-ming and the Chinese Dilemma of Modernity* (Berkeley: University of California Press, 1986), pp. 283–292.
50. Cf. Charles W. Hayford, *To the People: James Yen and Village China* (New York: Columbia University Press, 1990), pp. 202–203, 213, 222–223. After assuming national power, the Communists officially distanced themselves from the MEM/RRM and other earlier reform movements and negated their influence. Starting in the 1980s, the contributions of James Yen and Liang Shuming to rural reform were officially acknowledged by CCP media; cf. "Liang Shuming zouwan jin bainian rensheng lucheng" [Liang Shuming Concludes the Almost Century-Long Journey of his Life], *RMRB*, July 8, 1988.

51. Paula B. Keating, *Two Revolutions: Village Reconstruction and the Cooperative Movement in Northern Shaanxi, 1934–1945* (Stanford, CA: Stanford University Press, 1997), p. 189, argues that many of the rural reforms initiated in the Communist base areas, in particular the cooperative movement, drew on models that had originally been sponsored by non-Communist reformers (including the KMT) and funded by Western missionary or philanthropic organizations.
52. Wang Xianming and Li Weizhong, "20 shiji 30 niandai de xianzheng jianshe yundong yu xiangcun shehui bianqian" [The County Administrative Reconstruction Movement in the 1930s and Rural Social Change], *Shixue yuekan* [Journal of Historical Science], No. 4 (2003), pp. 90–104.
53. Liu Haixi, "30 niandai," pp. 77–81.
54. Jia Shijian, "Qianxi Nanjing guomin zhengfu de xianzheng shiyan" [A Sketch of the Nanjing Nationalist Government's Experiments in County Administration], *Tianzhong xuekan* [Journal of Tianzhong], Vol. 18, No. 1 (2003), pp. 84–87.
55. An astute analysis of why Deweyan reformers failed can be found in Barry Keenan, *The Dewey Experiment in China: Educational Reform and Political Power in the Early Republic* (Cambridge, MA: Council on East Asian Studies, Harvard University, 1977).
56. *Taihang dangshi ziliao huibian, di san juan*, pp. 260–262.
57. For important Deng statements on experimentation, see *Deng Xiaoping wenxuan, 1975–1982* [Selected Works of Deng Xiaoping, 1975–1982] (Beijing: Renmin chubanshe, 1983), p. 140; *Deng Xiaoping wenxuan, disan juan* [Selected Works of Deng Xiaoping, Vol. 3] (Beijing: Renmin chubanshe, 1993), pp. 78, 130, 373.
58. For a collection of Chen Yun's quotations on experimentation in economic policy making, see Wang Jiayun, "Chen Yun jingji juece de shi da yuanze" [Ten Major Principles Pursued by Chen Yun in Economic Decision-making], *Huaiyang shifan xueyuan xuebao* [Journal of Huaiyang Teachers College], No. 3 (1998), p. 33. From his time as chief economic policy maker in the Northeast prior to the founding of the PRC, Chen Yun had consistently stressed the importance of prudent experimentation.
59. Li Zhining, *Zhonghua renmin gongheguo jingji dashidian 1949.10–1987.1* [A Dictionary of Major Economic Events in the PRC, October 1949–January 1987] (Changchun: Jilin renmin chubanshe, 1987), p. 453.
60. See *Chen Yun wenxuan* [Selected Works of Chen Yun] (Beijing: Renmin chubanshe, 1995), Vol. 3, p. 279.
61. CCP Central Committee Documents Research Office, ed., *Guanyu jianguo yilai dang de ruogan lishi wenti de jueyi zhushiben* [Annotated Edition of the Resolution on Certain Questions in the History of Our Party since the Founding of the State] (Beijing: Renmin chubanshe, 1983), p. 57.

62. Lei Meitian, "Jianli Makesi zhuyi shehui shiyan de xin guandian" [Establishing a New Standpoint on Marxist Social Experimentation], *Nanjing zhengzhi xueyuan xuebao* [Journal of Nanjing Political College], No. 6 (1994), pp. 38–41.
63. Yang Luo, "Lun shidian fangfa," pp. 3, 5.
64. *Constitution of the Communist Party of China* (bilingual Chinese-English edition) (Beijing: Foreign Languages Press, 2003), pp. 26–27. On the insertion of the experimentation paragraph in 1992, see the brief comments in *Zhongguo gongchandang lici dangzhang huibian (1921–2002)* [A Compilation of All Previous Constitutions of the CCP, 1921–2002] (Beijing: Zhongguo fangzheng chubanshe, 2006), p. 389. The first post-Mao party constitution in 1982 did not mention experimentation, nor did any of the previous party constitutions.
65. A number of instructive case studies on failed local administrative-reform experiments is contained in Fu Xiaosui, *Zhongguo xingzheng tizhi gaige fenxi* [Analysis of China's Administrative System Reform] (Beijing: Guojia xingzheng xueyuan chubanshe, 1999), pp. 153–168.
66. In his comments during the conference on "Adaptive authoritarianism: China's party-state resilience in historical perspective," held at Harvard University, July 14-16, 2008, Barry Naughton emphasized this argument on the generalized information effects of experimentation. Seen from such a depoliticized systemic perspective, the aggregate informational advantages of broad-based experimentation clearly outweigh the potential injustices brought about by an uneven distribution of costs and benefits among various experimental sites. In experimental practice, however, political and legal conflicts frequently are due to demands to compensate the losers from the experiments.
67. World Bank, *East Asia Decentralizes: Making Local Government Work* (Washington, DC: World Bank, 2005); Yongnian Zheng, *De facto Federalism in China: Reforms and Dynamics of Central-Local Relations* (Singapore: World Scientific Press, 2007).
68. Elizabeth J. Perry, "Studying Chinese Politics: Farewell to Revolution?" *The China Journal*, No. 57 (2007), p. 6.

## Chapter 3

1. Peter Evans, "Development as Institutional Change: The Pitfalls of Monocropping and the Potentials of Deliberation," *Studies in Comparative International Development*, Vol. 38, No. 4 (2004), pp. 30–52; Peter Evans, "The Challenges of the 'Institutional Turn': Interdisciplinary Opportunities in Development Theory," in Victor Nee and Richard Swedberg, *The Economic Sociology of Capitalism* (Princeton, NJ: Princeton University Press, 2005), pp. 90–116.

2. Charles E. Lindblom, "Still Muddling, Not Yet Through," *Public Administration Review*, Vol. 39, No. 6 (1979), p. 521.
3. Evans, "Development as Institutional Change," p. 30.
4. Sarun W. Mukand and Dani Rodrik, "In Search of the Holy Grail: Policy Convergence, Experimentation, and Economic Performance," *American Economic Review*, Vol. 95, No. 1(2005), pp. 374–383.
5. Douglass C. North, *Institutions, Institutional Change and Economic Performance* (Cambridge: Cambridge University Press, 1990), pp. 80–81; Douglass C. North, *Understanding the Process of Economic Change* (Princeton: NJ: Princeton University Press, 2005), p. 154.
6. Valerie Bunce, *Subversive Institutions: The Design and the Destruction of Socialism and the State* (New York: Cambridge University Press, 1999).
7. Friedrich A. Hayek, *The Constitution of Liberty* (Chicago: University of Chicago Press 1978); North, *Institutions, Institutional Change and Economic Performance*; Gérard Roland, *Transition and Economics: Politics, Markets, and Firms* (Cambridge, MA: MIT Press, 2000); Mukand and Rodrik, "In Search of the Holy Grail," pp. 374–383.
8. Frederick Mosteller, "New Statistical Methods in Public Policy. Part I: Experimentation," *Journal of Contemporary Business*, No. 8 (1979), pp. 487, 496. Reprinted in Stephen E. Fienberg and David C. Hoaglin, eds., *Selected Papers of Frederick Mosteller* (New York: Springer, 2006), pp. 487–498.
9. Roger Jowell, *Trying It Out: The Role of "Pilots" in Policy-Making* (London: Government Chief Social Researcher's Office, 2003).
10. Frederick Mosteller, "Experimentation and Innovation," *Bulletin of the International Statistical Institute*, Vol. 47 (1997), pp. 479–480. Reprinted in Fienberg and Hoaglin, eds., *Selected Papers of Frederick Mosteller*, pp. 473–485; Frederick Mosteller, "New Statistical Methods in Public Policy. Part I: Experimentation," *Journal of Contemporary Business*, Vol. 8 (1979), pp. 492–496. Reprinted in Fienberg and Hoaglin, eds., *Selected Papers of Frederick Mosteller*, pp. 487–497.
11. Charles E. Lindblom, "The Science of 'Muddling Through,'" *Public Administration Review*, Vol. 19, No. 2 (1959), pp. 79–88; Lindblom, "Still Muddling, Not Yet Through," pp. 517–526.
12. Thomas G. Rawski, "Implications of China's Reform Experience," *The China Quarterly*, No. 144 (1995), pp. 1150–1173; Yuanzheng Cao, Yingyi Qian, and Barry Weingast, "From Federalism, Chinese Style to Privatization, Chinese Style," *Economics of Transition*, Vol. 7, No. 1 (1999), pp. 103–131; Roland, *Transition and Economics*; Yingyi Qian, "How Reform Worked in China," in Dani Rodrik, ed., *In Search of Prosperity: Analytic Narratives on Economic Growth* (Princeton, NJ: Princeton University Press, 2003), pp. 297–333.

13. Roland, *Transition and Economics.*
14. Gabriella Montinola, Yingyi Qian, and Barry Weingast, "Federalism, Chinese Style: The Political Basis for Economic Success in China," *World Politics,* Vol. 48, No. 1 (October 1995), pp. 50–81; Dali Yang, *Beyond Beijing: Liberalization and the Regions in China* (London: Routledge, 1997).
15. Susan L. Shirk, *How China Opened Its Door* (Washington, DC: Brookings Institution, 1994); Wing Thye Woo, "The Real Reasons for China's Growth," *The China Journal,* No. 41 (1999), pp. 115–137; Hongbin Cai and Daniel Treisman, "Did Government Decentralization Cause China's Economic Miracle?" *World Politics,* Vol. 58, No. 4 (2006), pp. 505–535.
16. Sebastian Heilmann, "From Local Experiments to National Policy: The Origins of China's Distinctive Policy Process," *The China Journal,* No. 59 (2008), pp. 1–30.
17. Rekha Wazir and Nico van Oudenhoven, "Increasing the Coverage of Social Programmes," *International Social Science Journal,* Vol. 50, No. 155 (1998), pp. 145–154.
18. David F. Pyle, "From Pilot Project to Operational Program in India: The Problems of Transition," in Merilee S. Grindle, ed., *Politics and Policy Implementation in the Third World* (Princeton, NJ: Princeton University Press, 1980), pp. 123–144.
19. Charles-Albert Morand, ed., *Évaluation législative et lois expérimentales* [Legislative Evaluation and Experimental Laws] (Aix-en-Provence: Presse Universitaires d'Aix-Marseille, 1993); David H. Greenberg, Donna Linksz, and Marvin Mandell, *Social Experimentation and Public Policymaking* (Washington, DC: Urban Institute Press, 2003); Konrad Hummel, *Recht der behördlichen Regelungsexperimente* [Law of Experiments in Administrative Regulation] (Berlin: Duncker and Humblot, 2003).
20. Peter H. Corne, "Creation and Application of Law in the PRC," *American Journal of Comparative Law,* Vol. 50, No. 2 (2002), p. 382.
21. Guojia xingzheng guanli xueyuan, ed., *Zhongyang zhengfu jigou* [Organs of the Central Government] (Beijing: zhongguo caizheng jingji chubanshe, 1998), pp. 466–469.
22. *Zhongguo jingji tizhi gaige nianjian (2005)* [China Economic Systems Reform Yearbook (2005)] (Beijing: Gaige chubanshe, 2005), pp. 50–54, 90–92.
23. State Council General Office, *Zhongguo jingji gaige kaifang shiyanqu* [China's Experimental Zones for Economic Reform and Opening] (Beijing: Zhongguo qingnian chubanshe, 1992), foreword.
24. Barry Naughton: *The Chinese Economy: Transitions and Growth* (Cambridge, MA: The MIT Press, 2007), pp. 406–408.

25. Jianwei Zhang, "Bianfa moshi yu zhengzhi wendingxing" [The Mode of Legal Reform and Political Stability], *Zhongguo shehui kexue* [Social Sciences in China], No. 1 (2003), pp. 140–141.
26. Wu Xiaoyun, "Chuangxin: Jingji tequ lifa de guihun" [Innovation: The Heart and Soul of Legislation in the Special Economic Zones], *Hainan renda* [Hainan People's Congress], No. 1 (2004), pp. 30–31.
27. David Zweig, *Internationalizing China: Domestic Interests and Global Linkages* (Ithaca, NY: Cornell University Press, 2002), p. 52.
28. Cao, Qian, and Weingast, "From Federalism, Chinese Style to Privatization," pp.124–125.
29. Vivienne Shue, *Peasant China in Transition: The Dynamics of Development toward Socialism, 1949–1956* (Berkeley: University of California Press, 1980), p. 88.
30. Silke Adamand and Hanspeter Kriesi, "The Network Approach," in Paul A. Sabatier, ed., *Theories of the Policy Process* (Boulder, CO: Westview Press, 2nd ed., 2007), p. 129.
31. Naughton, *The Chinese Economy*, p. 97.
32. Edward S. Steinfeld, *Forging Reform in China: The Fate of State-Owned Industry* (New York: Cambridge University Press, 1998).
33. Murray Scot Tanner, *The Politics of Lawmaking in Post-Mao China* (Oxford: Clarendon Press, 1999), pp. 167–205.
34. Jinglian Wu, *Understanding and Interpreting Chinese Economic Reform* (Mason, OH: Thomson/South-Western, 2005), p. 155; *Zhongguo jingji tizhi gaige nianjian (1995)*, pp. 138–141; *Zhongguo jingji tizhi gaige nianjian (1996)*, pp. 222–226.
35. Susan Young, *Private Business and Economic Reform in China* (Armonk, NY: M.E. Sharpe, 1995), pp. 13–14; Naughton, *The Chinese Economy*, p. 95.
36. David L. Wank, "Bureaucratic Patronage and Private Business: Changing Networks of Power in Urban China," in Andrew G. Walder, ed., *The Waning of the Communist State: Economic Origins of Political Decline in China and Hungary* (Berkeley: University of California Press, 1995), pp. 153–183.
37. Young, *Private Business and Economic Reform in China*, pp. 9–10, 16.
38. Kristen D. Parris, "Local Society and the State: The Wenzhou Model and the Making of the Private Sector in China," PhD Diss., Indiana University, 1991.
39. Yang, *Beyond Beijing*, pp. 54–55.
40. Zweig, *Internationalizing China*, pp. 82–84.
41. Shirk, *How China Opened Its Door*, p. 42.
42. Yang, *Beyond Beijing*, pp. 48–49.
43. Jae Ho Chung, "Preferential Policies, Municipal Leadership, and Development Strategies," in Jae Ho Chung, ed., *Cities in China: Recipes for Economic Development in the Reform Era* (London: Routledge, 1999), pp. 106, 111.

44. Zweig, *Internationalizing China*, p. 50.
45. Shirk, *How China Opened Its Door*, p. 55.
46. Carl E. Walter and Fraser J.T. Howie, *Privatizing China: Inside China's Stock Markets* (Singapore: Wiley, 2006), p. 4.
47. Stephen Green, *The Development of China's Stock Market, 1984–2002: Equity Politics and Market Institutions* (London: RoutledgeCurzon, 2004), pp. 61–62.
48. Cf. Walter and Howie, *Privatizing China*, p. 166.
49. Esther Duflo, Greg Fischer, and R. Chattopadhyay, "Efficiency and Rent-Seeking in Local Government: Evidence from Randomized Policy Experiments in India," paper presented at the Harvard Institute of Quantitative Social Science, December 2006.
50. Yuanli Liu, William C. Hsiao, and Karen Eggleston, "Equity in Health and Health Care: The Chinese Experience," *Social Science & Medicine*, Vol. 49, No. 10 (1999), pp. 1349–1356; World Bank, "Rural Health in China," China Rural Health Analytical and Advisory Activities, *Briefing Note*, No. 6 (2005).
51. Wang Shaoguang, "Zhongguo gonggong zhengce yicheng shezhi de moshi" [Patterns of Public-Policy Agenda-Setting in China], *Zhongguo shehui kexue* [Chinese Social Sciences], No. 5 (2006), pp. 92–93.
52. Ministry of Land and Resources, "Wenbu tuijin zhengdi gaige" [Advance the Reform of (Compensation for) Land Expropriations with Steady Steps], at www.mlr.gov.cn/pub/gtzyb/gtzygl/tdzy/gdbh/t20040625 _13553.htm, accessed March 15, 2006.
53. Jamie P. Horsley, "The Rule of Law in China: Incremental Progress," in C. Fred Bergsten and Eve Cary, *China: The Balance Sheet in 2007 and Beyond* (Washington, DC: Center for Strategic and International Studies, 2007), pp. 93–108.
54. Joan Kaufman, Zhang Erli, and Xie Zhenming, "Quality of Care in China: Scaling Up a Pilot Project into a National Reform Program," *Studies in Family Planning*, Vol. 37, No. 1 (2006), p. 18.
55. Andrew Wedeman, "Looters, Rent-Scrapers, and Dividend-Collectors: The Political Economy of Corruption in Zaire, South Korea, and the Philippines," *The Journal of Developing Areas*, Vol. 31, No. 4 (1997), pp. 457–478; Mushtaq H. Khan and K.S. Jomo, eds., *Rents, Rent-Seeking and Economic Development* (Cambridge: Cambridge University Press, 2000).
56. Shirk, *How China Opened Its Door*, p. 5.
57. Lawrence J. Lau, Yingyi Qian, and Gérard Roland, "Reform without Losers: An Interpretation of China's Dual-Track Approach to Transition," *Journal of Political Economy*, Vol. 108, No. 1 (2000), pp. 121–122.
58. Zhao Liu, Wang Songqian, and Huang Zhanfeng, "Lun gonggong guanli shijian zhong de 'shidian' fangfa" [On the Pilot Method in the Practice

of Public Management], *Dongbei daxue xuebao* [Journal of Northeast University], Vol. 8, No. 4 (2006), p. 281.
59. Lindblom, "Still Muddling, Not Yet Through," p. 521.
60. Steinfeld, *Forging Reform in China*, pp. 165–224.
61. Heilmann, "From Local Experiments to National Policy," pp. 1–30.
62. Justin Yifu Lin, Fang Cai, and Zhou Li, *The China Miracle: Development Strategy and Economic Reform* (Hong Kong: Chinese University Press, 2003), p. 327.
63. Xining Pan, "Gaige shidian cheng bai bian" [Discussing the Success and Failure of the Experimental Points for Reform], *Fazhan* [Development], No. 2 (1995), pp. 26–29; Shuguang Li, "Li Shuguang jianyi quxiao gaige shidian" [Li Shuguang Proposes to Abolish the Experimental Points of Reform], *Jinrong xinxi cankao* [Financial Digest], No. 5 (1997), p. 32.
64. Jean C. Oi and Han Chaohua, "China's Corporate Restructuring : A Multi-step Process," in Jean C. Oi, ed., *Going Private in China: The Politics of Corporate Restructuring and System Reform* (Stanford, CA: Walter H. Shorenstein Asian-Pacific Research Center, 2011), pp. 19–38.
65. Marshall W. Meyer, "Notes on China's Second Economic Transition," paper presented at the China Institute for Policy Studies, Beijing, January 27, 2007.
66. Corne, "Creation and Application of Law in the PRC," p. 375.
67. William Stanley Jevons, *Experimental Legislation* (Hitchin: Garden City Press Ltd., 1904 [1880]), p. 9.

# Chapter 4

1. Fan Gang and Wing Thye Woo, "The Parallel Partial Progression (PPP) Approach to Institutional Transformation in Transition Economies: Optimize Economic Coherence, Not Policy Sequence," *Modern China*, Vol. 35, No. 4 (2009), pp. 352–369.
2. Wang Shaoguang, "Adapting by Learning: The Evolution of China's Rural Health Care Financing," *Modern China*, Vol. 35, No. 4 (2009), pp. 370–404.
3. Philip C.C. Huang, "China's Neglected Informal Economy: Reality and Theory," *Modern China*, Vol. 35, No. 4 (2009), pp. 405–438.
4. Fan and Woo, "The Parallel Partial Progression (PPP) Approach to Institutional Transformation in Transition Economies," pp. 352–369.
5. Gérard Roland was a major contributor to the debate. In his *Transition and Economics: Politics, Markets, and Firms* (Cambridge, MA: MIT Press, 2000), pp. 42–50, he presents formal models of reform sequencing that are designed to shed light, retrospectively, on "the observed regularities in the sequencing of reforms" and to account for the numerous factors that constrain policy makers. The prescriptive value of these models remains extremely vague.

6. David Braybrooke and Charles E. Lindblom, *A Strategy of Decision: Policy Evaluation as a Social Process* (New York: The Free Press, 1963).
7. Dani Rodrik, *One Economics, Many Recipes* (Princeton, NJ: Princeton University Press, 2007).
8. Thomas Carothers, "The End of the Transition Paradigm," *Journal of Democracy*, Vol. 13, No.1 (2002), pp. 5–21.
9. Charles E. Lindblom, "The Science of 'Muddling Through,'" *Public Administration Review*, Vol. 19, No. 2 (1959), pp. 86, 88.
10. Horst Rittel and Melvin Webber, "Dilemmas in a General Theory of Planning," *Policy Sciences*, Vol. 4, No. 2 (1973), pp. 155–169; Tom Ritchey, "Wicked Problems: Structuring Social Messes with Morphological Analysis," *Acta Morphologica Generalis*, Vol. 2, No. 1 (2013), pp. 1–8, at http://www.swemorph.com/pdf/wp.pdf, accessed November 18, 2017.
11. Jon Elster, Claus Offe, and Ulrich K. Preuss, *Institutional Design in Post-Communist Societies: Rebuilding the Ship at Sea* (New York: Cambridge University Press, 1998).
12. Rodrik, *One Economics, Many Recipes*, pp. 100, 104–105, 117.
13. Wang, "Adapting by Learning," pp. 370–404.
14. Sebastian Heilmann, "From Local Experiments to National Policy: The Origins of China's Distinctive Policy Process," *The China Journal*, No. 59 (2008), pp. 1–30.
15. An attempt to put such an open-ended processual analysis into practice and extract an experimentation-based policy cycle can be found in Heilmann, "From Local Experiments to National Policy," pp. 1–30.
16. Nassim Nicholas Taleb, *The Black Swan: The Impact of the Highly Improbable* (London: Penguin, 2008), p. xxi.
17. Michael Howlett, M. Ramesh, and Anthony Perl, *Studying Public Policy: Policy Cycles and Policy Subsystems* (Toronto: Oxford University Press, 3rd ed., 2009).
18. Wang, "Adapting by Learning," pp. 370–404.
19. Huang Yasheng, *Inflation and Investment Controls in China* (New York: Cambridge University Press, 1996); Hongbin Cai and Daniel Treisman, "Did Government Decentralization Cause China's Economic Miracle?" *World Politics*, Vol. 58, No. 4 (2006), pp. 505–535.
20. Barry Naughton, "Singularity and Replicability in China's Developmental Experience," *China Analysis*, No. 68 (2009).
21. Fritz W. Scharpf, *Games Real Actors Play: Actor-Centered Institutionalism in Policy Research* (Boulder, CO: Westview, 1997), pp. 197–198.
22. Hyman Minsky, *Stabilizing an Unstable Economy* (New York: McGraw-Hill Education Ltd., 2008).
23. Major early protagonists of ordoliberalism are Wilhelm Roepke, Walter Eucken, Alfred Mueller-Armack, and Franz Boehm. Comprehensive

treatments of ordoliberal thinking in English can be found in Alan Peacock and Hans Willgerodt, eds., *Germany's Social Market Economy: Origins and Evolution* (London: Macmillan, 1989); Peter Koslowski, ed., *The Theory of Capitalism in the German Economic Tradition* (Berlin: Springer, 2000); Rolf Hasse, ed., *Social Market Economy: Principles and Implementation* (Berlin: Adenauer Foundation, 2008). Chinese translations of important ordoliberal works include Walter Eucken [Ao Ken], *Jingji zhengce de yuanze* [Principles of Economic Policy] (Shanghai: Renmin chubanshe, 2000); Carsten Herrmann-Pillath [He Mengbi], ed., *Zhixu ziyouzhuyi* [Ordoliberalism] (Beijing: Zhongguo shehui kexue chubanshe, 2002).

24. Huang, "China's Neglected Informal Economy," pp. 405–438.

## Chapter 5

1. Peter J. Boettke, ed., *The Collapse of Development Planning* (New York: New York University Press, 1994); Michael P. Todaro and Stephen C. Smith, *Economic Development* (Harlow/London: Pearson, 10th ed., 2009).
2. CCP Central Committee, "Decision of the CCP Central Committee on Some Issues Concerning the Establishment of a Socialist Market Economic Structure," *Xinhua News Agency News Bulletin*, No. 16388 (November 17, 1993); Gui Shiyong et al., eds., *Zhongguo jihua tizhi gaige* [The Reform of China's Planning System] (Beijing: Zhongguo caizheng jingji chubanshe, 1994), pp. 72–76.
3. Zhang Zhuoyuan and Lu Yao, "Di shige wunian jihua de zhiding he shishi" [Formulation and Implementation of the 10th Five-year Plan], in Liu Guoguang, ed. *Zhongguo shige wunian jihua yanjiu baogao* [Rescarch Report on Ten Chinese Five-year Plans] (Beijing: Renmin chubanshe, 2006), pp. 661–703.
4. Yang Weimin, ed., *Fazhan guihua de lilun he shijian* [The Theory and Practice of Development Planning] (Beijing: Qinghua daxue chubanshe, 2010).
5. Daniel I. Okimoto, *Between MITI and the Market: Japanese Industrial Policy for High Technology* (Stanford, CA: Stanford University Press, 1989), pp. 9–12, 36–37.
6. Somsak Tambunlertchai and S.P. Gupta, "Introduction," in Somsak Tambunlertchai and S.P. Gupta, eds., *Development Planning in Asia* (Kuala Lumpur: Asian and Pacific Development Centre, 1993), p. 5.
7. Yoichi Nakamura, "Economic Planning in Japan," in Tambunlertchai and Gupta, eds., *Development Planning in Asia*, pp. 21–22.
8. Il Sakong, "Indicative Planning in Korea," *Journal of Comparative Economics*, Vol. 14, No. 4 (1990), pp. 678–679.
9. Okimoto, *Between MITI and the Market*, pp. 24, 228.

10. Terence J. Byres, ed., *The State, Development Planning and Liberalisation in India* (Delhi: Oxford University Press, 1998), pp. 1–35.
11. Sebastian Heilmann and Elizabeth J. Perry, eds., *Mao's Invisible Hand: The Political Foundations of Adaptive Governance in China* (Cambridge, MA: Harvard University Asia Center, 2011).
12. Harro von Senger, *Moulüe: Supraplanung* [Supra-Planning in China] (Munich: Hanser, 2008).
13. Dani Rodrik, *One Economics, Many Recipes* (Princeton, NJ: Princeton University Press, 2007), p. 99.

## Chaper 6

1. Joseph C.H. Chai, ed., *China: Transition to a Market Economy* (Oxford: Oxford University Press, 1998); Long H. Liew, *The Chinese Economy in Transition: From Plan to Market* (London: Edward Elgar, 1997); Loren Brandt and Thomas G. Rawski, eds., *China's Great Economic Transformation* (New York: Cambridge University Press, 2008); Yasheng Huang, *Capitalism with Chinese Characteristics* (New York: Cambridge University Press, 2008); Barry Naughton, *The Chinese Economy: Transitions and Growth* (Cambridge, MA: The MIT Press, 2007); Gregory C. Chow, *China's Economic Transformation* (Malden, MA: Blackwell, 2007).
2. For individual, yet rather dated, exceptions, see Barry Naughton, "China's Experience with Guidance Planning," *Journal of Comparative Economics*, Vol. 14, No. 4 (1990), pp. 743–767; Robert C. Hsü, "The Political Economy of Guidance Planning in Post-Mao China," *Review of World Economics*, Vol. 122, No. 2 (1986), pp. 382–394.
3. Chris Bramall, *Chinese Economic Development* (London: Routledge, 2009), pp. 473–474; Oliver Melton, "Understanding China's Five-year Plan: Planned Economy or Coordinated Chaos?" *China Insight Economics* (GaveKalDragonomics), November 9, 2010, pp.1–19.
4. Barry Naughton, *Growing Out of the Plan: Chinese Economic Reform, 1978–1993* (New York: Cambridge University Press, 1995).
5. Tian Jinjian, "Guihua zhibiao de sheji yu cesuan" [Designing and Calculating Plan Targets], in Yang Weimin, ed., *Fazhan guihua de lilun he shijian* [The Theory and Practice of Development Planning] (Beijing: Qinghua daxue chubanshe, 2010), pp. 145–161.
6. This instruction, given by Wen Jiabao in 2003–4, was not published after the meeting but it was independently confirmed by several high-ranking interviewees. The instruction was immediately regarded as a boost for the power of the planners within the NDRC and other economic ministries.
7. Li Pumin and Li Bing, "'Jiu wu' shiqi woguo jihua tizhi gaige huigu" [A Retrospective on the Reform of the Planning System in Our Country

during the "9th Five-year Plan" Period], *Hongguan jingji yanjiu* [Macroeconomic Research], No. 2 (2001), pp. 24–26.
8. Cf. Michael P. Todaro and Stephen C. Smith, *Economic Development* (Harlow/London: Pearson, 10th ed., 2009), p. 518; Rakesh Mohanand Vandana Aggarwal, "Commands and Controls: Planning for Indian Industrial Development, 1951–1990," *Journal of Comparative Economics*, Vol. 4, No. 14 (1990), p. 682; Zhong Qifu, *Zhong Qifu zi xuanji* [Selected Works of Zhong Qifu] (Beijing: Zhongguo renmin daxue chubanshe, 2007), pp. 52–59; Xiang Wei, "Dui shier wu guihua bianzhi de sikao" [Reflections on Drafting the 12th Five-year Plan], *Hongguan jingji guanli* [Macroeconomic Management], No. 1 (2009), pp. 38–40.
9. Susumu Yabuki, *China's New Political Economy* (Boulder, CO: Westview Press, 1995), pp. 32–34; Chen Xian, ed., *Jihua gongzuo shouce* [Handbook on Planning Work] (Beijing: Zhongguo caizheng jingji chubanshe, 1984).
10. Hsü, "The Political Economy of Guidance Planning in Post-Mao China," p. 383; Naughton, "China's Experience with Guidance Planning," pp. 743–744; Liu Rixin, *Xin Zhongguo jingji jianshe jianshi* [A Brief History of Economic Construction in New China] (Beijing: Zhongyang wenxian chubanshe, 2006), pp. 145, 347–349.
11. Gui Shiyong et al., eds., *Zhongguo jihua tizhi gaige* [The Reform of China's Planning System] (Beijing: Zhongguo caizheng jingji chubanshe, 1994); Shi Qingqi et al., "Changing Patterns of Development Planning in China," in Somsak Tambunlertchai and S.P. Gupta, eds., *Development Planning in Asia* (Kuala Lumpur: Asian and Pacific Development Centre, 1993).
12. CCP Central Committee, "Decision of the CCP Central Committee on Some Issues Concerning the Establishment of a Socialist Market Economic Structure," *Xinhua News Agency News Bulletin*, No. 16388 (November 17, 1993); Li Pumin and Li Bing, "'Jiu wu' shiqi woguo jihua tizhi gaige huigu," pp. 24–26.
13. Gui Shiyong et al., eds., *Zhongguo jihua tizhi gaige*, pp. 72–76.
14. Detailed records on how top-level policy makers engaged in the post-1993 planning process can be found in the memoirs of Chen Jinhua, *Guoshi yishu* [Recollections on State Affairs] (Beijing: Zhonggong dangshi chubanshe, 2005); Li Peng, *Shichang yu tiaokong: Li Peng jingji riji* [Markets and (Government) Controls: Li Peng's Economic Diaries] (Beijing: Xinhua chubanshe, 2007).
15. Li Peng, *Shichang yu tiaokong*, pp. 1206–1208.
16. Chang Xin, "Di jiuge wunian guihua de dingzhi he shishi" [Formulation and Implementation of the 9th Five-year plan], in Liu Guoguang, ed., *Zhongguo shige wunian jihua yanjiu baogao*, p. 658.

17. Zhang Zhuoyuan and Lu Yao, "Di shige wunian jihua de zhiding yu shishi" [Formulation and Implementation of the 10th Five-year Plan], pp. 665–667, 674–677.
18. Though Zhu Rongji was appreciated as a forceful economic policy maker by NDRC interviewees, he was seen as constantly curtailing the administrative powers of the former State Planning Commission. Zhu Rongji, who had been dismissed from the Planning Commission in the 1950s due to "rightist" deviations, apparently "never again set foot in the building of the Planning Commission" when he served as vice-premier and premier between 1993 and 2003 (interviews with State Planning Commission [SPC]/NDRC officials).
19. The formula was based on an internal NDRC research report that suggested giving top priority to these five challenges so as to put into practice the party's "scientific developmental view." This information comes from interviews with officials at the NDRC and researchers at the Academy of Macroeconomic Research (AMR) of the NDRC. Cf. CCP Central Committee, "Guanyu wanshan shehui zhuyi shichang jingji ruogan wenti de jueding" [Decision on Some Issues Concerning Improvement of the Structure of the Socialist Market Economy], October, 14, 2003, at http://www.people.com.cn/GB/shizheng/1024/2145119.html, accessed March 16, 2017.
20. Ma Kai, "'Shiyi wu gangyao' de bianzhi guocheng he dingwei" [Drafting Process and Orientation of the "11th Five-year Plan Outline"], *Jingji ribao* [Economic Daily], April 18, 2006; Hu Angang et al., "Guojia 'shiyi wu' guihua gangyao shishi jinzhan pinggu baogao" [Evaluation Report on the Implementation and Progress of China's 11th Five-year Plan Outline], *Hongguan jingji guanli* [Macroeconomic Management], No. 10 (2008), pp. 13–17; Zhu Zhixin, ed., "'Shiyi wu' guihua shishi zhongqi pinggu baogao" [Mid-term Evaluation Report on Implementation of the 11th Five-year Plan] (Beijing: Zhongguo renkou chubanshe, 2009); Xu Lin, "Guihua bianzhi chengxu he pinggu zhidu" [Plan Drafting Procedures and Evaluation Institutions], in Yang Weimin, ed., *Fazhan guihua de lilun he shijian* [The Theory and Practice of Development Planning] (Beijing: Qinghua daxue chubanshe, 2010), pp. 163–179.
21. The old term continues to be used for the annual planning exercises that still form a core routine of the policy-making cycle and also for the five-year periods in certain "traditional" hierarchical planning areas such as the railway system.
22. Yang Weimin, "Woguo guihua tizhi gaige de renwu ji fangxiang" [The Mission and Direction for Reforming China's Planning System], *Hongguan jingji guanli* [Macroeconomic Management], No. 4 (2003), pp. 4–8; Yang Weimin, ed., *Fazhan guihua de lilun he shijian*.
23. State Council, "Guowuyuan guanyu jiaqiang guomin jingji he shehui fazhan guihua bianzhi gongzuo de ruogan yijian" [State Council

Opinions on Strengthening the Drafting Work for the National Economic and Social Development Plan], October 22, 2005, http://www.gov.cn/zwgk/2005-10/26/content_84417.htm, accessed March 16, 2017; Yang Weimin, ed., *Fazhan guihua de lilun he shijian*.

24. Yang Weimin, ed., *Fazhan guihua de lilun he shijian*; Cheng Siwei, "Lun Zhongguo shehui zhuyi shichang jingji zhidu xia de fazhan jihua" [On Development Planning under China's Socialist Market Economic System], *Gonggong guanli xuebao* [Public Management Studies], No. 2 (2004), pp. 4–11.

25. Pioneering works on particularistic contracting in China are Susan L. Shirk, *The Political Logic of Economic Reform in China* (Berkeley: University of California Press, 1993); Yang Dali, *Beyond Beijing: Liberalization and the Regions in China* (London: Routledge, 1997).

26. Sebastian Heilmann, Lea Shih, and Andreas Hofem, "National Planning and Local Technology Zones: Experimental Governance in China's Torch Program," *The China Quarterly*, No. 216 (2013), pp. 896–919.

27. On core definitions and principles of macro-regional planning, see the AMR of the NDRC, "Woguo zhuti gongneng qu" [Development Priority Zones in Our Country], *Hongguan jingji guanli* [Macroeconomic Management], No. 4 (2007), pp. 3–10. There were many attempts at interprovincial coordination of development and infrastructure policy during the early and mid-1990s. But almost all these early efforts were regarded as failures by the planners who participated in the drafting process. Cf. Du Ping, "Quyu guihua de yanbian yu zhanwang" [Evolution and Prospects of Macro-regional Planning], in Yang Weimin, ed., *Fazhan guihua de lilun he shijian*, pp. 79–97.

28. Jae Ho Chung, Hongyi Lai, and Jang-Hwan Joo, "Assessing the 'Revive the Northeast' Programme: Origins, Policies and Implementation," *The China Quarterly*, No. 197 (2009), pp. 108–125.

29. Interviews with planning officials and advisers in Guangzhou and Shenzhen, 2009, 2011.

30. Interviews at the Guangdong DRC, 2010.

31. Interviews at the NDRC and Chongqing DRC on the process of Chongqing's 2007–9 elevation to a national experimental zone. See also Wu Hongying, "Zong gaicheng Chongqing 'lianghui' chong zhong zhi zhong" [Comprehensive Reform: Top Priority of the "Two Sessions" in Chongqing], *21 shiji jingji baodao* [Twenty-first Century Business Herald], January 10, 2009; State Council, "Guowuyuan guanyu tuijin Chongqingshi tongchou chengxiang gaige he fazhan de yijian" [Opinions of the State Council on Furthering Urban-Rural Integrated Reform in Chongqing Municipality], February 5, 2009, at http://www.gov.cn/zwgk/2009-02/05/content_1222355.htm, accessed March 17, 2017.

32. Interviews with the NDRC, Guangdong DRC, and Shenzhen government officials and advisers, 2009, 2011.

33. Peng Sen, "Duo cengci gaige shidian geju jiben xingcheng" [Pattern of Multi-level Reform Pilots Basically in Place], Xinhua News, June 7, 2010, at http://news.xinhuanet.com/politics/2010-06/07/c_12192753.htm, accessed March 10, 2017.
34. Chung, Lai, and Joo, "Assessing the 'Revive the Northeast' Programme," p. 125.
35. CCP Central Committee, "Decision of the CCP Central Committee on Some Issues Concerning the Establishment of a Socialist Market Economic Structure," *Xinhua News Agency News Bulletin*, No. 16388 (November 17, 1993).
36. Zhu Baozhi, "Guojia zhuanxiang guihua de bianzhi yu guanli" [Drafting and Administering National Special Plans], in Yang Weimin, ed., *Fazhan guihua de lilun he shijian*, pp. 99–109.
37. State Council, "Guowuyuan guanyu jiaqiang guomin jingji he shehui fazhan guihua bianzhi gongzuo de ruogan yijian" [State Council Opinions on Strengthening the Drafting Work for the National Economic and Social Development Plan], October 26, 2005, at http://www.gov.cn/zwgk/2005-10/26/content_8441, accessed March 14, 2017.
38. This estimate is based on the documents listed under the 11th Five-year Plan's Special Plans tab on the NDRC's website and similar lists from provincial DRCs, at http://www.sdpc.gov.cn/fzgh/ghwb/115zxgh/default.htm, accessed January 21, 2013.
39. Mark D. Levine et al. found that during the 2006–8 period, China had met roughly one-third of its five-year goals in this area. See Mark D. Levine et al., "Assessment of China's Energy-Saving and Emission-Reduction Accomplishments and Opportunities During the 11th Five-year Plan," April 2010, at https://china.lbl.gov/sites/all/files/lbl-3385e-11fyp-accomplishments-assessmentapril-2010.pdf, accessed March 14, 2017; Yao Rosealea and Arthur Kroeber, "Energy Efficiency: Damned Statistics," *China Economic Quarterly*, Vol. 14, No. 3 (2010), pp. 6–8; State Council, "Guomin jingji he shehui fazhan di shierge wunian guihua gangyao" [The 12th Five-year Plan for National Economic and Social Development], March 16, 2011, at http://news.xinhuanet.com/politics/2011-03/16/c_121193916.htm, accessed March 10, 2017.
40. This section draws on Melton, "Understanding China's Five-year Plan," pp. 10–14.
41. Premier Wen Jiabao noted the failure to fully implement energy-efficiency policies or to assign responsibilities sufficiently amid deteriorating energy consumption efficiency, leading Beijing to implement a strict evaluation and responsibility program. Cf. Levine et al., "Assessment of China's Energy-Saving and Emission-Reduction Accomplishments and Opportunities During the 11th Five-year Plan," April 2010, at https://china.lbl.gov/sites/all/files/lbl-3385e-11fyp-accomplishments-

assessmentapril-2010.pdf, accessed March 14, 2017, p. 8; Zhao Xiaohui, "Zhongguo tuixing yange de jieneng jianpai wenze zhi" [China to Strictly Carry Out Energy Efficiency and a Pollution Reduction Responsibility System], Xinhua News, April 28, 2007, at http://news.xinhuanet.com/politics/2007-04/28/content_6041195.htm, accessed March 17, 2017.

42. State Council, "Zhonghua renmin gongheguo jingji he shehui fazhan di shiyige wunian guihua gangyao" [China's 11th Five-year Plan for National Economic and Social Development], March 16, 2006, at http://www.gov.cn/ztzl/2006-03/16/content_228841.htm, accessed March 11, 2017; State Council, "Guanyu luoshi 'Zhonghua renmin gongheguo guomin jingji he shehui fazhan di shiyige wunian guihua gangyao' zhuyao mubiao renwu gongzuo fengong de tongzhi" [State Council Notice on the Division of Major Targets and Responsibilities for Implementation of "China's 11th Five-year Plan for National Economic and Social Development"], August 24, 2006, at http://www.gov.cn/gongbao/content/2006/content_413969.htm, accessed March 11, 2017.

43. State Council, "Guomin jingji he shehui fazhan di shierge wunian guihua gangyao" [The 12th Five-year Plan for National Economic and Social Development], March 16, 2011, http://news.xinhuanet.com/politics/2011-03/16/c_121193916.htm, accessed March 11, 2017.

44. NDRC, "Jieneng zhongchangqi zhuanxiang guihua" [Medium- and Long-Term Energy-Conservation Plan], July 11, 2005, at http://www.sdpc.gov.cn/fzgggz/hjbh/jnjs/200507/t20050711_45823.html, accessed March 11, 2017.

45. Levine et al., "Assessment of China's Energy-Saving and Emission-Reduction Accomplishments and Opportunities During the 11th Five-year Plan," April 2010, at https://china.lbl.gov/sites/all/files/lbl-3385e-11fyp-accomplishments-assessmentapril-2010.pdf, accessed March 14, 2017, pp. 15–16.

46. See fn. 42.

47. Levine et al., "Assessment of China's Energy-Saving and Emission-Reduction Accomplishments and Opportunities During the 11th Five-year Plan," April 2010, at https://china.lbl.gov/sites/all/files/lbl-3385e-11fyp-accomplishments-assessmentapril-2010.pdf, accessed March 14, 2017, p. 59.

48. Ibid., p. 59; NDRC, "Jieneng zhongchangqi zhuanxiang guihua" [Medium - and Long-Term Energy-Conservation Plan], July 11, 2005, at http://www.sdpc.gov.cn/fzgggz/hjbh/jnjs/200507/t20050711_45823.html, accessed March 11, 2017.

49. See also Administration of Quality Supervision, Inspection and Quarantine, "Guanyu guanche luoshi 'qian jia qiye xingdong shishi fang'an' de tongzhi" [Notice on Implementation of the "Implementation

Plan for the 1,000 Enterprises Energy-Conservation Program"], April 26, 2006, at http://www.chinabaike.com/law/zy/bw/gwy/zl/1373103.html, accessed March 17, 2017); NDRC, "Guanyu yinfa qianjia qiye jieneng xingdong shishi fang'an de tongzhi" [Notice on the Issuance of the Implementation Plan for the 1,000 Enterprises Energy-Conservation Initiative], April 7, 2006, at http://hzs.ndrc.gov.cn/newzwxx/t20060413_66111.htm, accessed March 17, 2017.

50. NDRC, "Jieneng zhongchangqi zhuanxiang guihua" [Medium- and Long-Term Energy-Conservation Plan], July 11, 2005, at http://www.sdpc.gov.cn/fzgggz/hjbh/jnjs/200507/t20050711_45823.html, accessed March 11, 2017; State Council, "Guowuyuan guanyu jiaqiang jieneng gongzuo de jueding" [Decision on Strengthening Energy-Conservation Work], August 23, 2006, at http://www.gov.cn/zwgk/2006-08/23/content_368136.htm, accessed March 11, 2017.

51. State Council, "Guowuyuan guanyu jiaqiang jieneng gongzuo de jueding" [Decision on Strengthening Energy-Conservation Work], August 23, 2006, at http://www.gov.cn/zwgk/2006-08/23/content_368136.htm, accessed March 11, 2017.

52. State Council, "Guanyu 'shiyi wu' qijian ge diqu danwei shengchan zongzhi nengyuan xiaohao jiangdi zhibiao jihua de pifu" [State Council on Approval of the Plan for the 11th Five-year Plan Period Regional Unit-GDP Energy Consumption Reduction Standards], September 17, 2006, at http://www.gov.cn/gongbao/content/2006/content_443285.htm, accessed March 11, 2017.

53. State Council, "Guowuyuan pizhuan jieneng jianpai tongji jiance ji kaohe shishi fang'an he banfa de tongzhi" [State Council Notice on the Approval of Methods for Implementing Energy Conservation and Emission Reductions Statistical Monitoring and Evaluations], November 23, 2007, at http://www.gov.cn/zwgk/2007-11/23/content_813617.htm, accessed March 11, 2017; Guangdong Province People's Government Office, "Yinfa Guangdong sheng danwei GDP neng hao kaohe tixi shishi fang'an de tongzhi" [Notice on Dissemination of the Implementation Plan on Methods to Implement Guangdong Province's Unit-GDP Energy-Conservation Evaluation System], April 7, 2008, at http://zwgk.gd.gov.cn/006939748/200909/t20090915_9506.html, accessed March 11, 2017.

54. Guangdong Province People's Government and Guangdong Province Economic and Trade Commission aimed to implement the State Council Decision on Strengthening Energy-Conservation Work, help meet the province's 16 percent unit-GDP power consumption reduction target, and follow through on the 1,000 Enterprises Energy-Conservation Initiative. See Guangdong Province People's Government, "Guanyu jinyibu jiaqiang Guangdong sheng jieneng gongzuo de yijian" [Opinions on the Progressive Strengthening of Guangdong Province's

Energy-Conservation Work], November 22, 2006, http://zwgk. gd.gov.cn/006939748/200909/t20090915_8944.html, accessed March 17, 2017; Guangdong Province Economic and Trade Commission, "Guanyu yinfa Guangdong sheng zhongdian haoneng qiye "shuang qian jieneng xingdong" shishi fang'an de tongzhi" [Notice on the Distribution of the Guangdong Province Key Energy Consuming Enterprises "Dual Implementation of the 1,000 Enterprise Energy-Conservation Initiative"], November 24, 2006, at http://www.gdei.gov.cn/zwgk/tzgg/2006/200612/t20061205_54132.html, accessed March 17, 2017. Another document of the Guangdong Province People's Government includes implementation responsibilities for a broad range of provincial-level energy-conservation programs to implement a comprehensive national work plan released by the State Council; see Guangdong Province People's Government, "Yinfa Guangdong sheng jieneng jianpai zonghexing gongzuo fang'an de tongzhi" [Notice on the Publication of a Comprehensive Work Plan for Guangdong Province's Energy Conservation and Emissions Reduction], July 19, 2007, at http://www.gd.gov.cn/govpub/zfwj/zfxxgk/gfxwj/yf/200809/ t20080916_67024.htm, accessed March 17, 2017; State Council, "Guowuyuan guanyu yinfa jieneng jianpai zonghexing gongzuo fang'an de tongzhi" [State Council Notice on a Comprehensive Work Plan to Implement Energy Conservation and Emissions Reduction], June 3, 2007, at http://www.gov.cn/jrzg/2007-06/03/content_634545.htm, accessed March 17, 2017.

55. Guangdong Economic and Trade Commission (2008) attachments 1–4 contain revised lists of centrally monitored companies within Guangdong province, companies monitored directly by the provincial government, and companies monitored by their city governments. See Guangdong Province Economic and Trade Commission, "Guanyu tiaozheng Guangdong sheng qianjia qiye jieneng xingdong qiye mingdan ji jinyibu jiaqiang jieneng jianguan de tongzhi" [Notice on Adjusting Guangdong Province's 1,000 Enterprises Energy-Conservation Initiative Enterprise List and Progressively Strengthening Energy-Conservation Supervision], August 26, 2008, at http://www.gdei.gov.cn/ywfl/jnhxhjj/201507/ t20150709_117774.htm, accessed March 11, 2017.

56. Cf. "Yue 21 dishi qianding jieneng 'jun ling zhuang' jiang hao mubiao jiang naru zhengji kaohe" [Guangdong's Twenty-one Prefectural Cities Sign "Military Order" Consumption Targets for Energy-Conservation that Will Enter Government Performance Evaluations], Nanfang wang, December 15, 2006, at http://www.southcn.com/ news/gdnews/nanyuedadi/200612150699.htm, accessed March 11, 2017; Guangdong Province People's Government, "Guanyu yinfa Guangdong sheng 'shiyi wu' qijian danwei shengchan zongzhi nengyuan

xiaohao jiangdi zhibiao jihua fenjie fang'an de tongzhi" [Notice on the Dissemination of the Target Allocation Plan for Guangdong Province's Unit-GDP Energy-Conservation Plan During the Eleventh Five-year Plan], December 17, 2006, at http://www.pkulaw.cn/fulltext_form.aspx?Db=lar&Gid=16895348, accessed March 11, 2017; Guangdong Province People's Government Office, "Yinfa Guangdong sheng danwei GDP neng hao kaohe tixi shishi fang'an de tongzhi" [Notice on Dissemination of the Implementation Plan on Methods to Implement Guangdong Province's Unit-GDP Energy-Conservation Evaluation System], April 7, 2008, at http://zwgk.gd.gov.cn/006939748/200909/t20090915_9506.html, accessed March 11, 2017.

57. NDRC, "Guanyu jiaqiang guding zichan touzi xiangmu jieneng pinggu he shencha gongzuo de tongzhi" [Notice on Strengthening Evaluations and Inspections of Energy Conservation for Fixed-Asset Investment Programs], December 12, 2006, at http://www.ncjnjc.org/Article/jnps/201107/108.shtml, accessed March 11, 2017; NDRC, "Guanyu yinfa guding zichan touzi xiangmu jieneng pinggu he shencha zhinan (2006) tongzhi" [Notice on the Dissemination of the 2006 Handbook on Evaluations and Inspections of Energy Conservations for Fixed-Asset Investment Programs], January 12, 2007, http://www.sdpc.gov.cn/zwfwzx/tztg/200701/t20070112_110731.html, accessed March 11, 2017.

58. Cf. Levine et al., "Assessment of China's Energy-Saving and Emission-Reduction Accomplishments and Opportunities During the 11th Five-year Plan," April 2010, at https://china.lbl.gov/sites/all/files/lbl-3385e-11fyp-accomplishments-assessmentapril-2010.pdf, accessed March 14, 2017; Yao and Kroeber, "Energy Efficiency: Damned Statistics," pp. 6–8.

59. See, for instance, Wang Yahua and Yan Yilong, "Shige wunian jihua de zhiding guocheng yu juece jizhi" [Drafting Processes and Decision Mechanisms for Ten Five-year Plans], *Hongguan jingji guanli* [Macroeconomic Management], No. 5 (2007), pp. 67–70; Barry Naughton, "The New Common Economic Program: China's Eleventh Five-year Plan and What It Means," *China Leadership Monitor*, No. 16 (2006).

60. The national guidelines, issued by the CCP Central Committee, are followed by similar documents issued by the local party committees in order of rank. The outlines are completed and released in reverse order by subnational governments: cities first, then provinces, and finally the national five-year plan outline, approved and publicized during the annual full session of the National People's Congress, usually held in mid-March. The inverted sequence of issuance of the plan outlines sometimes leads to confusion, as targets released in provincial or city outlines may subsequently be overruled by targets released in the national outline.

61. Peter Evans, *Embedded Autonomy. States and Industrial Transformation* (Princeton, NJ: Princeton University Press, 1995); Sebastian Heilmann,

"China's Core Executive in Economic Policy," paper presented at the conference on "Power in the Making: Governing and Being Governed in Contemporary China," Oxford University, 2012.
62. The national 11th Five-year Plan had three outside reviewers—the World Bank, the Development Research Center of the State Council and Tsinghua University's Center for National Conditions—that conducted mid-term evaluations (cf. "'Shiyi wu' guihua shishi zongti jinzhan lianghao jingji shehui fazhan zhuyao zhibiao daduo dadao yuqi jindu yaoqiu" [Implementation of the "11th Five-year Plan" is Progressing Well: The Majority of Major Economic and Social Development Targets are on Schedule], Xinhua News, December 24, 2008, at http://news.xinhuanet.com/newscenter/2008-12/24/content_10554035.htm, accessed March 11, 2017. Guangdong's Academy of Social Sciences conducted a third-party evaluation of the five-year plan alongside the review led by the Guangdong DRC; cf. "Guanyu Guangdong sheng 'shiyi wu' guihua gangyao zhongqi pinggu ji bufen mubiao tiaozheng caoan de baogao" [Report on the Mid-Term Evaluation of Guangdong Province's 11th Five-year Plan Outline and the Draft Target Adjustments], presented by Commission Chairman Li Miaojun to the Seventh Plenary Meeting of the Standing Committee of the Eleventh People's Congress of Guangdong Province, at http://www1.rd.gd.cn/wjf/new/2008/newrd161.htm, accessed March 11, 2017. See also Lai Rui, "Gengjia kaifang zixin de Zhongguo: 'Shier wu' guihua xiang quanqiu qu jing" [A More Open Self-Confident China: The 12th Five-year Plan Looking to the World for Ideas], *Renmin ribao haiwai ban* [Overseas Edition of *People's Daily*], February 3, 2010, at http://cppcc.people.com.cn/GB/34952/10916092.html, accessed March 11, 2017; Yu Donghui, "Lianghui qianzou: 'Shi wu' jihua shi zenyang zhiding chulaide?" [Prelude to the Two Sessions: How Was the "10th Five-year Plan" Formulated?], Zhongguo xinwen wang, February 26, 2001, at http://www.chinanews.com/2001-02-27/26/73800.html, accessed March 11, 2017.
63. This information is based on interviews at national- and provincial-level DRCs.
64. Information on informal, small-scale central-provincial economic policy meetings is scattered throughout the two volumes of Li Peng, *Shichang yu tiaokong*.
65. Cf. Xu Lin, "Guihua bianzhi chengxu he pinggu zhidu."
66. This is based on NDRC and AMR interviews.
67. Guangdong Province People's Government, "Guangdong sheng guomin jingji he shehui fazhan shiyi wu guihua gangyao" [Guangdong Province 11th Five-year Plan for Economic and Social Development], March 10, 2006, at http://www.gd.gov.cn/govpub/fzgh/sywgy/0200607260010.htm, accessed January 18, 2013.

68. This is based on individual interviews held with NDRC and Guangdong DRC officials.
69. Interview with economic historian Wu Li, 2009; see also Wu Li, "Zhonghua renmin gongheguo shishi jihua guanli de jichu he tiaojian" [Foundations and Conditions for Implementing Plan Administration in the PRC], in Liu Guoguang, ed., *Zhongguo shige wunian jihua yanjiu baogao*, pp.1–51.
70. CCP Central Organization Department (COD), ed., *Jianli cujin kexue fazhan de ganbu kaohe pingjia jizhi shier jiang* [Twelve Statements on Creating a Cadre Appraisal Mechanism to Promote Scientific Development] (Beijing: Zhongguo fangzheng chubanshe, 2009); Li Guangcun, *Ganbu kaohe* [Cadre Appraisals] (Beijing: Dangjian duwu chubanshe, 2009).
71. Interviews with NDRC planning officials, 2009, 2010, 2011.
72. Interviews at Chongqing DRC, 2009. See also the documents issued by the General Bureau of the Chongqing Municipal Government, No. 184 (2006), No. 30 (2007), No. 44 (2008), and No. 111 (2009), in which realization of the binding plan targets contained in the municipal 11th Five-year Plan are established as benchmarks for local government and cadre performance evaluations, and they are repeated or modified in annual planning so as to ensure implementation of the overall five-year plan targets. Party and government organizations, personnel, and supervisory bodies are explicitly ordered to incorporate the binding targets in their cadre evaluations.
73. In the State Council document ("Notice on the Division of Major Targets and Responsibilities for the Implementation of 'China's 11th Five-year Plan for National Economic and Social Development'"), arable land preservation, energy- intensity targets, and pollution controls were added to the leading cadre performance evaluation systems. Local implementation efforts in Guangdong exceeded these three targets for cadre evaluations since the mid-term evaluations included revisions to increase Guangdong's pollution and energy-intensity targets and a special appendix to address shortcomings in meeting the three priority restrictive targets. Cf. Guangdong DRC, "Report on the Mid-Term Evaluation of Guangdong Province's 11th Five-year Plan Outline and Draft Target Adjustments."
74. Another State Council notice ("Notice on the Approval of Methods for Implementing Statistical Monitoring and Evaluation of Energy Conservation and Emissions Reductions") approved three implementation plans for evaluating and monitoring energy consumption and three methods for evaluating and monitoring emissions of major pollutants issued by the NDRC and the State Environmental Protection Administration. A document issued in Guangdong states that for leading city-level government groups and leading cadres, failure to meet the energy-

conservation targets specified in Guangdong Document No. 125 would constitute a veto criterion in the performance evaluations, the relevant cadre would not attend the annual awards ceremony, and approval of high energy-consuming investments would be blocked in their respective districts. Individual enterprises, particularly state-owned or state-controlled firms, would face similar restrictions and incentives; see Guangdong Province People's Government Office, "Notice on the Dissemination of the Implementation Plan on Methods to Implement Guangdong Province's Unit-GDP Energy-Conservation Evaluation System."

75. Sebastian Heilmann, "Economic Governance: Authoritarian Upgrading and Innovative Potential," in Joseph Fewsmith, ed., *China Today, China Tomorrow: Domestic Politics, Economy, and Society* (Lanham, MD: Rowman & Littlefield, 2010), pp. 109–126.
76. Cf. Genia Kostka and William Hobbs, "Local Energy Efficiency Policy Implementation in China: Bridging the Gap between National Priorities and Local Interests," *The China Quarterly*, No. 211 (2012), pp.765–785.
77. Sebastian Heilmann, "Making Plans for Markets: Policies for the Long Term in China," *Harvard Asia Quarterly*, Vol. 13, No. 2, pp. 33–40.
78. This assessment is based on a series of interviews with NDRC planning officials, 2007–2011.
79. Cf. NDRC, "Guanyu yinfa cujin zhongbu diqu jueqi guihua shishi yijian de tongzhi" [Notice on the Dissemination of Opinions on the Implementation Plan for Promoting Western Development], August 12, 2010, at http://www.sdpc.gov.cn/zcfb/zcfbghwb/201008/t20100825_585474.html, accessed March 11, 2017.
80. Interviews in the Planning Division of the NDRC, 2009, 2011.
81. Provincial-level DRC interviews, 2009, 2010, 2011. On the basic mechanisms of beautifying or standardizing cadre evaluations, see Richard McGregor, *The Party: The Secret World of China's Communist Rulers* (New York, Harper, 2010), pp. 70–103.
82. Hu Angang and Yan Yilong, *Zhongguo: Zouxiang 2015* [China: Heading Toward 2015] (Hangzhou: Zhejiang renmin chubanshe, 2010), p. 28.
83. Interviews with NDRC planning officials, 2009, 2010, 2011.
84. The most systematic statement on this is given by Michael Howlett, M. Ramesh, and Anthony Perl, *Studying Public Policy: Policy Cycles and Policy Subsystems* (Toronto: Oxford University Press, 3rd ed., 2009).
85. Interviews in the Planning Division of the NDRC, 2011.

# Epilogue

1. Sebastian Heilmann, *Das politische System der Volksrepublik China* [The Political System of the PRC] (Wiesbaden: VS Verlag für Sozialwissenschaften, 2nd rvsd. ed., 2004).

2. Nassim Nicholas Taleb and Gregory F. Treverton, "The Calm Before the Storm: Why Volatility Signals Stability, and Vice Versa," *Foreign Affairs*, Vol. 94, No. 1 (2015), pp. 86–95.
3. Chalmers Johnson, *MITI and the Japanese Miracle: The Growth of Industrial Policy, 1925–1975* (Stanford, CA: Stanford University Press, 1982); Meredith Woo-Cumings, *The Developmental State* (Ithaca, NY: Cornell University Press, 1999); Sebastian Heilmann, "Das Modell des ostasiatischen Entwicklungsstaates in der Revision" [Revising the Model of the East Asian Developmental State], in Verena Blechinger-Talcott, Christiane Frantz, and Mark R. Thompson, eds., *Politik in Japan: System, Reformprozesse und Aussenpolitik im internationalen Vergleich* [Politics in Japan: System, Reform Processes, and Foreign Policy in International Comparison] (Frankfurt am Main: Campus, 2006), pp. 103–116.
4. Stefan A. Halper, *The Beijing Consensus: How China's Authoritarian Model Will Dominate the Twenty-First Century* (New York: Basic Books, 2010); Joshua Cooper Ramo, *The Beijing Consensus* (London: Foreign Policy Centre, 2004).
5. Ian Bremmer, *The End of the Free Market: Who Wins the War between States and Corporations?* (New York: Portfolio, 2010).
6. Sebastian Heilmann, "Economic Governance: Authoritarian Upgrading and Innovative Potential," in Joseph Fewsmith, ed., *China Today, China Tomorrow: Domestic Politics, Economy, and Society* (Lanham, MD: Rowman & Littlefield, 2010), pp. 109–126.
7. Martin Jacques, *When China Rules the World: The Rise of the Middle Kingdom and the End of the Western World* (London: Penguin, 2nd ed., 2012).
8. Daniel A. Bell, *The China Model: Political Meritocracy and the Limits of Democracy* (Princeton, NJ: Princeton University Press, 2015).
9. Pan Wei, *Zhongguo moshi: Jiedu renmin gongheguo de 60 nian* [The Chinese Model: Decoding 60 Years of the PRC] (Beijing: Zhongyang bianyi chubanshe, 2009).
10. Hu Angang, *Zhongguo 2020: Yige xinxing chaoji daguo* [China in 2020: A New Type of Superpower] (Hangzhou: Zhejiang renmin chubanshe, 2012); Hu Angang, Tang Xiao, Yang Zhusong, and Yan Yilong, eds., *Zhongguo guojia zhili xiandaihua* [Modernization of Chinese National Governance] (Beijing: Zhongguo renmin daxue chubanshe, 2014).
11. Chen Jinhua et al., eds., *Zhongguo moshi yu Zhongguo zhidu* [The China Model and the Chinese System] (Beijing: Renmin chubanshe, 2012).
12. Ding Xueliang, ed., *Zhongguo moshi: Zancheng yu fandui* [The Chinese Model: Pros and Cons] (Hong Kong: Oxford University Press, 2011); Zheng Yongnian, ed., *Zhongguo moshi: Jingyan yu kunju* [The China Model: Experiences and Dilemmas] (Hangzhou: Zhejiang renmin chubanshe, 2010).

# ABBREVIATIONS

| | |
|---|---|
| ADB | Asian Development Bank |
| AMR | Academy of Macroeconomic Research (of the NDRC) |
| AQSIQ | General Administration of Quality Supervision, Inspection and Quarantine |
| CCP | Chinese Communist Party |
| CFELSG | Central Financial and Economic Leadership Small Group |
| COD | CCP Central Organization Department |
| DRC | Development and Reform Commission |
| GONGO | government-organized non-governmental organization |
| KMT | Kuomintang |
| MCS | "modern company system" |
| MEM | Mass Education Movement |
| NBS | National Bureau of Statistics |
| NDRC | National Development and Reform Commission |
| NEP | New Economic Policy |
| NGO | non-governmental organization |
| PRC | People's Republic of China |
| *RMRB* | *Renmin ribao* |
| RRM | Rural Reconstruction Movement |
| SARS | severe acute respiratory syndrome |
| SASAC | State-owned Assets Supervision and Administration Commission |

| | |
|---|---|
| SEZ | special economic zone |
| SME | small and medium-sized enterprise |
| SOE | state-owned enterprise |
| SPC | State Planning Commission |
| USSR | Union of Soviet Socialist Republics |
| WTO | World Trade Organization |

# GLOSSARY

*changjiang sanjiaozhou diqu quyu guihua*      長江三角洲地區區域規劃
*cujin zhongbu diqu jueqi guihua*      促進中部地區崛起規劃

*dianmian jiehe*      點面結合
*dianxing jingyan*      典型經驗
*dianxing shifan*      典型示範
*dianxing shiyan*      典型試驗
*diaoyan*      調研
*dongbei diqu zhenxing guihua*      東北地區振興規劃
*dongbei pian, xibei pian*      東北片、西北片

*fang'an*      方案
*fangfa*      方法

*ganbu kaohe*      幹部考核
*ganbu zhibiao*      幹部指標
*gangyao*      綱要
*gebie zhidao*      個別指導
*gongzuo fang'an*      工作方案
*guan hongtou wenjian de hongtou wenjian*      管紅頭文件的紅頭文件
*guihua*      規劃
*guihua si*      規劃司
*guojia fenjie zhibiao dao ge ge sheng*      國家分解指標到各個省

| | |
|---|---|
| *hongguan tiaokong* | 宏觀調控 |
| *hukou* | 戶口 |
| *jihua* | 計劃 |
| *jingji tequ* | 經濟特區 |
| *jizhong liliang* | 集中力量 |
| *jueding* | 決定 |
| *lingdao ganbu* | 領導幹部 |
| *meiyou guihua jiu bu pi xiangmu* | 沒有規劃就不批項目 |
| *mingmai* | 命脈 |
| *mofan xingguo* | 模範興國 |
| *quyu guihua* | 區域規劃 |
| *rushi* | 入世 |
| *shangfang baojian* | 尚方寶劍 |
| *shidian* | 試點 |
| *shishi fang'an* | 實施方案 |
| *shixian ji* | 市縣級 |
| *shixing tuiguang* | 試行推廣 |
| *shiyan zhuyi* | 實驗主義 |
| *shiyanqu* | 實驗區 |
| *shiyanxian* | 實驗縣 |
| *shuoming* | 說明 |
| *sige pian hui* | 四個片會 |
| *wuge tongchou* | 五個統籌 |
| *xianjie* | 銜接 |
| *xianxing xianshi* | 先行先試 |
| *xibu dakaifa "shiyiwu" guihua* | 西部大開發「十一五」規劃 |
| *xinxing chaoji daguo* | 新型超級大國 |
| *xinxing fazhan jihua tizhi* | 新型發展計劃體制 |

| | |
|---|---|
| *yi dao qie* | 一刀切 |
| *yi piao foujue* | 一票否決 |
| *yiban haozhao* | 一般號召 |
| *yidian daimian* | 以點帶面 |
| *yijian* | 意見 |
| *yindi zhiyi* | 因地制宜 |
| *yiqie dou cong shiyan xiashou* | 一切都從實驗下手 |
| *yiqie jingguo shiyan* | 一切經過試驗 |
| *you dian dao mian* | 由點到面 |
| *yucexing zhibiao* | 預測性指標 |
| *yueshuxing zhibiao* | 約束性指標 |
| | |
| *zhengce baozhang* | 政策保障 |
| *zhengce shiyan* | 政策試驗 |
| *zhengzhi guashuai* | 政治掛帥 |
| *zhibiao zhu ji fenjie* | 指標逐級分解 |
| *zhidao jihua* | 指導計劃 |
| *zhongchangqi fazhan guihua* | 中長期發展規劃 |
| *Zhongguo moshi* | 中國模式 |
| *zhu ji fenjie* | 逐級分解 |
| *zhuanxiang guihua / jihua* | 專項規劃/計劃 |
| *zonghe peitao gaige* | 綜合配套改革 |
| *zuo jihua de xin fangfa* | 作計劃的新方法 |
| *zuofeng* | 作風 |

# INDEX

## A

adaptive authoritarianism 68, 70, 75
adaptive capacity 27, 28, 34, 40, 42, 68, 75, 123, 124, 125
adaptive Governance 17, 27, 145
adaptive planning 187
administrative coordination 31, 96
administrative Integration 68, 143, 144
"agency point of view" 178
aggregate balancing 133, 152
"anticipate-and-regulate" 34
Art of War 36
Asian Financial Crisis 18, 96, 102, 109, 120, 153, 202

## B

"Beijing consensus" 212
binding targets (*yueshuxing zhibiao*) 8, 134, 135, 136, 150, 155, 167, 180, 181, 184, 190, 191
Bolshevik 56
Book of Change 36
bottom-up 26, 49, 50, 74, 88, 97, 98, 106, 112, 122, 124, 143, 188, 210
Braybrooke, David 117

## C

cadre evaluation 12, 169, 171, 183, 184, 185, 192, 193, 194
cadre performance (*ganbu kaohe*) 12, 13, 184, 194
cadre system 10, 12, 29, 140, 185, 189
Cao Yuanzheng 91
Central Finance and Economics Leadership Small Group (CFELSG) 175, 176, 177
central-local interaction 35, 37, 39, 47, 69, 70, 79, 91, 148
checks and balances 2, 14, 70, 79
Chen Yun 48, 55, 65, 66
command economy 24, 137, 185, 196
"commanding heights" 20, 151
"comprehensive complementary reform" (*zonghe peitao gaige*) 119
comprehensive coordination 133, 134, 152, 154
comprehensive plan/planning 54, 83, 134, 138, 154, 156, 164, 165, 166, 180, 188
contractual planning (contract-based planning) 159, 186, 187
consultative authoritarianism 212

"coordinative plan" (*guihua*) 154
correction mechanisms 3
corrective mechanisms 42, 132, 138, 139, 145, 188
corporate governance 103
crisis mode 198, 200, 201, 202, 203, 204, 205
cross-provincial plan 159
cross-sectoral coordination 131
Cultural Revolution 38, 204

## D

decentralized experimentation 45, 46, 47, 68, 70, 86, 108, 11, 163, 187
Deng Xiaoping 38, 48, 51, 55, 64, 65, 99, 201, 203, 208, 210
"dependent clientelism" 97
development planning 7, 8, 9, 10, 131, 132, 133, 139, 141, 142, 144, 145, 146, 147, 148, 150, 152, 180, 186, 188, 192, 196, 212
"developmental state" 20, 140, 196, 200, 212
Dewey, John 57, 58, 59, 63
drafting group 90, 175

## E

Eastern European 17, 26, 41, 214
Elizabeth Perry 69
Embedded Autonomy 177, 179
Evans, Peter 73, 74
*ex ante* coordination 133
"experimental counties" (*shiyan xian*) 50, 60, 62
experimental county 60, 61, 62, 64
"experimental extension" (*shixing tuiguang*) 60
"experimental points" /"experimentation point" (*shidian*) 5, 46, 47, 66, 80, 82, 83, 84, 88, 89, 95, 103, 110, 163

experimental programs 5, 6, 45, 47, 63, 64, 78, 79, 86, 87, 94, 104, 105, 106, 110, 119, 141, 188, 195
experimental regulations 6, 81, 85, 92, 122
"experimentalism" (*shiyan zhuyi*) 58, 59, 75
experimentation under hierarchy 70, 75, 79, 111, 159, 188
"experimentation zones" / experimental zones (*shiyan qu*) 5, 80, 84, 85, 86, 162, 163, 188, 210
*ex post* coordination 133

## F

fact-finding tours (*tiaoyan*) 179
Fan Gang 117, 118
"Five Comprehensive Coordination" (*wuge tongchou*) 134, 154
"four modernizations" 32
"four slices meetings" (*sige pian hui*) 178
fragmented authoritarianism 198
"Freiburg School" 127
"from point to surface" (*you dian dao mian*) 6, 46, 47, 51, 53, 66, 67, 68, 79, 82, 88, 89, 108, 109, 122

## G

"go ahead of the rest and try new things out" (*xian xing xian shi*) 162
Gorbachev 41, 209
"government promises" (*chengnuo*) 135, 155
"Great Leap Forward" 23, 38
"guerrilla-style policy-making" 4, 26
guerrilla policy style 4, 5, 31, 32, 34, 35, 36, 38, 40, 41, 42
guidance planning (*zhidao jihua*) 135, 151

## H

"hard targets" 37, 190
harmonization (*xianjie*) 179, 180, 181
Henan 50
Hu Angang 177
Hu Jintao 198, 201, 203, 204, 207
Hu Shi 58
Hu Yaobang 32
Huang, Philip 127, 128

## I

"imperial sword" (*shangfang baojian*) 160
imperative plan/planning 139, 151, 154, 155, 189
"in accordance with local circumstances" (*yin di zhi yi*) 79
indicative targets (*yuce zhibiao*) 8, 131, 134, 155, 156
institutional adaption 8, 131, 134, 155, 156
institutional arrangement 40, 41, 73, 98, 151
interagency coordination 168

## J

Jiangsu 62
Jiangxi Soviet 48, 49, 50
Jiang Zemin 150, 203, 207, 210

## K

Kaldor-improving effects 110
Keynesianism 127
Khrushchev 41
Kuhfus, Peter 53

## L

"laboratories of federalism" 47, 86
Lanxi 62
leading small group 168, 172, 173
Lenin 55, 56
Leninist 20, 24, 25, 26, 55, 56, 185
"level-by-level subdivision of plan targets" (*zhi ji fenjie*) 185
Li Peng 179
Liang Shuming 62
lifelines (*mingmai*) 151
Lindblom, Charles 74, 78, 118
Liu Shaoqi 61
long-term coordination 134

## M

MacFarquhar, Roderick 68
"macro-management" 9
macroeconomic stability 100, 150
macro-regional development plan 156, 159, 161, 176, 188
macro-structural shift 142, 193
making of general policy appeals (*yiban haozhao*) 66
major proportional relationship (*zhongda bili guanxi*) 152
mandatory planning 186
Mao Zedong 17, 22, 28, 48, 49, 57, 58, 62, 203
Marcuse, Herbert 58
marketization-cum-privatization paradigm 20, 115
Marx 55, 58, 66
Marxist 55, 56, 66
Marxism 66
"mass line" 32
Mass Education Movement (MEM) 60
"maximum tinkering" 27, 115, 123, 124, 126, 129

May Fourth period 58
medium and long-term development planning 8, 9
meritocracy 212
middle-income trap 199
"mobilization-style" 88
"model demonstration" (*dianxing shifan*) 50, 53, 71, 80
"model experiment" (*dianxing shiyan*) 6, 46, 49, 51, 53, 64, 66, 67, 68, 88, 89, 107
"model villages" 48, 52
"model Soviet governments" 49
"modern company system" (MCS) 88, 95
Mosteller, Frederick 77
Mukand, Sharun W. 74
multi-city regional planning 159
multiple plans/planning 156, 164
multi-year plans/planning 8, 143, 149
Munro, Donald 55

## N

Nathan, Andrew 23, 43
"national champions" 103
Naughton, Barry 23, 29, 149
New Economic Policy (NEP) 58
"new socialist countryside" 86
new-style development planning 132, 133, 150, 152
"new type of superpower" (*xinxing chaoji daguo*) 213
*Nomenklatura* 23, 183
non-command segments 149
"normal mode" 200, 201, 204, 205
North, Douglass 27, 75

## O

Okimoto, Daniel 136
Oksenberg, Michel 35

one-size-does-not fit all 121
one-size-fits-all 52
open-ended approach 29
open-ended process 2, 74
ordoliberalism 127, 128, 129
"overall guidance" 152

## P

"Parabellum paradigm" 36
Pareto-improving effects 110
performance evaluation 169, 175, 184, 192, 253
"permanent revolution" 5, 26, 32
plan-cadre nexus 151, 155, 183, 185, 194
"plan lock-in" 179, 182
plan-market dynamics 149
planning cycle 173, 187, 194
planning processes 147, 166
planning system 10, 133, 134, 141, 142, 148, 149, 150, 151, 152, 154, 155, 159, 171, 178, 180, 182, 190, 192, 194, 195, 196
plan-updating process 166
plasticity 29, 37
policy analysis 3, 77
policy areas 9, 10, 45, 105, 107, 110, 123, 124, 126, 194, 198, 203, 205
policy authority 150, 175, 185
policy authorization 162, 163
policy capital 162
policy coordination 9, 131, 132, 140, 145, 147, 150, 189, 195
policy cycle 7, 75, 79, 86, 87, 88, 90, 173, 196
policy departures 78, 99, 113
policy entrepreneurs 69, 100, 110, 112
policy environment 113, 121
policy experimentation 5, 7, 40, 46, 47, 48, 51, 53, 55, 57, 64, 66, 71,

73, 76, 77, 78, 80, 81, 86, 87, 90, 91, 94, 106, 107, 108, 110, 11, 112, 116, 139, 189, 210
policy formulation 45, 77, 106, 109, 173
"policy grabs" 100
policy learning 75, 107, 109, 112, 116, 120, 122
policy incentives 166, 188
policy innovation 4,5,7, 39, 45, 46, 55, 65, 67, 68, 70, 81, 86, 88, 89, 99, 108, 122, 125, 150
policy instruments 6,14,37,46, 47,49, 63,64,70,102,120,129,132,145,187,188
policy-making process 14,166,195
policy-making community 89,94
policy objectives 37,46,51,64,68,164,166,185
policy paradigm 94,105
policy parameters 69,99,103,109
"policy pivots" 178
policy prioritization 116
policy process 1, 3, 4, 13, 14, 26, 31, 40, 45, 46, 47, 48, 54, 68, 70, 71, 74, 76, 77, 86, 90, 91, 92, 106, 107, 111, 112, 118, 121, 122, 123, 124, 129, 140, 168, 177, 188, 196, 197, 209, 218
policy regime 96, 101
policy repertoire 93, 94
policy re-prioritization 76
policy safeguards 162
policy sequencing 117
"politics in command" (*zhengzhi guashuai*) 34, 40
policy target 6, 151, 213
policy tools 56, 86, 125, 137, 185
point-to-surface 46, 48, 49, 52, 54, 55, 56, 57, 60, 64, 65, 66, 69, 86
post-law experimentation 95
post-Mao 5, 18, 20, 21, 29, 30, 32, 34, 35, 38, 65, 66, 67, 60, 70, 82, 148, 149
post-revolutionary 25
post-socialist 117, 198
preconceived regime 2, 3
"proceeding from point to surface" (*you dian dao mian*) 46, 47, 51, 53, 66, 67, 68, 79, 82, 109
Profit-seeking 104, 106, 107, 110, 112
Prognostic-indicative 153
protective policy styles 40
"push-and-seize" style 34

**Q**

Qian Yingyi 91
Qu Qiubai 56, 61
quantitative targets 11, 13, 133, 135, 152

**R**

Red-letterhead document 139, 162
"reform and opening" 5, 29, 32, 58, 65, 85, 122
regional planning 159, 180
regulatory state 140, 196
rent-seeking 75, 104, 106, 107, 110, 112
resilience 1, 21, 23, 24, 26, 27, 29, 42, 68, 121, 140, 149, 206, 207, 208, 209
Rodrik, Dani 28, 73, 121
Rule of law 34, 40, 43, 86, 111, 218
rural decollectivization 6, 45, 87, 104
Rural Reconstruction Movement 59, 60

**S**

Scharpf, Fritz 125,126

Schwartz, Benjamin 56
"seeking truth from facts" (*shi shi qiu shi*) 55
"segmented deregulation" 101
sequencing model 117
Shambaugh, David 23
Shanxi 50
short-cycle 144, 145
social experimentation 59, 60
social goods 103, 104, 186
social management 212
"social science laboratories" 66
social welfare planning 138
"socialist construction" 5, 29, 32
"Socialist Market Economy" 5, 30, 32, 99, 102, 133, 136, 152, 164
soft budget constraints 96
Soviet Union 1, 2, 8, 24, 26, 41, 46, 54, 56, 99, 120, 209
soviet-style 132, 149, 150, 153, 188
special plan 156, 164, 165, 166, 173, 174, 180, 188
"spontaneous" 55, 88
Stalin 55
Stalinist 41
State Planning Commission 152
state sector restructuring 45
"states as laboratories" 80
strategic policy coordination 9, 132
strategic coordination 163
strategic emerging industries 213
state-sponsored experimentation 106
structural reform 73, 81, 83, 109, 120, 154, 199, 211
subplan 155, 156, 179
Sunzi 36
"symbiotic clientelism" 97
synoptic models 116, 117

T

Taihang Base Area 50, 64

"Take markets as the foundation" 133
Taleb, Nassim 1, 27, 123
technology planning 138, 215
Three Gorges Dam area 162
tinkering 27, 28, 54, 78, 93, 94, 96, 115, 116, 119, 120, 121, 122, 123, 124, 125, 126, 129, 188
top-down 26, 56, 88, 125, 138, 143, 180, 191, 205, 209, 210, 211
top-level 46, 88, 89, 108, 120, 124, 135, 139, 141, 145, 160, 171, 189, 195
"top-level design" (*dingceng sheji*) 81, 209, 211
transformative governance 5, 32, 40
trial and error 51, 57, 76, 126, 188
tried-and-tested 46
Tsai, Kellee 24
Tsai, Lily 24, 68

U

uniform targets (*yi dao qie*) 182

V

"[a] veto" (*yi piao fou jue*) 185, 253

W

Walder, Andrew 23
Wang Shaoguang 121, 123, 124
"Washington consensus" 212
Weingast, Barry 91
Wen Jiabao 134, 150, 154, 171, 190, 198, 201, 207
welfare state 116, 127
World Bank 9, 177, 190
work on individual issues (*gebie zhidao*) 66
"work-style" (*zuofeng*) 30, 50
Woo Wing Thye 117, 118
Wu Jinglian 178

## X

Xi Jinping 197, 198, 200, 201, 203, 205, 206, 207, 208, 209, 210, 211, 215, 217
"Xingguo Model" (*mofan Xingguo*) 49, 50

## Y

Yan'an 48, 50, 62
Yan Xishan 50
Yan Yangchu (James Yen) 60, 61
Yang, Dali 23
Yu Yingshi 58

## Z

Zhejiang 62
Zhu Rongji 107, 133, 134, 150, 153, 154, 207